Darrell Cleveland

The New World of Education

The New World of Education

A Philosophical Analysis of
Concepts of Teaching

Marc Belth

Queens College
of the
City University of New York

Allyn and Bacon
Boston

Library of Congress Catalog Number: 73–109597

Printed in the United States of America

To the memory of

Samuel and Bertha Caro Belth

*Even in the greatest of traditions
there is to be found a sense of the
future which makes it congenial to
the advent of new worlds*

Contents

Preface

IN July of 1968 I was privileged to be invited to conduct a Seminar
in Vancouver under a special grant made available by joint spon-
sorship of Simon Fraser University and the British Columbia Teacher's Federation. The students enrolled in the Seminar were a group
of men and women who had just been appointed members of the
Faculty of Education at Simon Fraser as Associates; several members
of the staff of the BCTF; people who were practicing teachers in
elementary and secondary schools in British Columbia; and at least
one member of the Faculty of the University of Victoria. In all,
there were twenty-four mature, intellectually vital, professionally
restless people who, without fail, spent more than three hours every
working day for the three week period in classes combining lectures
and seminars.

I was given freedom in the choice of the content of the Seminar
as well as of the format for its presentation. I chose to begin with a
fairly brief survey of some of the basic concepts of the work I had
been doing until then in the development of a discipline of education.
From that point I moved more fully into the development of ideas
that had not yet been worked out publicly. The original title of the
Seminar was "An Adventure in the Philosophy of Education," and
the content of this book is the thoroughly revised version of the informal lectures that I gave.

The New World of Education is presented as an effort to re-
examine the most familiar of educational problems within a context
of ideas that, unhappily, are rarely used to analyze and evaluate these
distinctly educational problems. This is a time of upheaval in education, an upheaval not matched since those late Medieval times when
the great universities of Europe were struggling for independence
from their theological origins, a struggle resulting in the great trials
of intellectual heresy of the twelfth and thirteenth centuries.

The present struggle is not altogether dissimilar. In both cases they can be seen as a struggle to obtain control of established power, control of the development of intellectual capacities in order to build and maintain a social-political force. And, in both cases, lost in that conflict are the very people for whom the whole establishment of education has been constructed. But lost as they may have been in this conflict, these individuals have themselves evolved into a third force of power—a power too often without political authority, but of overwhelming legitimacy. It is the legitimacy of the learner who has found his voice. He demands to know what the significance of this struggle between authority groups is for the actual internal teaching—learning processes, and for his own developing powers. Certainly it should also be the legitimate demand of the teacher whose profession is being shaped.

At present, these demands are not being made in the elementary level of education, and only insignificantly at the secondary level. But at the college and university levels the third force is becoming so great that its effects will soon reach down to these earlier levels. It is at this higher level that questions arise, questions seeking not only an account of the uses of power as such, but also an account of how power in education is being used to penetrate deeply into the processes of that education; how it can make available to the individual learner all of the force the modern world has made available to all who would learn. But it is all too rare that such account is ever offered.

Much of the discontent began with dissatisfaction concerning the use of authority, administrative and otherwise, in the educational process. Tradition has long decreed that a Board of Education, or a Board of Trustees should sit in judgment over the curriculum, the distribution and collection of monies, and the employment and the disbarment of administrators, teachers, and students. Suddenly the teachers' and administrators' forces are challenging the heretofore unquestioned use of authority by such Boards. Further, these professional educators are demanding the right to participate in the decision-making process.

And now, outside the windows of the council halls, can be heard the voices of the students, demanding an account from all of these decision-makers. How have the judgments been made? What are these judgments? What criteria have been used to determine, for example, who shall teach, and who shall learn? What other activities shall the school be allowed to embark upon?

Once these demands have been made, the demand for further clarification of the legitimacy of the control and the pursuit of educational process will follow. Are the criteria used until now valid criteria for the world coming to be? Is there nothing to rely on beyond the purer passions and good will of men when attempting to define the learning and teaching situation? Do not the more structured approaches of the philosophies of science and the more recently developed disciplines of anthropology, sociology, genetics, and astrophysics make available whole areas to be explored, new methods to be analyzed, allowing a reformulation of the process of education into something more estimable than a struggle for power among politically oriented groups?

Is there nothing in the educative process to identify the teaching act, setting it forth as a most imperative force for legitimizing educational decisions? Is there nothing other than the written contract and the bylaw to determine what is effective in education? Is there no way to objectively and formally ascertain if a student is deprived, even though his teacher may have attended scrupulously to every paragraph of the contract, every sentence of the law and charter? Is it reasonable to continue to believe that even when there is a bad teacher in the room, the learner can continue to go forward on his own? Are romantic assumptions and quasi-mystical beliefs always to form the foundations for carrying out the educational process?

Much of this lack of orientation and definition results from the curious historical division of education into practice and study, a division projected into the present in a distressingly sterile form. As a practice it has been involved in social-political-economic dominions, from which it has been expected, even obligated, to take its cues and directions. As a field of study, it has been shaped to be consonant with all of the beliefs, presuppositions, and assumptions constituting current philosophical doctrines of worth, existence, and purpose, and also with the conclusions about human behavior derived from biology, psychology, anthropology. Thus, in the field of practice choices must be consistent with the choices of our public policy makers; in the field of study, education has had to prove itself consistent with the theoretical and metaphysical systems used to describe the fundamental meanings of life.

When education is studied in terms of the *processes* entailed in developing the power to penetrate into the very decision-making operations and conditions of our political leaders and analysts, and into the modes of the logical inquiries of metaphysicians, psychologists, anthropologists and the rest, then it must be seen as a field of inquiry that cannot be reduced to a particular metaphysical doctrine or political commitment.

As this work develops, it will be observed that no specific metaphysical commitment is required in order to explore and to shape for use the educational models being presented here. One does not need to hold the metaphysical belief that there are no problems which defy complete resolution in order to be able to recognize the role of a particular model for nurturing the capacity of learners to cope with problems for which no empirical evidence is available, and whose solutions require intellectual agreement.

So with an educational model of exploration of structures. One does not need to believe in the existential character of the "body politic," in fact one might even recognize the metaphoric extension of the human body, and still maintain educational integrity in applying such a model to the exploration and explanation of materials to be exposed and made comprehensible to those who come to learn some things which they would normally not be able to perceive.

One is not required to believe a particular set of doctrines, nor to stand committed to a given view of the universe, of the nature of the child, or of man, in order to recognize the effectiveness of the educational models set forth in this work, any more than one has to believe in the doctrine of the absence of free will in order to develop the skill of the use of certain instruments by means of which a recognized series of responses may be produced in those who come to learn.

The study of education must achieve the level of sophistication demanded in this time. We have no longer the right to luxuriate in education as a romantic undertaking, of freeing human beings to their inherent wonders of freedom and personal privilege, as if nature had already prepared men with the purest and wisest, most courageous and penetrating of powers. We have by this time passed through that phase of civilization's development. Unless we go beyond it consciously now, we stand in danger of becoming quaint in our own time. But such quaintness, if it ever was charming, is not so any longer. There is nothing charming about the perpetuation of intellectual or emotional ghettos, any more than there was ever anything charming about racial-political-religious ghettos.

It is only when we free education itself from the total subservience it has had for almost all of its existence to the political doctrines of the moment, or to the metaphysical dominations of an age, that all the rest of our civilization will free itself from the high walls built by timid men for the spurious certainty of mind.

As to this work, the intention is to present an analysis of a small, but growing vocabulary for a discipline of education, the conception of which I had begun to work out in an earlier book. The line of argument begins in the first chapter with a consideration of the role of symbols and symbol systems in sorting out what is experienced in any human undertaking. The next three chapters move to a consideration of the tendencies toward degeneration in such symbol systems. The clichés for sorting experiences, their ascribed meanings no longer vital or viable, have become ineffectual in making full meanings available in newer encounters. It is shown that a discipline such as mathematics creates the possibilities of new worlds of experience by creating new worlds of thought. These new worlds of thought are symbol systems produced through continuing development. In these terms, each new system can be seen as, first, a sorting system for ideas and things encountered, and second, the means by which our comprehensions and our responses to our worlds are expressed.

This new world is created, then, in the models of new symbol systems. These systems of models enable us to sort out educating from expressing (Chapter Three), teaching from learning (Chapter Four), and the different models of education from each other. The final four chapters are devoted to an explicit development and analysis of five models in this new world of education. These models make it possible to teach students to think together in an effort to reach clarity and definition where none would otherwise exist; to think as another has thought; to think introspectively; to think in and of the terms of what is already known; to think of what has not been thought before. These are, respectively, the models of Dialectic, Didactic, Monologue, Paradigm, and Projective education. In this continuing analysis I have attempted to explore the distinctive methods used by the teacher, the types of materials each model is limited to considering, the kinds of knowledge each seeks to attain, and the kinds of thinking each is designed to foster in those who come to learn. In the final chapter I have attempted to illustrate how it is possible to integrate these educational models and shape them into a lesson plan that is definable within a curriculum of the models to be used in nurturing ways of thinking.

I have included a brief appendix, consisting of four essays written by former students of mine. In each case the essay is so clear an illustration of how the use of a model shapes description, explanation, and analysis, that I could not resist using them here. For as all teachers know, and most admit, it is from the student who pursues the limits of an idea that we learn the most.

Acknowledgements

I would be remiss if I did not at the outset offer a special note of gratitude to those who have helped to make this project possible, and the rewriting of it which followed.

First, to Mr. C. D. Ovans, General Secretary of the British Columbia Teachers' Federation, who helped develop the Seminar, and who worked closely with many facets of the work as it developed.

To Dean Archie R. MacKinnon of the Faculty of Education at Simon Fraser University, who joined with Mr. Ovans by making a grant available, and by arranging for his new Associates to participate in the work.

To Mr. A. J. Spragge who had charge of the general activities which were organized, and kept the work going smoothly.

To Professor Ayres Bagley of the University of Minnesota, who read an early version of the entire manuscript and made a number of valuable recommendations which have been incorporated in the final version of the text.

In addition, Professor R. S. Peters of the University of London, has read parts of the earlier version of this work, and made some demanding observations. If I have not met all his criticisms, it cannot be accounted his failure, but mine.

Professor Paul Hirst, also of London, made some valuable if indirect contribution by allowing me to explore some of the ideas of private knowledge in work we shared at the University.

Each of these has been of invaluable assistance, though none of them can be held to account for the directions this work has taken. They may, each in his own way, support some or all of the ideas developed here, but in his own way each is much more temperate in his visions of what is to come.

To Mr. Harold P. Bernstein, to whom I first set forth the basic ideas of this book on a drive between Annecy and Geneva, and who, I hope, will think this work touches matters of importance in that public mind so much a matter of concern to him.

My thanks to Miss Judith Fiske of Allyn and Bacon, Inc., who guided the manuscript through the various stages of production and to Mr. John Dwyer who prepared the index. I appreciate their fine efforts.

Finally, my wife, with her angelic patience and diligence, has prepared the manuscript, and has sustained me with infinite tolerance throughout the period of the lectures and the writing.

To all, my deep appreciation. And to the men and women who were members of the Seminars in which this work had its origins and to the students whose work I have included here my greatest respect for their eager and enthusiastic participation.

The New World of Education

CHAPTER 1

Disciplines and Symbol Systems: A Philosophical Consideration

I AM some of the possibilities of my world of education made real. My failures condemn that world, my successes honor it. To judge myself is to judge a distillation of that old world which strives constantly to renew itself. And contrariwise, as Alice might say, to judge that old world, to penetrate its mysteries and open them to wide consideration is but to judge myself, and to open myself to the scrutiny of all who read and listen.

I am not describing a particular type of schooling, but the education that sums up each person. My concern is for the qualities of our thoughts, and for the effect control of these qualities has upon our sensitivities, our dispositions, our powers of vision, our force of communion and communication. Our biographies are a critique of the education that forms us. And thus, to inquire into education is to inquire into the molding of lives. By presenting a critique of a new world of education just being born, I shall be writing a biography of our future selves. For the effort to define the new world of education is also the effort that will produce a new world altogether.

THE ROLE OF THE SYMBOL

The inquiry delimited. There are aspects of the educational process that will not be explored in this work. It is not that those

1

aspects are uninteresting. It is, rather, that it is not possible to explore everything that falls within the category of education, and yet remain disciplined. But then, one of the great problems that education has always faced is that it never has made an adequate evaluation of its intrinsic limitations. As a result, most studies try to do too many things simultaneously, with no guidelines for what can actually be accomplished.

Without a doubt every teacher, even one who has taught for only a month, has had the experience of being called upon, sometimes against his wishes, to be psychiatrist, psychologist, school nurse, economist, and statistician in addition to quasi-parent, friend, and confidante. This takes place not only at the elementary level, but also at the high school level. Those who teach at the college level are not less broadly and vaguely involved, though by this time students themselves are not always so congenial to the idea. Even the students have been led to believe the teacher is some general practitioner capable of dealing with every possible distress however vaguely school-contracted. Indeed, at least one acknowledged basis for the great student unrest in today's universities is the instructor's abandonment of the student who needs and clamors for personal contact.

If there is to be a basis for limiting this inquiry, it would be well to begin with a discussion of what constitutes a discipline—any discipline. Every serious study seeks to define itself by some disciplinary characteristics. In doing so it is setting forth the rules, relationships, and defining traits by which it can be comprehended. Such claims are not primarily intended as synthetic but analytic statements. That is, to claim that such and such a study is a discipline is not like saying that studying mathematics is tiresome (which is proven or disproven in our experiences), but rather like saying "the study of mathematics is the study of symbol relationships." Refinements or rejections are not made by counter examples, but by logical distinctions and definitional extensions. Thus, clarification is achieved, not by empirical examinations, but by logical analysis of the extended concepts that are entailed in the statement itself. If ultimately the analysis is tested in experience, it is because all concepts come, as Peirce once said, to have the meanings of their directive force in experience.

The best way to begin is with the simple truism that we all share traits of being human. As humans, we are primarily concerned with the ways of the world, for we need to make a go of things. But more often than not, we do this intuitively, out of habits that were developed long before we had even begun to talk or to walk. Researchers, scholars, and scientists have shown that it is possible to describe the pattern of these developments, not only in observable behavior, but in concept formation and in concept employment. At this point in history, the pattern of these developments is a familiar one to most of us.

At the earliest stage we learn by mimicry. We learn to do things because other people have done them. Very often we do things for no other reason than that other people are doing them. We seem, often without being aware of it, to envy everyone who does things competently and with enjoyment. We love the world of action. We imitate it, hoping that in the imitation we will partake of the world our guardians and lovers are part of, and that in some remarkable way we will enjoy the world that they are enjoying. Clearly this is at least one basis for mimicry. It begins with the desire to know what others know in order to appear as others appear. Yet curiously, the fulfilment of this desire does not end the pattern of development.

It does not take us long to recognize that the world is full of at least two types of events. It is full of things that go, or that can be made to go—that can be pushed, or that can be wound up, set down, and permitted to run. And it is also full of the symbols of things that go, of the symbols of the furniture of our world.

It takes no great insight to point out that most people discover quickly how much easier it is to control the symbols of things than to control the things themselves. When we learn this we have taken the first step in the direction of human intervention into the natural ways the world operates. That intervention is not just a matter of placing oneself in the midst of the events themselves and partaking of them. It is more a matter of trying deliberately to control events; of standing back a little, discovering the symbol system by means of which things are identified, and then learning to control those symbols. "The train is running," is a systematic set of symbols, logically connected so that some symbols denote things or processes in the world ("train," "run") and some ("the," "is," ". . . ing") refer to the way one is expected to see the relationship between actual things in time, sequence, and condition.

All this is a symbolic notation of a thing occurring—a train running. By means of such symbol systems we are able to move away from the physical, or tangible part of the world. In fact, we learn about the world and its particulars more effectively and economically as we move deliberately closer in our attention to the symbols of the world. In doing this we mature and become more thoroughly human. For the result of such a move is that we learn to control rather than to continue to be controlled by the world around us. Moreover, as we become more critically concerned with the symbols of things, we move into a disciplined capacity to control, to predict and to reconstruct the world that we are trying to understand. The degree of this discipline marks the degree we can come to grasp the traits and powers of this world.

The role of experience in education. In the Western world experience is viewed as the best and often the only teacher. There is devotion, often extreme, to the precept that the only way children ever learn is by being given direct, immediate opportunity to confront the world with their own experiencing. Experience is seen not as having a *role* in education, but as *being* education.

Put this way (and so often it is put in some form such as this), this view is utterly without merit. This does not mean, of course, that we are ready to dismiss experience. On the contrary, in the context of our concern with a rising discipline, we need to give to experience a new character, one that will serve us even more promisingly and prominently in the study of education, though very differently.

Consider, then, the thesis that experience is not so much the source of learning as it is the outcome and thus the test of it. If this were so, then intelligence, maturity, developed capacities for control, for penetration, would not simply arise from experience, but rather from a direct tuition, a critical analysis, of the symbols that represent the things of the world, and which give meaning to experience. If we were to accept this view, we would have to make a great many changes in our beliefs, in fact, restructure much of our belief system.

To understand this thesis of experience it is important to make clear the difference between a thing, and that which symbolizes a thing. This difference can be seen in the field of science. Although historically science has been recognized as the discipline of experience, this is not the reality. Many have come to recognize that the scientist as scientist improves as he gets further and further away from experience and even from experiment. It is held that a scientist is one who has learned how to construct the world he wants by learning the character, the range, and the significance of the symbols which have been established to represent segments of reality.

A meteorologist who is trying to predict the weather for this afternoon or tomorrow does not approach his task directly. He would not get into an airplane and fly about searching for storms, but would use data gathered from instruments on satellites, and so on. Even if he did use the plane, he would have to have some symbolic system to operate on and with. For it is only in terms of some such system that he can observe cloud formations, temperatures, currents, wind velocities and directions. When he records, he records notations of characteristic behavior recognized as symbolic of certain events.

He predicts not by looking at an event directly, but by reasoning through the symbols that he has recorded, which now take the form of some paradigmatic case. It will not do just to go up in a plane and glance about. His symbol system has become so precise that nature itself has become something like an intrusion upon his scientific undertaking. In order to make it obedient to his inquiry, he constructs an instrumentation that translates the actuality of the heavens into an entire symbolic notational system which he views, in this case, on a radar screen. By observing the radar screen (which is designed to sort out and illuminate what is otherwise not easily noticed) the eye can encompass in a narrow area what it could not possibly have seen from an airplane. It becomes possible to make deductions from these symbolic notations and, on the basis of these, predict the weather. In fact, if direct experiential observations are made possible, it is only because this kind of symbolizing has been done first.

Analogously, experience results from the developed radar screen; it is the outcome of symbol-making; it tests the functioning of the symbol system that has been made and used. When there is a recognized failure in an experiment or an experience, the very first assurance must be that there has been no failure in the explanatory function of the symbol system in use. This might be the case when the symbol system is both vague and ambiguous. Failures indicate that there must be more precise and more inclusive or exclusive representation of the datum of reality in order to make explanations within controllable compass. What cannot be turned over physically, can be turned over verbally, and explained.

Some illustrations. As it translates physical reality more exhaustively and more coherently into a symbol system, the discipline of physics becomes an increasingly sophisticated undertaking. It is understandable why so much is made of the seemingly absurd fact that Einstein never performed any of the experiments that are part of the literature of the theory of relativity. It seems such a defiance of common sense expectation. Moreover, when others, coming after him, put Einstein's theories to the test, what were they doing?

Within the realm of science the word *test* means an inspection of the explanatory character of the symbol system being recommended. They were testing, not so much whether the theory was true, but whether the theory could be used to make sense out of the behavior of things. Looking at actual events within the context or framework of Einstein's notational system, were all parts and all operations given meaning? The test indicates failure if events keep occurring for which there are no notations and, therefore, no meanings or explanations. The test validates that system (that theory) when everything that occurs can be explained, or given a meaning coherent and consistent with every other thing in the context being explained.

To give another illustration—Einstein's notational system was predicated on the familiar idea that causal laws govern the behavior of all atomic events. So long as the experimenters used Einstein's system of observation, measurement, and testing, the one thing they were required to look for was the causal law that would account for change and motion. In a continuing dispute between Einstein and Niels Bohr, a "thought experiment," recommended by Einstein to determine the time and change of even a single photon with absolute certainty, was contradicted when Bohr applied aspects of Einstein's own theory that had been overlooked. The very symbol system (theory) in use verified that causal laws did not explain the facts. The story is told that Einstein was defeated but unconvinced.[1] What was he puzzled about? It is possible that he was puzzled about how nature deceives us. But if he was really puzzled about this, he would have directed his attention to the character of a theoretical structure that did not enable him to take account of the fact that acts that appeared to be reflecting some natural law revealed other behaviors when the theory was more closely applied.

One more illustration—this time in the more familiar field of psychology. Teachers seem unable to avoid becoming pseudo-psychologists. That is, they practice in one field while confidently using the language of another. When the teacher sees a child acting up in class, he might glare at him. But how much staring time is

---

[1] The story is told with charm and excitement in Friedrich Waismann's "The Decline and Fall of Causality" in *Turning Points in Physics,* ed. Alistair C. Crombie (Amsterdam: North Holland Publishing Co., 1950), Ch. 5.

required before the basis for this bad behavior will be revealed? And is it a special kind of a glare? Staring at the child is not generally accepted as a sound means of discovering the basis for bad behavior. Even if one were to ask directly, "Johnny, why did you hit and scratch Mary?" would his answer in fact indicate his motive? Would he really know the motive himself? And if this is not the way, how are motives determined? The face may give clues, but are these standard, established clues?

How does one study psychology? By simply observing children? Too often this has been presented as the only possible approach, when it really is one aspect of one method of study. It is used in the hope that the behavior of the children will demonstrate the validity of a notational system (which becomes the explanatory instrument) that some psychologist had already invented and that was "given" by verbal communication in some teaching situation.

Intelligence and experience.   Although intelligence is manifest in behavior, it first arises in some formal or informal symbol situation. In such a setting there is transmitted a context of notations that is learned and applied to an actual situation. This accomplishes two things—first, the discovery of the fuller explanation of the notations themselves (that is, seeing what it is they refer to); and second and more important, the illustration in an actual situation of the meanings of children's behaviors. Thus, behavior is given an account, and the symbols are given meanings in actual behavior.

A Freudian psychologist might say, "You know that all behavior is primarily sex motivated. No matter what you think you see when you see children's behavior, you must look more deeply into what is apparent to discover motives. From the symbols which denote the sexuality of being human we can deduce the causes and purposes of the behavior." Thus, to take any one of a number of situations that have occurred recently, in Canada, in America, in England, in France, where young men and women students have decided that they would no longer be willing to accept the affront of administrators in the conduct of the university, and apply this Freudian explanatory system, would yield an interesting account and interpretation of the ensuing denunciations and upheaval. One interpreter commenting on a great disturbance at Columbia University identified it as a manifestation of sexual repression on the part of students, a release of repressions that had been growing for a long time. Conditions in our present time are such, he argued, that young people, male and female, are no longer frustrated by one another. The sexual revolution has produced absence of restraint. The consequence is that young men and women now have to look for other areas where great restraints still obtain, within which they will be certain to be frustrated. Since they get anything they want from their classmates, they need much more challenging obstacles. This is why there is rebellion against the administration, against the Board of Trustees, against the police. The building of such rebellious pressure marks the dynamic of being involved and alive, and growing increasingly aware of their bodies and their passions. So goes the explanation.

To accept this symbol notation, and the character of order implied in it, then, is to accept that it is the id making itself manifest in the straining and stretching, the shouting and exhibiting. But intelligence, which is the conscious explaining and controlling power, also arises here. For the world of the superego against which this id will press reacts sharply until finally, in the heightened conflict, the ego appears. It is when this occurs that the students become self-conscious and assert a governing balance between the two. In this system, meanings can be ascribed to the individuals who manifest various types of behavior. The exhibitionists are id-dominated; the reactionaries, superego-ridden; the cautious are ego-alive, or *self-conscious*, intelligent.

If a behaviorist psychologist were to offer an explanation he would probably say that all behavior is simply the manifestation of electrical discharge produced by the tensions of the overloading chemical stimuli. What the machine needs is a governor. What each individual needs is a channel for the release of that overload. Viewed in this context, the human organism is a machine which needs a governor lest it overload the connections providing the flow of energy required to run this machine. If the connections are destroyed, the entire machine runs down. Whenever students perform as they have at San Francisco State, at Berkeley, or at Columbia University, the behavior can be explained; energy was continuously building up, and there were no safety channels, no governing devices to allow for the escape of this increasing excessive energy. The clear channels needed for the continuing flow of energy were being filled up. The net result was a breakdown and the machines were thereafter unable to function at all. Examination of the kinds of behavior that students reveal will be necessary in order to construct that type of governor which will prevent this from happening again. But it would not have been possible to ask this question without the use of the symbol system that, say, a Skinner or a Watson had constructed. By its means children can be studied without actually sitting before them, talking to them, or observing their conduct to discover its cause. All that is needed is the symbol system, and the symbolic representation of the data constituting the situation and the behaviors.

To conclude: intelligence arises from our construction and/or use of symbol systems, and is manifest and tested in experience.

From these considerations one further point can be made. The more we cast our symbol systems into the forms of mathematical notations, the less likely we are to suffer the deceptions that often victimize us. Of course there is always the possibility that we want to be fooled, that what we dearly want or do not want to see happen has happened, or has not happened. To overcome such objective threats to truths of actuality every discipline eventually moves in the direction of a mathematization, where the possibility of strictest denotation increases. Only in this way can we reduce the problems of a subjectivity created by value judgments. By this system we eliminate the ambiguities and the vagaries, the connotative overtones, the romantic, distorting convictions that we tend to drag along with us while trying to understand with precision the structure and the function of the world and its people. There is no room for any of these beclouding passions in mathematical notation.

This, of course, distresses a great many. But when it does people ought to accord themselves the dignity of recognizing that they do not want to be any more disciplined than they absolutely have to be. They just do not want to be any more intellectually precise than they need to be, lest they lose some of the nameless wonder of their worlds; nameless, but very gratifying.

It does take time and maturity to see the wonder and warmth in the uses of mathematical precision, which scientists see. The beauty of intellectual power and penetration takes acclimatization, for it is strictly a conceptual affair, and it is very hard to remain in this realm for too long.

THE SCIENTIFIC MODEL

The tangible and the intangible, the explained and the explaining.   In the discussion so far I have tried to make the point that the confrontation of the symbol system is the most meaningful and most significant confrontation of reality, if not the only one. Outside of some symbol system all we have is ebb and flow in the world. It is surely real, this ebb and flow, as real as a pinprick on your skin is real. It is as real as the headache it produces when the flow continues to threaten and there seems to be no way of controlling its threat of inundation.

But we cannot limit ourselves to talking about that kind of reality. As teachers we also talk of the reality that we cannot put our hands on—the mind of a child, his values, his happiness, his anguish. We cannot hold these. We cannot turn them around, nor can we inquire into them just by looking at the child, then choosing to chop off some small segment of him in order to slide it under a microscope. These are also realities, although intangible ones. Where would we find his values? Yet we do admit that he has values and anguish; that he has intelligence; that he suffers when he recognizes inadequacies, that he has this something we may call *recognition*. But where would his recognition be?

It would seem that as we talk about human beings, these are the things that are at least as significant as any of the physical elements that we might be concerned with. This is not to suggest that the physical are distinct from these conceptual phenomena, but to point out that the *base* of something is not the whole of it. And the physical may be only the base, or the basis of these intangibles. The only way to approach these other matters—the fostering of intelligence, the nurturing of refined sensibilities, the improvement of appreciations, the capacity for balancing oneself under the pressures of achievement—is through the symbol systems which make their identification possible. We have only words for these. But, as many philosophers have argued, it is a debatable matter whether or not these words actually refer to any thing.

But whether they refer to things or not, what we know, we know only in our confrontations of symbols; and only through these confrontations do we know their significance. For example, saying certain words to children alters not only their behavior but their dispositions. This overt behavior can indeed be observed, but where does one go and at what does one look in order to observe a disposition? At a face? A shoulder? A position of the body? A gesture? A disposition is reducible to none of these. But it is true that a word will alter a disposition for better or for worse. A certain type of conversation with a child will suddenly motivate him to do things he never thought he would want to do. As he is observed, he can be seen to be doing things, but can the *motivation* be seen? Or the disposition? In every such case the explanatory statement is confused with the thing being explained. For "disposition" is really a symbol to *explain* what is tangible—it is not the tangible thing itself.

Concepts and percepts in education.   It is imperative to recognize that inevitably teachers are conceptually bound and their profession is conceptually born. All the work begins and ends at the level of the conception, however much it passes through the realms of behavior. This may seem very abstract and very removed from the teacher's everyday classroom activity, and in one sense it is. It is as far removed from daily activity as the classroom of the prospective surgeon is removed from the actual surgical theater. But, as it is absurd to expect the surgeon to be able to operate without having gone through the classroom, then it may also be recognized that it is equally absurd for the teacher to operate in the classroom without having gone through the symbol world of education. For without having gone through this long and sometimes despairing period of preparation nurtured in the confrontation of concepts, perceptions of education become impossible. Indeed, it is a serious question whether one who is called upon to nurture intelligence can even be expected to know what is being asked of him unless he has first made this conceptual universe his own.

A more familiar example will clarify this problem. There has been in recent educational history a curious dispute as to whether teachers teach subjects or children. This is as good an illustration of symbol systems being misunderstood or mistaken as could be found. In the past fifty years much moral denunciation has accompanied the dispute, for a choice of one appears to be a callous abandonment of the other.

More revealing than the nature of the dispute itself is the discovery of where the battles were fought. They were fought not in classrooms but in conference rooms, and the combatants were adherents of different conceptual systems. As far as the practitioners in the schools were concerned, it didn't really matter who won. Those who say that they do not teach subject matter but children inevitably must teach something to the children. It is that *something* (even when it is called "problem solving" or "thinking") that turns out to be subject matter. And those who stoutly insist that they do not really teach children (since, as Socrates seemed consistently to hold, there is no such thing as teaching), will finally admit that although they must be concerned primarily with subject matter, the subject matter that they transmit, the transmission is directed to the children. In the confusion of symbol systems battles took place too often without the recognition that the protagonists were in different worlds, talking about different paths, with different concepts of perfection. When they finally came to establishing common ground in a common symbol system, they often continued to dispute, but the truce had actually been signed.

This same kind of a problem has ever been what the philosopher has confronted. And anyone who seeks to approach a solution to this conceptual-perceptual dilemma is obliged to begin to develop the skill of asking philosophical questions, even about the most ordinary educational statements.

What do categories categorize? Philosophy long ago was divided, and still is, for that matter, into four major fields: Epistemology, which is a theory of knowing; Logic, which is a theory of reasoning; Metaphysics, which is a theory of being; and Ethics, which is a theory of acting. Obviously, all of these require a study of abstractions. To become adept in philosophy we are expected to study Being-as-such, Knowing-as-such, Reasoning-as-such, and Acting-as-such.

But the world has gotten very impatient with all of these abstractions, primarily because doubts arose as to what was actually being studied, the language of philosophy, or philosophy. We have come to look at the world as an on-going business of particular events in transaction, as William James called it.[2] What we really want to know is this: What do people do, under what conditions? On what basis do they do it? This obliges us to turn from a study of being, of knowing, etc.-as-such, to a study of the particulars which, when organized into consistent classes of events, become the distinctive disciplines or fields of knowledge we now know. In the light of the classifications we turned also to a study of the rules for organizing or creating these categories, these modes of being, of knowing, of reasoning, and of acting. What was the study of abstractions from doubtful entities became the study of abstractions from quite specific, determinate processes. The result of the shift is that today philosophy seems to be more appropriately divided into such fields as the philosophy of science, the philosophy of law, the philosophy of psychology, the philosophy of sociology, the philosophy of anthropology, the

---

[2] William James, *Pragmatism* (Cleveland: Meridian, 1955), esp. lectures 1 and 2: "The Present Dilemma in Philosophy" and "What Pragmatism Means."

philosophy of mathematics, and sometimes reluctantly, sometimes eagerly, the philosophy of education.

In each case the distinction is made between the study of some objective event and the exploration of the *rules* and the *grounds* for such a study. Consider this time a primitive scientist. If he were going to measure the rate of acceleration of falling objects, he would say, "I am going up to the top of that tower there. I will stand on top while you hold a stopwatch. At the moment that I let go of what I am holding, let the stopwatch run. We will see by this timing how fast it came down.

"The first thing I will drop is a pound of lead. Then I will drop a pound of feathers. What I want to see is whether there is any difference in the falling time."

The assistant agrees to the plan. But the philosopher in his untroubled garden, out of harm's way, and unable to intrude on serious business, propounds his characteristically word-chopping questions. "I think I understand what is meant by saying the scientist is going *up* there. He is going to mount a series of steps and he will end at a level higher than the head of the assistant by several degrees, or inches, or feet. But why does he use the word 'up'?"

Knowing what any scientist would say to such a question, the philosopher addresses it only to students, thereby assuring that philosophy is only a common garden or schoolroom affair.

"I'll tell you why I worry," he explains to the students who will listen. "Let me show you a picture. I often worry about things like this. It is true, isn't it, that we live on a round place? And it stays put, so to speak, as I understand it (because I am not a scientist, all I know is what scientists tell me) because it spins very rapidly. And the reason that *we* stay in place is that it spins at such a speed that centrifugal force holds us to the spots on which we stand. Now, at whatever place I stand, where my head is, is considered up. Where my feet are is considered down. Just think of that for a moment. If I were standing up there," (pointing to British Columbia on a scrawled simulation of a map) "my head is up there" (pointing out above it). "But how about a man down here in Australia? His head is in that direction," (pointing out *under* it, as seen from British Columbia). "Is not that *up* to him? If this is *up* for him, and that is *up* for me, then I don't think I understand the rules for the word *up*. And certainly I don't understand the use of the word *down*. It is curious, isn't it? Such a little word."[3]

[3] Susanne Langer used such an illustration for this problem in her essay "Why Philosophy?" *The Saturday Evening Post* 234 (1961):34.

Any scientist would testily advise such a questioner to please go find another philosopher and pursue this nonsense with him.

But there is something quite interesting at stake here. How did the words *up* and *down* become the accepted symbols in this business?

In theologically rooted literature *up* means some area where heaven might be found and *down* means the other place. Earth and heaven were thought of in terms of planes, not circles or spheres. Yet we know now that we live on a globe. Do the people down under have their heads up? To keep talking this way is to produce more than just philosopher's jokes and confusions, for the rules are quaint.

When people down under die and go to heaven, do they have to come to the northern hemisphere? Is God a Northern Hemisphere inhabitant? This surely sounds parochial. And yet, how distressing to discover that this is precisely what was meant when the terms *up* and *down* were earlier introduced in history. The earth was considered to be the very center of the universe. All things dark and evil lived down and all things bright and noble lived up. Yet, as innocent and as amusing as this sounds, further examination yields the discovery that science has long remained dominated by the lingering vestiges of a language with theological references. It should then not be surprising to see how much of science has continued to be cast into the language, the symbolic notations, of theology. Small wonder that a Soviet cosmonaut enjoyed the derision of his own announcement to the press that during his flight around the world he had looked about carefully, but he had not seen God in the heavens he was cruising through. The old category sorted out matters other than those to which they are applied today.

Philosophers and scientists, as categorists.   Taken more seriously, and in the more sophisticated context of a complex scientific problem, the philosopher of science does play a seminal role. His participation involves the identification, clarification, even the construction of the categories, or the ideas that are the instruments of science, and that lead to the attainment and evaluation of scientific goals.

The philosopher, of course, is not a scientist. Yet without the philosopher, there would be no science. It is the philosopher who, if he does not create the categorial language of science, reveals, or creates, the conceptual necessity for refining that language. In a sense he cleans up the dictionary of the scientist and even on occasion adds words to that dictionary.

So, too, with the philosophy of psychology. In exactly the same manner, consider once again a Freudian psychologist as he talks about an ego, an id, and a superego. The philosopher may be impressed with the ingenuity of these terms, but he has his own service to perform. He must ask what the categories categorize, what the terms refer to. The answer usually given is that the id is the principle of motion, aggression and pleasure. The superego is the principle of restraint. And ego refers to that which develops when there is confrontation and stress established between id and superego. The philosopher says, "But this sounds like the description of a hydraulic system. Energy from one source conflicts with energy of another source and produces a third source of energy."

The Freudian defends himself against this by saying that it sounds more mechanistic than he intended, for he does not think of man as a mechanism.

"Well, if he is not a mechanism," asks the philosopher, "what do you mean when you talk about *principle* (as pleasure *principle,* pain *principle*)? Are you saying that there is internal operation, but not mechanism?"

"Yes, the id is a term for the way in which blood motion and sex impulses (which are both innate) respond to the events of the world, chemically, not mechanically."

"Well, now, you are talking in a curious sort of way," the philosopher says. "You are talking as if these were organic elements."

"Ah, but they are!"

"Well," continues the philosopher, "I understand that organic elements, if they exist, exist in some quantity, and if they exist in some quantity, they must be measurable. Does that mean I can measure an id?"

"An id is not to be measured."

"Not to be measured? Well, how can you claim it exists if it is not to be measured?"

The dilemma is apparent. The questions that the philosopher again raises are questions that attempt to identify the rules as to how far a concept can be used. These questions are also concerned with how clear the concept is, how consistent it is with others that are used, and what the concept is really expected to refer to.

Now these are very simple, even innocent illustrations of the function of the philosopher in the realm of the science of physics and in the realm of the science of psychology. There are more abundant illustrations, but these will be sufficient. The insights gained can now be applied to the problem of education.

Every educator has some symbol system, more or less developed and clear, which he uses constantly. Moreover, he uses it with the same unguarded confidence that scientists often use their symbols. The philosopher, then, will have as vital a role in this important area of activity as in any other. This may not accord with the familiar view that the philosopher should be concerned with the ends, or purposes, or objectives of education; but it is at least a more respectable view, if only because it is a less pretentious or pompous occupation without being less responsible. If those who insist on seeing the philosopher as the wise speculator in visions of the future need reassurance, they should consider that before objectives can be evaluated, we ought to be clear about what it is we are presently doing and saying. It is no less imperative for the educator than it is for the scientist, the historian, and the artist to equip himself to cope with the vagaries and the ambiguities of his symbol system. Educators surely need to be prepared to analyze the meanings, the range of significance, the tenability of what they are saying and doing in their professional pursuits, no less than others. Thus, if there are philosophers of science, art, and history, there must be philosophers of education.

If the clichés and the bandwagon jargon that have stunted the development of education and the educational symbol system in this and in previous centuries were abandoned, there is no doubt educational matters would be pursued more fruitfully.

The intention of this work. This is one of the responsibilities which this work has undertaken: to offer insight into what equipment of critical instruments will be needed and is available for destroying the clichés that strangle our thinking about and our participation in the processes of education. The objective is to explore and construct a unique symbol system that will enable us to create a new world of educational endeavor and to control the contributions of other disciplines, which until now have been borrowed or been given without any inquiry as to whether or not they really fit the world of education.

For example, there should be a careful examination of the symbol system that makes up the field of mathematics or history or science or art. But in order to examine any symbol system, there must be yet another symbol system. It cannot be done in a vacuum, or from some divine, self-sustaining perch. If a uniquely educational symbol system can be constructed and defined, it might be used to examine the educational character of history as a field to be studied, of science as an area to be taught and learned, of art as an area of human value to teach in order to nurture certain specific powers among children. To build this new system is, in the metaphor used, to build a new world of education whose rules and structures will give to all the known disciplines and all the prevailing values and aims a definitive place in the new geography.

But since we are not gods, but rather over-dependent earth-clods, we cannot create a new world out of nothing. We have no alternative but to begin with words that are already familiar in some sense. But we will have to use many of these words in other than their usual meanings. We will in all probability find ourselves selecting meanings that enable us to see qualities in events that are rarely identified in the familiar terms. In this way we can identify, organize, and describe processes in the very terms which we have used to explain our more familiar worlds. Consider, as but one example, the familiar word "clock." Its referent is the object on the wall, or shelf, whose function it is to show the time, day and night. This it does by means of a process of interacting gears, cogs, wheels, springs, hands, and so on. But this familiar word "clock" applied to the interactions of the human organism, enables us to talk about describable differences between biological, psychological, sociological, and intellectual interactions, or "clocks."

Science, as a further and different kind of an example, is a logically developed and directed, empirically focussed, explanatory system concerned with the nature that sustains the existence of each of us. But the system is not drawn from some source of perfection. Science is no more determinate in its activities than are the interactions of nature itself. Nature itself does not determine what shall be said about it, nor does any predisposition in the mind of man. Indeed, there is a peculiar aspect to the interactions in nature. At any given moment the substances that are involved in the interaction are only partly altered by the interaction. If observations produced descriptions showing that these substances were totally altered from their previous condition, then nature itself would be evidence of how impossible it is to say anything firm and final about nature. In the interaction whatever occurs, occurs. All that could be said about it and all that can be done about it is to describe it. But we will cling, as long as possible, to some insistence on partial unchangingness. More important, from these descriptions an attempt can be made to construct a generalization that could be accepted as a law, or a statement of lawlike behavior of nature. In terms of this law, it should be possible to predict the behavior of nature in some later interaction. The aim is less a matter of producing description or at proving unchangeableness than of writing laws of behavior.

When we come to man, the perplexity is enormously compounded. Men transact with one another—here Dewey's term is important. In one way or another men consciously and unconsciously relate to one another for purposes more or less clear to them. In this transaction the lives of all of the human beings alter in a cumulative way, though at different rates, and in varying degrees. New dimensions will appear in the persons who were involved in the transaction.

Dewey called it a transaction in order to point out that it is an activity in which men have in some way agreed to partake. Nature does not agree to partake of any interaction. A gust of warm wind does not agree now to interact with a cumulous cloud flying fairly low, so that together they will produce rain for the farmers who live in the area below. But men can transact with one another in a situation hoping that they will produce something they have agreed to try to bring about. They can draw upon nature in order to determine which transaction, among what elements, would be most desirable or most effective. They can also agree on the kinds of transactions they should avoid undertaking, in light of the undesirable consequences which they can anticipate. No such thing again can be said about choice-making among elements of nature.

The difference between interaction and transaction must be stressed, because if one claims that nature is a transacting event, then one must also claim pre-existent purpose for it, or a purposing mind in nature itself. Further, there would have to be proof that all its patterns, objectives, and goals are consistent. Thus, a man would sooner or later have to be able to see what will occur, what must occur, in order that nature's effort to maintain itself in a desirable balance could be shown. But the curious thing about nature is that it does not really care whether it maintains itself in balance or not. Nature (speaking again in an advisedly animistic manner) would just as soon create a typhoon as to create a balmy summer evening. But man, when he chooses to create a typhoon, chooses to do so because he is convinced that certain conditions not now existing ought to exist, even if it is only to satisfy his curiosity or to amuse himself.

Nature, culture and education.   In a very interesting way culture, as man creates it and lives in it, is the sum total of all of the "oughts" that he has established in transaction with other human beings, the result of the experiences they each have undergone. On that basis a more interesting and more fruitful definition of how culture functions can be found. Whether all philosophical systems would agree with this or not is not particularly pertinent at this moment. At some other time it might be, but the concern here is to suggest a theory of how culture comes into being. And such a theory is necessary because nature does not by choice present observing man with the knowledge about itself that he wants or needs. If man is to force nature to reveal more of its potentialities, he is obliged to establish a system of transactive relationships which give nature's operations a meaningful, created context. From this variety, men choose what will benefit all who are involved.

If this is conceded, then culture can be identified as the system of knowledge and belief that has become the instrument by which we shape the dynamic and passive elements of nature into congenial living environments. Further, in that culture the educative process is a fundamental instrument for organizing the symbols of that environment in order for children to learn to use them in creating their own experiences and shaping their futures. This is man's way of perpetuating his accomplishments, of enabling the next generation to take advantage of what the previous generation has already accomplished. In this sense too, culture is a binding force, an adhesive that makes human achievement on this planet cumulative; a force that makes it possible for each generation to learn about the instruments which have been developed out of the experiences of all those who have lived before them.

To continue the examination of this concept of culture, certain behavioral aspects that seem to characterize every culture can be set forth to determine how these separate elements operate as the culture's ethical rules of conduct. First of all, intrinsic to every cultural system there is a symbol system. Second, there is a series of beliefs of different kinds—beliefs about the world as it is, which are more or less demonstrably true, and beliefs about a world which ought to be, which can only be validated against some theory of ethics. Third, every culture contains within itself a systematic means of creating continuity between the generations. Within that system of means exist systems of dress, of worship, of earning a living, of building, of communicating, of educating oneself and others, and so on.

The transaction of these three aspects of culture that I have identified: that culture is characterized (1) by a symbol system;

(2) by the two types of beliefs mentioned; and (3) by a series of means for establishing both continuity between the past and future through the present and of binding the given members of the present into some kind of a harmonious and integrated series of social relationships, reveals a process which can be better understood when the process of science as intelligence organizing nature is used as a model. In this model science grows in power and precision as its symbol systems are refined, as intelligence is improved. Both culture and science can be construed as the product of man's contribution to the growth of his world and his own self. It is this same scientific model that will provide the model for the new educational world.

THE MODEL OF MAN

The acculturating force of symbols.   Symbols are the necessary means of communicating or establishing communion. Without symbols there could be no shaped culture. Without symbols human existence, which is characterized by and dependent upon intellectual economy, would not be possible. Without symbols any generation of living creatures must begin anew to construct a culture, to control its environment, only to have it die with them.

Without symbol systems the ethical rules by means of which any group functions must necessarily be both private and totally unique to each individual member of the group. By contrast the beliefs that we live by are evidence of how far we have gone in our efforts to understand and direct the ways of nature and of men. These include the beliefs forming the integrated symbol systems which are the ethical rules by which we live. These are the means— the instruments—that create our cultural continuities, and are themselves manifestations of how far a society has moved beyond its primitive character.

As these symbols, beliefs, and instruments are made to operate in the form of models and become more refined, more complex, more sophisticated, more subtle, more complete, more sensitive, more effective, culture itself becomes more forcefully directive of the lives of the human beings. And as it comes to dominate the lives of men, the rules by which life is to be lived become more and more determinate, and more and more determining. Within the increasing inflexibility of the culture patterns the ethics by which we live become equally rigid. Because of this characteristic development of rigidity in the controlling of systems of things and beliefs, it can be said that every revolution begins as a scientific-epistemological and ethical revolution. The systems of belief on which the culture has rested have lost their hold. New systems of beliefs have been projected from some newly constructed symbol system and are finding acceptance. The struggle of group against group in order to expand or to restrict cultural opportunities is but a reflection of the struggle of disparate models for living against one another. The fury of the revolution is the measure of the resistant force that every culture reveals in its attempt to perpetuate itself. The development of a new world of education should take into account this resistance, a resistance that tends to corrupt its own members; the concern must be for a different quality of function, for both science and ethics.

Symbol-making and environment-making—the thinking act.   I will conclude here with a rather sweeping, but hopefully not pretentious statement. I have taken much care in arguing the role of the symbol in the fashioning of the culture—the environment for human existence. It is man alone who is the symbol-maker. The presence of symbols marks the presence of man, either man the maker or man the discerner of those symbols. For man is, of all creatures in nature, the symbol-maker and symbol-user. Indeed man is defined by the functions of symbol-making. But in spite of this, the function itself requires a great deal of nurture and refinement. To the degree that this native power is refined, and brought to a level of development which in principle, but rarely in fact, he can reach by himself—to that degree does his environment improve, and greater possibilities for living, achieving, creating, become possible for him.

For nature is most cautiously conceived as event upon event, (just one thing after another, Bertrand Russell once wrote[4]) and interactions between events which would produce outcomes of no significance were it not for the signifying creatures present. Nature may truly be the source of whatever environment each man lives in and with. But it is man's developed and developing capacity to create and to use symbols which takes nature as it is and reshapes it until it becomes a living and liveable environment.

This operation of symbol-making and symbol-using I choose to call the act of thinking. Simply to identify thinking in this way, however, is to say very little. Yet it is enough to suggest that when, in a

[4] Read Bertrand Russell, *Our Knowledge of the External World* (New York: W. W. Norton and Co., 1929), lecture 4, for a careful analysis of this notion.

later chapter, I will explore in greater detail what enters into the activities of symbol-construction and symbol-use, it will be a setting forth of a more detailed conception of how it is possible to continue to think about thinking. But we must recognize why this is important and therefore, why it is necessary to identify the act of thinking with an activity which can be nurtured and literally brought into existence where it did not exist before. For, if we live human lives to the degree that we shape a raw nature into a human environment, and if neither nature outside of us nor our inner human potential determines, according to any known laws, what that environment shall be, then our lives do indeed depend upon our developing power to make and to use symbol systems; hence upon our power to think.

Although this may sound cosmic and lofty, perhaps even grandiose, it is a statement of intellectual economy and frugality. It suggests we turn away from the quest to find in nature, or in any other source but our developing capacity to think, the reasons for our existence, the purpose for our lives. To relate the growing capacity to think to the growing control of symbol systems as categorizing instruments is to suggest that from the smallest, or most immediate confrontations with nature and other men, to the broadest and the most abstract problems of culture as such; from the accounts given of man's stretching into purely conceptual realms, where art and science abide, to the very immediate rules which direct his games of golf and tennis, the symbol system constructed and used is the very basis of the process which marks as his a segment of his living environment.

The new world of education of which we speak is the world in which symbol-making and symbol-using are both the fundamental function and the basic substance used.

CHAPTER 2

The Old World:
What Keeps It Old

TWO purposes will dominate this chapter, the first to analyze further the conception of education introduced at the end of the last chapter, and the second to examine critically how symbol-systems become the substance of the study of education. For, if models determine and direct thinking within every discipline, then educational models will provide the instruments for a structuring of the teaching-learning activity. They must be employed to develop this required controlled environment.

Moreover, it will be observed that the connection between these two purposes will serve as the basis for the description and analysis of a new world of education.

DEFINITIONS

The function of definition. The rather precarious definition of education offered earlier must be examined again. It might, however, be valuable to consider the problem of definition itself first, in order to understand what is being attempted. Definition is, of course, a familiar philosophical problem.[1] Are definitions derived from close

[1] The reader might look into Richard Robinson's *Definition* (Oxford: Clarendon Press, 1962), esp. Ch. 1.

scrutiny of some *thing* in nature or do they leap out at us when we watch some thing or some act? Are they hypothesized at the outset of some investigation, and then proven right or wrong, adequate or inadequate after they have been put to the test of observation and experiment? Is a definition intrinsically connected to the thing it defines? Or are there two distinct worlds, the world of facts and the world of ideas, with definition belonging only to the latter?

Any standard textbook in logic will give examples of several *kinds* of definitions. But in keeping with the basic premises on which this work is being developed, I will consider not *kinds* of definitions but definition-as-such. From within this context it can be suggested that definitions are part of the intellectual effort involved in developing the categories by which we sort out the things of the world. It is to be assumed, of course, that these do not sort themselves out.

This further suggests that the purpose, or at least one major purpose of every experiment, analysis, investigation, or inquiry, is to conclude with a recommendation for a definition. For the experiment, analysis, or inquiry has led to the view that the events of any future encounter exhibiting certain marks or characteristics will become more manageable if they are so named or categorized. Equipped now with a definition which is the outcome of some previous inquiry, we have a classifying term, or system, for sorting out the materials we may yet encounter, expectedly or unexpectedly.

This also suggests that any definition with which we begin an investigation, or which we intrude into the midst of an investigation, has no absolute status for testing what we have achieved or even if we are right so far. Rather, it is the instrument for helping us to discover *where* we are relative to the symbol notations which bespeak some past experiment or experience. This is the service which conventional definitions always perform. They are like maps which we lay over otherwise unconnected points, giving them meanings and connections.

An operational illustration. Suppose we were to decide to make a careful examination of some newly arisen problem in a situation we previously thought not a problem at all. Suppose we were to respond to one such problem that is of interest right now, the question of what constitutes death. This is a problem which has suddenly become a deeply significant and difficult one, now that medicine has made such progress in the matter of heart transplants. Somewhere during the course of inquiry we will find ourselves applying familiar, earlier definitions (categorizing terms or ideas), such as the one that states that death occurs at the arrested beating of the heart. If a heart has stopped, and then begun to beat again, for any reason, we say it was a temporary cessation, indicating serious danger. We may even say that a man died and came back to life again. With the development of the ability to perform heart transplants successfully, however, the definition remains as a part of the history of previous beliefs or ways of speaking about such things. But given the new abilities, such a definition leaves us unable to make important distinctions and decisions in speaking about such events consistent with ways of speaking about other events. For, if a heart has stopped and we assume death has occurred, then why should we accept this as final for the patient, while continuing to speak of an organ of this patient as a possible mechanism to restore another to life?

We would clearly need a newer, more critical definition of life and death in order to be able to make more defensible judgments in just such cases. We would have to explore further, seeking a better basis for making a judgment between cases that seem similar but are indeed not.

In medicine, recent analysis has led to a consideration of the consequences of the restoration of health, that is, of the life functions. It has been discovered that the function of the heart, once considered so crucial in the judging life and death, can be replaced in whole or in part, or brought back to full function by means of mechanical devices. Thus, according to newly developed powers, the fact that the heart stops beating is of itself no longer proof of death. In fact, at present this becomes the condition for undertaking certain of those new activities. But we still need to know, in the case of transplants, when a person is *truly* dead if we are to use his heart without impunity to bring another man back to full function. At the moment the decision seems to be to define death in terms of the cessation of brain waves. But perhaps that is because we have not yet been able to restore the function of brain waves.

The important thing for us to observe is the fact that it is our definitions which allow certain judgments to be made. And such judgments mark the momentary limits of our powers. Thus we might construe definition as a statement of momentary limitations, some of which are readily overcome, some of which seem quite final. In politics our definitions are in constant change (as, for example, with the term "democracy"). An indication of the fact that no statement of limitations (or definitions) is final is that we cannot find an illustration exactly contrary to what we find in considerations of politics. We would only find areas in which definitions change more slowly.

The point of this digression is quite simple. The first steps of shaping raw nature into human environments are those that lead us to constructing definitions. From these definitions events are sorted, connected, and given form and meanings. To learn to think is to learn to define and to use definitions, as I will show in greater depth in the latter part of this book.

CURRENT DIFFICULTIES

The character of prevailing definitions of education.   A loose definition makes for loose speech, loose thinking, and loose writing. This is nowhere as evident as it is in the consideration of the definition of education.

We may either deny that there is or ever could be a clear definition, or we may insist that education is adequately defined as the transmission of knowledge and the attendant development of character. This transmission and development are the same thing to those who argue that we are what we know; for those who argue that we are not what we know, being indeed far more than our cognitions, there is no limit set upon critical comments to be made on the work of the institutions of education. This is because we really do not know the limits of the powers that transcend the cognitive effects of the educative process. Where either view prevails, then everyone assumes himself a proper critic of education, for he assumes knowledge of the limits in the process, even while he may admit little knowledge of the process. What is more to the point, with such a definition the institutions could not possibly be successful in their undertakings. The definition of education in this case would depend upon the further definition of the development of character and of the transmission of knowledge, additional processes whose functional limitations are assuredly not known. The former is all but undefinable, the second prone to categorial confusions. Developing character has no limit or final end, and thus the education designed to reach it has great difficulty in being measured finally, or along the way. The concept of transmitted knowledge is a source of dissatisfaction when it is discovered to be always on the verge of being erroneous and requiring definitional revision.

Perhaps because of this dilemma, education finds itself the constant center of critical, carping storms, with no way of establishing a defense.

In the introductory essay of *The Concept of Education,* Richard Peters[2] argues much as I have here, although rather more implicitly than explicitly. He writes that we talk about education in such a way that it prevents us from delimiting what we are talking about and prohibits us from coming to an agreement upon definitions. He argues that we have not been able (I prefer to add that we have not even been willing) to identify the specific task or field of activities to which the term education can be applied. As a result, analysis, discussion, inquiry, become all but hopeless.

Peters moves in the direction of a solution by recommending that we use the term *education* as we use the term *reform,* as an outcome word. The suggestion is a useful one, for it enables us to speak of education in a more limited, specific, and meaningful way. (One might wonder if this is the only path to such needed limitations.)

Clearly it is the actual recommendation he has made that is readily acceptable. The fact that we need to delimit the arena of examination recommends this view. But the specific suggestion that we ought to treat the term *education* as an outcome word presents other problems. Having said so much, we would still need to agree upon what we ought to look at. We cannot assume the very thing we are trying to discover. We must identify the outcome in order to prove that it is an outcome word, and so we have not moved very far in the direction of refinement and delimitation.[3]

One of the problems of education is precisely the fact that we cannot distinguish outcome from cause or motive from anticipation. Because we cannot establish such a relationship readily we are victims of any definition constructed by any observer, critic, or supporter of education whatsoever. Usually this turns out to be completely private, and produces more mischief than clarification and agreement.

What should be clear is that in such a complex event as education, any definition is going to be postulated for purposes of organizing certain of our experiences and deriving consistent and coherent

[2] Richard S. Peters, ed., *The Concept of Education* (London: Routledge Kegan and Paul, 1968).
[3] Israel Scheffler, *The Language of Education* (Springfield, Ill.: C. C. Thomas, 1960), Chs. 4 and 5. Scheffler's argument is more cogent because he identifies teaching as the achievement (or outcome) term, not the more general term education.

meanings from them. But just recommending definitions is only the beginning of this complicated activity. What now should be done is to use the definition—for talking about, thinking about, and examining those activities that seem to have been a fairly constant part of the familiar activity ordinarily called education; being on guard, however, to recognize that not everything carried on in its name is usefully called education.

A way not to go about defining aspects of education. A good way to proceed is to begin to analyze what happens when we do not attempt to distinguish the variety of activities that take place in educational situations. For example, what is the result of the acceptance of the idea that everything going on in the school is what is meant when we talk about education?

The first thing that becomes evident is that the failure to make distinctions within a broad life-activity leaves education the victim of vigorous, often cruel, and certainly demoralizing criticism. We are witness, in such cases, to "evaluations" which are not evaluations at all. Worse, these provide journalists, who have little awareness or understanding of a process that is open to and in need of examination, with the conviction that it is perfectly acceptable for them to impose their own expectations or desires and utilize categories of their unexamined social inheritance as the basis of comments.

What is worse, when newspaper men hear educators producing the same kind of superficial, sloganizing evaluations of education, what more do they need to make good copy out of it? It takes no great research to find newspaper articles which one might quote as evidence of this practice. What is ironic is the fact that while we recognize that scholars and students need to make a great issue of the press in education, the newspapers and popular journals themselves have become increasingly the primary arbiters of educational conceptual problems, not only for the public, but also for the profession itself. One day we find a director of a human resources council, which is identified in the press as an educational venture, confidently telling a room full of principals that fewer regulations and rules will result in better student behavior and performance. Such statements are seasonal and can be found in the daily press anywhere in the world, I predict. This becomes the basis of the view that he will present without further evidence, that there is a direct, comprehensible, and common sense relationship between the rules and regulations that constitute the proper conduct of a school and that learning process that we call education. Ambiguity is no deterrent. Indeed, it is a security for the speaker to assure his listeners that he is really not advocating schools without discipline. He is only looking for a different kind of discipline. Thus, the ambiguities pile up.

Now, one does not need to be an educator to make this kind of a comment at this level of precision and warrant. Any newspaperman could; any parent could; any political figure could; and it is to be suspected, even a television comedian could, if he wanted to make it part of a pattern of jokes on misbehaving children and despairing and confused parents. At this level the school director's comment has about as much merit and reveals about as much insight into what constitutes the act of educating as any one of these other persons. To urge that schools discontinue all examinations while nevertheless trying to measure student performances and potential is like urging someone to measure height without using a rule of any kind, or not to measure at all since measurement should be recognized as being self-revealing. It is to assume that growth is unfailingly self-evident at every moment. At best, tests in education measure thought applied to the resolution of both behavioral and intellectual problems. At worst, they measure inured habits of response or the mere ability to parrot previously memorized materials. The urging of abandonment of examinations rests on the assumption that either education is a self-evident set of acts and outcomes, or that neither of these really constitutes education. But if these do not, then what does constitute education? Inescapably we come back to the problem of definitions.

The growth of education depends on critical definitions.   It is interesting to observe how infrequently speakers offer genuine alternatives, or counterinstances, to what they are criticizing. And again, one can only assume that this failure is tied to the disposition taken toward the situations surrounding education; to the superficial notions that the ordinary man in the street can quickly understand and quickly respond to. It is taking advantage of the fact that support, meaning the public support, which the schools require, usually demands sloganizing. And, distressing as it may be to the committed, all too often the career of education depends upon these slogans.

It must be evident that the absence of limiting definitions continues to promote this pejorative criticism of education, compensated for only, when it is compensated for at all, by meaningless sentimentality about children.

We know, of course, that no discipline, no human undertaking dare be kept free of critical analysis. If one wanted deliberately to destroy the power of education, he need only to keep it from being treated critically. The history of authoritarian societies proves this. But there is a marked difference between that criticism whose purpose it is to analyze what constitutes the inner operation of events such as education, and the carping remarks that appear as the opinions of someone who has merely dredged up some idle image to satisfy his own yearning. There are no directives that can be examined and evaluated from such images.

This continues because leaders in education who participate in this kind of a game have spent too little effort in understanding what it is that they are about, and too much in issuing pronouncements which are meant to sound sage and statesmanlike. Administrative industry is, far too frequently, the only cover needed to protect this kind of sagacity.

It is the easiest thing in the world to criticize someone else's direction simply because it is not your direction. But this only leaves each of us open to being criticized by the man who speaks next in a sequence. At this point no agreement of any worth could possibly be reached. It is a mark of their status in the public mind that educators make assertions, pronouncements, or denunciations. They have learned that for the moment, and for many long moments until now, the way to power and to the headlines is through denunciation, or the cheerful assurance of breakthrough. For to praise education today seems to identify the speaker as a selfish person defending an undertaking in which he has a vested interest, or as someone who has not been able to see the handwriting on the wall, or both. And not to announce a breakthrough means you are not sincere in your concern for children.

Sometimes the criticism has within it the taint of an inappropriate cynicism. This is the joyless pronouncement of the fervent nihilists who seem to know the effect of this kind of denunciation on the public mind. It might appear as a prediction that no teaching is ever possible. The teacher's job in the future, it is argued, will be to direct pupils to the places where knowledge can be found. Thus, the teacher-dispenser will disappear. The logic of such an utterance is of no importance, only its safe iconoclasm. It is of no significance to them that the second part of such a pronouncement is already entailed in the first, which they are now denying, and thus words have merely been shifted around, for purposes of effect. What is said is that the teacher will tell the children what they should know by telling them where to go to find out what they will need to know. This is tautological—it must be because there is really only one process here, with several phases. Any difference is one of sequence. Education never *has* called for the kind of dispensing such a critic thinks it did. And certainly directing someone to a source *does* require imparting knowledge, unless we are playing blind man's buff.

Telling and finding.   But somehow as it is pronounced, there does appear a great difference. It is thought that if the teacher gives the boy the definition of a word, he is not educating him. But if he tells him to go to the dictionary and look it up for himself, then he is.

Should this be accepted as serious criticism? Should this be accepted as the insight of an educator peering into the very process that is involved? Should we allow the act of opening a book, and running down a list of words until one finds the one he wants, to define the act of education? The definition would thus include a book's revealed meanings, but exclude the teacher telling the student the meaning. Is education a matter of ocular but not oral experience? In either case teachers would be progressively less able to satisfy their pupils' desire for knowledge as the body of knowledge increases and the store of information expands. But this has ever been the case.

There were very few Renaissance men—men who supposedly knew everything that was to be known—in the Renaissance. All the rest, even in the best of times, struggled with limited knowledge and the severer limitations of common sense. In that day, too, people had to be educated. They, too, had to learn to read and to become proficient in science, and not all of them did. Nor is it hard to believe that in any age a teacher would suddenly come up with the rather tricky little idea of not telling the students anything, of allowing them to find out for themselves.

But what does this signify? What occurs when the child finds out for himself? He comes back to the class and he tells the teacher what he has found. Two things can then happen. The teacher listens appreciatively, but without comment, which would be absurd. Or he listens and tells the pupil truthfully that he is right, lending his authority, or that he is wrong, that he looked in the wrong place. The child would then have a perfect right to say: "If you thought I was likely to look in the wrong place, and the answer is so important, why didn't you tell me so right from the start and save me all this difficulty?" The teacher might say, "I wanted to see if you could do it right," or "You learn best by the mistakes you make." In spite of what is known today as the principle of reinforcement, this is a questionable way of teaching, for it seems to make education an unfair contest. The child is the recipient of penalty, and the penalty is for erring. His aim becomes avoidance of error, and the absence of error means the absence of conscious understanding. In the absence of consciousness of understanding there is also an absence of the consciousness of error. Thus, whatever is learned and not challenged by adults is learned and reinforced, even if this is negative reinforcement. It is in this way that so much that is absorbed becomes a block of further learning.

Teaching and guiding—a specious disjunction. But more and more we hear the argument that teachers should no longer teach. We are thus treated to the argument that teaching is really not teaching but guiding. But what is guiding? What can we point to that is like guiding? Some of the analogies that are created to show what is meant are just as coercive as the coercive teaching being avoided.

It was said that Socrates was not really a teacher, but a midwife. He said so himself, many times. But we recognize that Socrates, at least, had great wit and that it is not always clear how serious he was about this. The result produces much confusion, for when our friends and leaders say the same thing, they apparently are very serious. Is it because they are victims of the belief that to teach is to transmit knowledge? Is it for this reason that they do not want teachers to teach? Is it because knowledge should not be received, but reached?

There can be found no better illustration of how little agreement there is of the meaning of *teaching* than that we now argue as to whether or not teachers ought to teach. What could it possibly be— this act of teaching—that the teacher is unable, or forbidden to do it? Taking this to its logical conclusion, then, schools will no longer school, and education will no longer educate.

What is left?

Guidance.

But this only produces the next obvious question: what is guidance, and how is the direction for it to be determined? The moment that the question of the meaning of guidance is raised, the outcome is inevitable. We find ourselves coming back to the question of which particular interpretation of teaching ought to be taken seriously and considered in clinical detail.

But why is there this confusion, which inevitably ends in pejorative statements? Perhaps it is because what we should have been examining in the term education is the one thing we have failed to look at. The teacher's role in the future, as it is now argued, will be to help pupils find the resources they will need. Surely this will have to include helping them individually and collectively to gather together their knowledge and skill into patterns, patterns that will help them lead full and rewarding lives within the present or future social-cultural contexts. Just suppose that the resources do not exist, and suppose the knowledge that is needed does not exist. And suppose the skill that is needed turns out to be the wrong skill or does not exist? Then what does the teacher do? Where does he lead the learners? Is it feasible to consider education critically and not consider these significant possibilities?

If all of the knowledge that we ever needed were already known, explicitly and implicitly, and all of the skills that we ever needed already existed, explicitly and implicitly, would there be the continuing perplexity that does exist? Is it not the case that this changing world seems always on the verge of getting totally out of hand, beyond the control of the knowledge, the skills and the instruments available? In the failure to make an accurate critical examination of what is being said, the teacher and the teaching profession as a whole absolve themselves of their fundamental responsibility and place responsibility on the child. Literally this is what is being said: There is so much knowledge in the world now that teachers cannot encompass enough to teach by, and therefore, the learner must find knowledge for himself. Of course, the question of why a learner can learn while a teacher apparently cannot is never raised, though perhaps it ought to be.

Apparently this line of argument does not hold up. There is really no need, and even less merit, in clinging to the premises that education is simply the transmittal of knowledge, and development of a character consistent with that prevailing fund of knowledge. With this approach to the educative process, what is there to hope for? In such an approach where shall we find sources for the criticisms of education such that the public might begin to understand the long hours and the most intensely diligent kind of intellectual competence required to make these criticisms? The dilemmas that education faces in a world constantly in change arise from rapidly accumulating knowledge, and not simply from mechanical breakdown in transmission. And this accumulation is itself dependent upon the invention of new, more refined categories and instrumentations by means of which our knowledge of the world and indeed the world itself is shaped.

The continuity between levels of education—between theory and practice. One further common criticism comes from the schools or school journals. There is a well-worn cliché that university faculty members should take a year off every few years and spend it in lower-school classrooms. Such a visit, it is argued, would bring them down to earth and give them a chance to reach past the ivory towers of theory into the genuine world of practice. This is an example of the most distressing failure to comprehend the relationship between what goes on at the university and what goes on in the classroom. In fact, it is simply a perpetuation of the notion that has been held for so long, that what the university does at its level has nothing to do with what the primary and secondary schools do at theirs. It is perpetuated in the inexcusable derogation that a young teacher sometimes hears when he appears for the first time at a school, prepared to teach, and the principal, in what must surely be intended as great comfort, says, "Glad to have you aboard. Now tell me, where did you do your university training?" "Oh, at Simon Fraser." (or "Queens College," or "Harvard University.") "Wonderful—great school. Now, let me tell you. Forget everything you learned. You are really going to learn to teach here in the school itself. All you got there is theory. But you had better forget the theory. Here you will really learn to teach."

If we are asked to take this seriously we find ourselves victimized, when, day after day throughout the year, newspapers print nothing but castigations of education and educators, because these denunciations are made upon a set of practices that are not theoretically based. And, distressingly, the louder voices in this castigation belong to those in positions of authority, the educational decision-makers who might have taken the time to understand the theoretical grounding of their daily activities, but who have failed to do so because it was too difficult or no longer seemed relevant.

The clay pigeon is the classroom teacher who has little means of defending himself. He has, by professional indifference or public indisposition, been deprived of the right to employ his theoretical grounding in giving an account of why he continues to do certain things in the classroom. How shall we treat the fact that he has been told by his superiors to "forget everything learned at the university"?

At its best such advice rests on the conviction that we do not learn to teach by thinking about preparing for teaching. We learn to teach by teaching. At its worst it is the advice of a frightened bankrupt. It is like telling a scientist that he will not learn science by thinking; that he will learn science only by doing experiments, through sheer trial and error. It is like telling the member of any profession or discipline not to think, but to do. If it is done often enough, one is led to believe, professional competence inevitably develops. There is, of course, a rough truth in this, but so rough as to be useless. There is so much more to any profession that at best such assertions are cruel oversimplifications.

But there is yet another side to all this. The odd assumption that educationists teaching at the university level have no contact with the classroom at the elementary or the secondary levels is obviously an argument designed to win a point, not to clarify any issue or idea. Before anyone makes a statement such as this, he ought to assure himself of what he is saying. Since he is making a claim that is factual and demonstrable, he really ought to present the evidence for his statements. One would be tempted to think that the most oppressive part of such a comment is its falsity. For almost all of this century the pattern of programs in teacher education in North America has obliged its faculty to maintain open channels with the lower schools. The increasing use of lower school faculty brought in to the university is a leaven for developing teacher-education curricula.

This uncritical insistence on making the separation between the university and the lower school is an unhappy portent for the future of education. Of course, one can understand this as well as one can understand that the social force of education seems to compel its leaders to make themselves heard through the public prints. Their pieties have to be known in terms that the general public can appreciate and find comforting. They must know that someone is on guard against every educational villainy, acting as the people's voice in the institutions of learning.

Public demands and professional responsibilities.   Yet it is not in such journals or newspapers that education develops, but in the pages of professional journals where the concepts are shaped, argued out, and refined. Most journalists would have difficulty reading the critical analyses that appear in professional journals and technical books. Impatient at what they consider needless complication, journalists often seek out some members of a panel or conference for an interview. With controlled impatience they ask simple questions because, after all, the public has to read what is written. Educators are too often flattered at the opportunity to appear in newsprint. The idea of becoming a leader is irresistible. If the newspaperman asks a fatuous question, the educator is quite prepared to give a fatuous answer. In the effort to make sure that the public understands the issue, the pronouncements made usually reduce education to nothing but a social-political affair. In the common eagerness to appeal to the community, it is all too apparent that the integrity of the idea of education is the expendable commodity.

But pandering to the public is significantly different from being sensitive to the public weal. The difference may be found in the fact that only in the latter does a disciplined profession apply continuous evaluative procedures to the way things function, not simply acknowledge the desires of the moment.

As with any complex profession these two levels of interest show strong contrasts and are often quite inimical to one another. Public pressures oblige us to seek simple, concise opinions in the form of conclusions. An advancing discipline seeks only the opportunity to explore more critically and analyze more cogently whatever ideas are offered. But in education the two levels are constantly being reduced to one in such terms that the concern for thoughtful definition and for more precise explanation is lost in the desire for public appeal.

In place of the intellectual independence, a fundamental necessity for the growth of any profession, there is a prevalence of bandwagon movements. In fact, educators in general are notorious bandwagoneers. A good slogan, a catchy phrase, will start a movement that can be kept going for a satisfying period of time. Sometimes the very idea of slogans is defended as performing a vital, unifying function of decision-making. But those who benefit are those who control the slogans, not those who follow them. For the latter there is the security of the patriot.

Let us consider briefly just one of the more recent bandwagon movements, the movement to expand involvement in writing a school or a class curriculum.

There is a current insistence that students must write the curriculum, as not too many years ago there was insistence that the community must help write the curriculum. But what *is* a curriculum that students are able to write it? Or a community? Consider the prospects of the democratization of medicine; of the patient telling the doctor what operation he wants and how he wants his operation to proceed. I summon my doctor and say, "Now you follow my plan because after all, this operation affects me. I have the right to make the decision about it. Besides, I know where the pain is."

Predicated on the same logical procedure a student writes his curriculum. Yet we know that this could never be seriously entertained in any fully developed discipline. You cannot ask the general public how a bridge should be built, or out of what materials, what length it should be, by how much tensile strength it should be supported. Perhaps the problem is an overextension of a reasonable approach. An automobile salesman may ask you what color you want the car to be. He may even ask what power the driver wants, what type of cooling system, and so on. You can, indeed, ask what shapes and colors in bridges most please the public, and where they might be built. But if the engineer-architect is going to put up a bridge, it is hardly rational to ask the public for preferences in matters in which preference is irrelevant. The public must, of course, approve appearances, select sites, decide the expenditures, even choose among accredited designers and builders. But in the technical matters of the materials to be used and how the bridge is to be suspended and how many pilings are to be sunk, and in what form, it would be the height of absurdity to ask the common man to make such decisions. The stories of graft and fraud in such undertakings, where money has been saved, pleasing the public but creating problems in function, attest to the need for something more than public approval.

In a mature discipline the very conditions for membership are publicized well enough so that even the public recognizes that to know the structure and the use of these materials requires some period of diligent study of the theories on which rest knowledge of such facts as the tensile strength of steel or cast iron, or the expandability of different kinds of cement and the relation of an arc to sustaining buttresses, and so on. The public generally recognizes that it lacks competence in such a field, and so is reluctant to intrude its advice upon those who have studied and become qualified. Nor is it the public but the profession itself which establishes and examines the qualifications for entry into a given profession.

But when leaders identify the significant level of comprehension that is required to understand education, and make common sense the expert voice in the field, then the discipline should worry more about its leadership than the public they are seeking to impress. Worse, it marks a condition of internecine conflict which must first be resolved before the discipline itself can grow to full and mature responsibility. Such leaders contribute nothing to the development of education as a field of study.

THE WAY TO THE NEW WORLD

Creating a discipline. The argument thus far is designed to point up the necessity of making a beginning in defining the field within which the study of education may be pursued. Of all the steps we might take to achieve this, the greatest impact would come from outlining controls for teaching practices. We need to demonstrate how lesson plans are created, what materials they must involve, and how the various levels of explanatory models permit different matters to transact with one another. We must explore how such ministerings make it possible for students to do things that they would otherwise never have been able to do. This is not a random matter, arrived at through endowed inspiration. It is a matter to be researched more and more intently until we come out with a reservoir of instrumental statistics and evidence of how the use of certain transacting models produces certain consequence. This is, at this point admittedly vague, but I trust it will become clearer as the work unfolds.

If such research were produced, education would never again be victimized by news-level analyses. It seems as if educators live in two totally different worlds. The first is the world of the public press, where we are constantly writing easy-to-understand condemnations—and all too often they must be condemnations—to appeal to the public, in order to let the public know that we are not taken in by ourselves or by our own comrades and colleagues. Beyond this there is the other, conceptual, world of education that sets upon us tasks of great intellectual complexity. Educators, just as well as anybody else, do know that what they are doing is often inept. But professional ineptitude is very different from what the uninitiated, who are after magical pathways to power and wealth, call inept. It must be shown that professionals have the courage to admit professional ineptitude. It is all too evident that gracefully appealing admissions of common sense failure will always be popular. But these accolades often distract from a concern for more significant inadequacies. Such easy "coin" creates a kind of a Gresham's Law within intellectual undertakings: bad ideas formed in abundance drive out the good.

The disposition for a discipline.   A discipline begins with the assumption that what is done is done honestly and must be examined with the same spirit. Within a discipline the primary disposition that must prevail is the appreciation of every member of the community for every other member of the community. If that does not exist, all that remains is lacerating personal warfare. Perhaps warfare is not the right term, perhaps it is more like a game in which we clash the empty covers of trash cans against one another, making loud noises and little sense. What we need to do is to turn our attention to the processes involved, and away from the personalities of the practitioners. We know, of course, that people are involved. But our more immediate concerns are the materials of experience that we possess, and the models by means of which we describe and explore, define and explain, and interpret and evaluate, those materials. When we learn to concentrate in this manner, some of the aggressions which are communicated as considered educational opinions may at last begin to dissolve.

Nor can there be envy in the practices of a genuine discipline. However much envy plays its psychological role in any human undertaking, intellectual disciplines grow only when respect and a kind of a loving appreciation obtains for whoever it was enabled us to see a little more, and understand a little more, than we could a moment ago, a week ago, or a year ago. What in the materials which have been presented has enabled us to see anything more than we saw a moment ago? Can you recall anything which you have read in the public prints, at the journalistic level, that has enabled you to see more than you see now, or has given you more than nugatory data and mere opinion? If this cannot be done, then news reporting stands as an even greater deterrent to the development of a profession or a discipline than an indifferent or rebellious community. If it can be done, then we must be grateful for the contribution, infrequent though it may be.

Must education, in its present amorphous state, remain only a near profession? Near, as a union organization is near? Or may it be transformed into an undertaking with a theoretical basis as the primary area of study and analysis, and with its processes under continuous inquiry so that the explanatory systems which identify it can be constantly improved?

Here lies the moral of the educational venture. Do we cater to people in positions of authority simply because they are the holders of the purse or because we do not know how to separate the realm of politics from the realm of intellectual development? Is there not a distinctive loyalty that a scholar must accept—loyalty to the work itself? Clearly this is a crucial question. An educator must recognize his moral obligation to his profession and to other educators. Entailed in this is the obligation not to gloss over the complexities of the inquiry in order to cultivate the good will of the general public.

The new world of education begins, for each future inhabitant, with the disposition to shape a discipline on the ground of a loyalty to intelligence, and to its continuing development.

With this in mind, the next chapter moves to a reconsideration of some of the problems already introduced, but at a much more critical level, and in a more disciplined language.

CHAPTER 3

Intimations of
The New World:
Educating and Expressing

PROCESS AND PURPOSE

Problems with the definition of education.   Consider now what has been construed to be the process of education. In any exploration whose purpose is the analysis of some complex task, there is the need for much clarification before the identity of the role of that task can be established. However, in this particular quest for definition there is, unfortunately, no agreed upon source of information. It is not to be determined as simply as the age of a tree can be read from the cross section of a tree trunk. If a dissection or cross section is in order, it will be strictly metaphoric. Not even a large dictionary can give a definition of education that is beyond argument or doubt. In fact, the "process of education" appears to be the kind of concept that we must create in deliberate agreement as we continue to relate to one another.

If agreement is required, we must make sure that the definition we establish is quite distinctive. We need to avoid reaching definitions that are ambiguous and vague. We must be able to talk about education in such a way that we know what is being included and what is being excluded.

Thus, we have two problems. First, we need to come to agreement as to what kind of an act can be called an educational act; and on the same basis, what kind of an act is not to be called an educational act, however much it may appear to us as educational.

Second, we need to determine the kind of activities to be included within the educational activity, and what kind of activities must be resolutely excluded.

The reason for these propositions is clear. We have grown up in what is loosely called a profession. We quite unspecifically call it "educational" when what appears to be desirable consequences are produced. Outcomes that seem to satisfy, add information, alter a habit and result in a better habit, or delight—all of these being, of course, willed and desirable—we eagerly call outcomes of the process of education.

If this is the case, then consider what else would have to fit within that definition. Going to a baseball game and watching our team win is an education, since it gives us great pleasure and is, therefore, quite desirable. In some emotional way we have identified with the team. Our dispositions and behaviors expand. However, if the team keeps losing, we are also being educated, because we are being frustrated and our frustrations enable us to appreciate our fulfilments. Thus, even frustration is beneficial.

What has been described is a variation of a much more significant and much more familiar activity. It is argued that just about anything that we do today that has the characteristic of a dignified undertaking has an educational consequence. Any involvement whatever with art really is education. It is not always clear how such a claim is made, but what seems to be meant is that going to the museum often enough and learning to enjoy pictures there can produce an educated man. It is hard to state precisely what one is being educated about, or for, or in, but the growing ability to enjoy pictures is given as evidence of being educated. In a similar manner, by learning to draw in order to express oneself one is being educated; for, in so doing there is opportunity to partake in the very act of expression.

But if we examine the language used in such assertions, we find, quite surprisingly, that mere absorption of certain material is presented as proof of the presence of educative process. But the last statement makes an additional claim, and thus adds much to the previous assertions. For, in the last view, education occurs only where what has been absorbed is manifested. Such claims, which do not follow logically from any previous assumptions, illustrate that there are certain unrecognized conditions present. By attaching random clauses to explain things that have not been accounted for, theory is avoided.

Education and modified behavior.   In all of us there are certain natural functions that form the pattern of our behavior, our development, and that are modified as a result of experience. Yet one of the most widely held definitions of education has made the consequences just mentioned a curious impediment to the understanding of the processes by which they develop. Education, it is claimed, is the modification of behavior. Logically, (because we are here dealing with equivalences) this means that whenever behavior has been modified, education has taken place. Otherwise we would have to say that some education does not modify behavior, or some modified behavior is not educationally derived. Now, we could hardly say that some modified behavior was not modified behavior, or that some education was not education.

But the very identification of education and behavior in the definition leads to difficulty, when the equivalence is accepted. For, we are aware that there are ways of modifying behavior that few would want to call educational. For example, if we are continuously threatened with being denied admission to the classroom for entering without saying "hello," in order to avoid being excluded we will develop the habit of giving the greeting. Since the threat modified our behavior, it must have educated us. But what is gained by calling this trivial outcome "education"? Moreover, what actually occurred that we were conscious of? The question we are left with is this: Do we want the word "education" to apply to that kind of outcome?

The sense of absurdity surrounding the concept of education has arisen because we have been unable to separate what might be called *natural* aspects of human development from what we deliberately do about that natural development. And curiously, because we have been unable to propound a logical separation, we have tended to consider them empirically identical. It is thus only a step to the view that anything that happens in life is educational. If it is, then the responsibility of teachers and of schools ought to be consistent with this notion. That would oblige us to ask why we need any kind of a formal structure if life itself educates. In fact, in the context of such beliefs formal structures must inevitably be less than genuine education. The education would be as artificial as the fictional categories that direct it. Moreover, since we also are convinced that it is nature which is harmonious and man who is anarchic and chaotic (as Rousseau argued), we cannot trust man to educate the child in the context of that most artificial of all constructs—society. We can only trust nature itself. Schools run by men could never equal in value the school of the forest. Let the child learn to read the signs in the trees and in the sky. Let him see what happens to the birds and the animals. In that way he will learn science, art, history, and medicine, as well. If he should ever climb a tree and fall out of it, he would, by natural intuition, learn how to bind up his wounds. And let the child's teacher also take the direction for his ministering from nature itself.

It may seem futile to argue this all over again. We ought not to waste time. And, indeed, this would be good advice were it not for the fact that in the lingering romantic haze that surrounds so many views of the human spirit, too many of us still cling to such a demonology. Nature (sometimes we put another "natural" word in its place: experience) will correct all the mistakes that, as teachers, we must inevitably make. For nature is purer than demon man, and is thus a better, more consistent teacher.

However, the role of teaching alters if we recognize that not every learned act of every individual can be meaningfully construed as an educated act. It is for this reason, that there is the need to define education more limitedly, and more precisely. We need to be able to sort out those acts which are evidence of education from those which are not. Curiously enough, agreement is quite easily reached, if an effort is exerted.

We must look for criteria for this distinguishing process. The first that usually occurs, considering our social coercions, is the moral criterion. We thus begin with the notion that education produces behavior and knowledge which can be characterized as good and virtuous. Not everything good that happens is educative, it will be argued, but everything educative is good. There can be no avoidance of an early consideration of education in terms of values. Education is a means of attaining what men consider good and desirable. In this it shares the quality of virtue that is also to be found in the practice of medicine. But the practice of medicine is understood to be a restorative virtue. One does not ordinarily go to a doctor unless one is not well, or suspects his health is failing, or is going into a situation where there will be a threat to health. Thus, medicine, when properly practiced, has the virtue of restoring the ill to good health or sustaining the health already obtaining.

The virtue of the practice of medicine is thus quite clear. In so far as it is practiced competently, it has the virtue of keeping us in good health or restoring us to good health.

But now consider. (I might be thought to be cribbing here from some of Plato's Dialogues, say, parts of the *Meno,* and of the *Protagoras,* so familiar is this line of reasoning.) In and of itself medicine, as an arena of study and research, has neither virtue nor lack of virtue. It is simply a process, a concern with expanding the understanding of the human condition and producing external conditions required for maintaining it at a level of normal functioning. It is in this sense that medicine has no intrinsic value. It has, rather, instrumental value, for it is that instrument which enables us to maintain the conditions required to do what we have decided needs to be done. As an area of study, then, medicine has no other than this instrumental value.

Is this also the case with education? Others, John Dewey, for example, have not been altogether clear on this. One would expect him to see the value of education as instrumental. Thus a discreet definition would suggest the necessity of making diagnoses first of the condition of those who come to learn, and second of the social, moral, economic, political conditions, within which the processes of learning and of teaching operate. But Dewey also wrote, with great emphasis, that education has no goal other than itself.[1] That would suggest that it is an *intrinsic* value. How, then, can we bring into harmony the instrumental aspect, which is that the use of education is to create certain conditions in the learner that would render him capable of choosing and performing acts that he desires, and that have value for him; and the intrinsic aspect, which is that the idea of education has a value in and of itself, not dependent on what external goals it attains.

This would seem nothing but a verbal dilemma, were it not for the fact that it is still the subject of dispute, especially in higher education. But if we approach the problem in terms, not of education, but of the act of educating, then perhaps what may appear to be a contradiction is not at all. (The same might also, afterward, be applied to the study of medicine. This would enable us to explain what we know to be the case anyway—namely, that medicine *is* studied for its own sake.) In the active sense, "educating" demands the study of a procedure, an examination of the purposes entailed in that very procedure just

[1] John Dewey, *Democracy and Education* (New York: Macmillan Co., 1916), pp. 59ff.

as medicine is studied for purposes entailed in the procedures of the medical undertaking. In this sense, education (using the noun as Dewey did in this case) has no goal other than education. But the "process of education" is translatable as "the nurture of human powers to a degree not otherwise attainable." And in this sense we might say, curious as it sounds, that at a certain level the study of education has an intrinsic value, sustained by the instrumentality of effectiveness.

The act of educating and the act of expressing.   If education is seen as a process for fostering abilities, we can say that it is possible to educate a person to produce a work of art. But the work of art itself is not the educative act. It is an expressive act. This difference between the act of education and the act of expression is of some importance. Education here is clearly of instrumental value. It is the means by which we achieve what we choose to achieve. It is even the means of making choices. But art, as the act of expression, is the manifestation, or the outcome, of what we have chosen to achieve. It is this difference between the achieving and the achievement, between the traveling and the arrival, that we must bear in mind. On the whole, education is far more fruitfully thought of as the former, the achieving, the traveling.

But what makes for some difficulty here is the fact that in principle we may accomplish whatever education produces, but without deliberate education. It is not likely, but it is at least possible. It is possible for an individual to develop the capacity to perform the most intricate surgery without ever going through the formal and formed educational process that is deliberately designed to enable him to do this. And, indeed, precisely because this capacity is not likely to develop without some special nurturing activities, we plan the procedures of education.

It is quite possible for a person to invent a new system of mathematics without ever having gone to school or studied mathematics. It is possible, of course, but not very likely. Physical theories are developed by physicists, not dancers.

Implicit in these illustrations are some of the intrinsic purposes of education, as well as some of the limitations which this same intrinsic quality imposes on it. There is a function of education which is concerned with making certain that human beings develop some capacities that might have developed by themselves had nature but had the wit and purpose to organize its own powers. This alone would be a respectable reason for the creation of schools. To foster what nature might foster and to do it in such a way that leaves us independent of the waywardness of an unconcerned nature is surely a good reason for education. Of course, this is not to say that man cannot and will not develop capacities *not* vouchsafed by nature. The point here is that *a* purpose of education is to produce the natural in an increasingly efficacious way.

One of the best illustrations of this is the one that Dewey uses in *Art As Experience*.[2] Most people are overawed by someone who seems to be an unquestioned genius. Such a person possesses, by nature, a power which seems to defy all the known rules of education. The man who is a brilliant dancer but never took a lesson in his life leaves us in a state of educational futility. The man who shows possession of a magnificent tenor voice and never took a lesson in his life is a living testimony to the limitations of deliberate education. And, of course, there is always poor hectored Mozart who, at the age of four, never having taken a lesson in his life, was already writing quite respectable music.

The more we consider these illustrations of geniuses who "never took a lesson in their lives" the more we seem to be denigrating education as a viable undertaking. No amount of education, we are advised, will produce a Mozart. We would have to redefine the term out of all recognition in order to show that Mozart's accomplishments were educational consequences. No amount of education will produce the great dancer or the great runner, or the mathematician. It is even pointed out from time to time, quite smugly, that Albert Einstein failed courses in mathematics in his college career.

The best we can conclude from such considerations is that education is a deterrent in the presence of genius. Genius must be freed in order to manifest itself in the great mathematicians, musicians, artists, scientists, and education does not facilitate that freedom. But again, we are too close to the confusion produced by the failure to distinguish between what education does and what expression does, to see that expression is a manifestation of one's educational nurture, formal or informal. It is the source for the further refinement of educative activities.

The effort to see the distinction may be better served if we take

<hr>

2 John Dewey, *Art as Experience* (New York: Minton Balch, 1934). One could find no more penetrating analysis of this whole problem than in this work, and particularly Ch. 4, where he analyzes "expression" more critically than I do here, for other purposes. Our conclusions differ somewhat, too.

a closer look at some of the connections between education and expression. Dewey points out that what a genius does intuitively is an illustration of what education seeks to accomplish deliberately and predictably. Left to its own devices, nature, which is not as dependable as Rousseau would have us believe, may leave a gap of a hundred years or more between the great mathematicians that it produces. Education is constructed in order not to have to wait that hundred years, only to produce *one* such mathematician.

Thus we find at least one connection between education and the expressions of genius. The ways of genius become models for the educative process. Yet it must be observed that any expression can be used to serve this function. The expression of genius serves as a purer and more economic model than most. It is said, and apparently quite correctly, that a reasonably good high school student in the middle of the twentieth century, knows more physics than did Galileo, for all his genius. This always appears to be a pretentious and absurd claim to many people, especially to those who have difficulty in separating the expression of genius from the function of education.

Genius is realistically considered as an intensification, almost an unbalanced capacity, to perform one particular act powerfully, rapidly, exclusively, precisely, or all of these at once. In this lies its economy. Thus, it would appear a joke to say that the average high school student in the modern world knows more about physics than Galileo ever did. But if we consider it for a moment, we discover the other strand of the connection between education and expression. Education, though it may not give birth to genius, undoubtedly gives shape or form to it. Compared with a modern student, Galileo had very few people whose work he could study. Ptolemy, Copernicus, Kepler, Tycho, Bacon, a few others, had come to grips with the problems of constructing rules and theories for predicting and explaining nature. And undeniably it was his study of these men that formed the quality and direction of Galileo's research and theory. But the modern high school student has not only Copernicus, Galileo, and the others, but all scientific knowledge accumulated since that time, the most numerous of its contributors being alive today. From all of this the modern student inherits an enormous reservoir of just those theories, rules and methods, as well as the experiments made possible by them, which characterize the intellectual furnishings of twentieth century civilization. With these instrumentalities an ordinary high school student would, if he had lived in the seventeenth century with Galileo, have been quite powerful, intellectually.

The educative processes, made consonant with the insights expressed in the workings of the occasional geniuses, produce thinkers whose capacity for intelligent selection is so great that the ordinary man of today would have been an incomparable genius three hundred years ago. Einstein made this same point in a wry and modest way. When he was being praised for his genius, he commented that the genius of one century is recognized as slightly below average two centuries later. And Newton, of course, stood on the shoulders of Galileo.

The sorting-out tools and procedures. Apparently our failure to determine with any precision an acceptable definition of education and to explore a model of the structure referred to by that definition deprives us of perspective in seeing what the educative process does with individuals from generation to generation. Our prevailing loose definitions oblige us to look for and to idolize genius, while we minimize the education of ordinary man. In the functioning of education we organize the components of the segments of the world experienced to order to give them coherence. To accomplish this, education must direct itself toward nurturing in every individual the capacity to understand, to organize, and to explain in his own way the world of his individual, often private encounter.

The outcome of education, once again, is expression. The educational act itself is not so much an expression as it is a concern for the nurturing of the *power* of expression. We are all of us congeries of quivering sensibilities. We know of five senses. Sometimes people insist upon the presence of a sixth sense, and beyond these perhaps extra-sensory powers. All of these face the wide, active world, the context of our living. The world pours in upon us through these sensibilities or sensitivities and we sort them out with the means available.

In the terms thus far described, we can deduce that the first function of the educative process is to make it possible to exercise selectivity upon the stimuli that keep pouring in. Of course, sometimes the physical organism undergoes arrest, shock, or pain. The powers of the body engaged in the sorting-out process are debilitated and are less able, or totally unable, to operate in sorting out stimuli. The categories simply cannot be used.

The disease known as aphasia, for example, which is a destruction of certain of the nerve receptors along the spine and in the brain, makes impossible the sorting-out of noises. It also makes it impossible to record stimuli. The absence of such recording makes recall impossible. Thus, people suffering from aphasia must finally protect themselves against noise since they cannot produce any order out of it. Most important, people suffering from aphasia suffer from lack of memory, which becomes manifest as a lack of the ability to identify the sounds heard even a moment ago. This explanation directs us to translate the whole physical process metaphorically into the conceptual, and we often speak of *intellectual* aphasia. The illuminating part of this is to be noted in the use we make of the physical process as a model for explaining a conceptual process.

But even when the organism is whole, this sorting-out power needs literally to be *brought* to an operating level, for it is a mental *act* we are considering. And it is in the educational system that the child learns to use the intellectual tools, called categories or classifications, made available to him. By means of them he sorts out external stimuli, giving distinctive meanings to them, meanings, incidentally, "embedded" in the sorting models used. When he sorts these out, the world makes "sense." The child who does not have control of these cognitive classifications or categorizing systems is said to live in a "senseless" (meaningless) world.

So education is designed to equip a child with classifying or categorizing systems. When a child listens to a piece of music and he is able to sort out the instruments of the orchestra, he is doing something which to begin with, or by nature, we might say, he was only potentially equipped to do. This potentiality becomes actuality when he learns to sort them out in some classroom where a teacher helped him to identify and employ categories, such as *piano,* and *violin,* and *cello,* and *flute,* and others. Although we do not usually think of these as categories, but as terms, this is precisely how they can be used.

When he has learned to employ these categories, he can listen to the piece of music and say that he has just picked out—which literally he did, in terms of sound quality—the piano. He may not yet have heard the flute. But the teacher, more competent in the use of this particular category, will know that it is there. The category may then be isolated and presented again until, in some peculiar way, perhaps very painstaking, perhaps very primitive, perhaps awkward, perhaps simply by repetition, the mind finally sorts it out of all the sounds he is hearing. Then suddenly the two phase together and the other sounds in this moment are trapped and separated out to leave only the flute sound for consideration. At that moment he does not hear the piano or the violin, only sound as such.

When we think of these events as categorial systems, as languages which are not verbal but tonal, we discover again the power to distinguish the metaphoric voice of a piano from the voice of a flute. And these are different voices that the children can be made to use. To understand what it means to equip a learner to recognize them as sorting-categories, and to enable him to use them to discover meanings in experience, is to understand the kind of thing that education does, and how it does it.

THE LEARNER EQUIPPED

The sorting-powers and control of experiences. So much for the moment, then, with the matter of equipping the child. Now let us consider briefly the child equipped. He is now the child in the world. He has achieved some more or less effective way of using categories enabling him to cope with a world that was until then quite beyond him. To see just how dramatic this can be, consider the change in a person who has to learn a new language in a new country. After a time, how gratifying it is for him to note that speech that was once so rapid, confusing and threatening, has become almost entirely comprehensible and, in fact, is quite luminous in its meaningfulness.

Anyone who has ever learned the language of a foreign country will know what is being described. A new world has come to take on a different character, certainly less alien and confusing. And it does so only because there has been developed a capacity to use categories that will sort out what had been unsortable, indeed, indiscriminable. We have all probably had the experience of talking to somebody who just barely spoke our language, and who said, "Do not talk so fast. Please speak more slowly." His problem is that where speech is too rapid, categorial controls are not efficient enough. Slowing up prevents too many stimuli from pouring in so that those which are received can be sorted out without missing sounds and meanings.

The consequences of sorting-out, and the limits of those consequences. It is in this sense that we may consider the learner equipped. Through use of a sorting-out system the ability to control experience has appeared. It is possible for one who is equipped to discover in the world qualities he did not know existed. The discoveries produce that human response which is each man's alone. They produce a desire to speak to a world that has been suddenly made intelligible, if not articulate. Need and capacity both appear. We are able to react to the world in its now observed facets. We can feel it, delight in it, and even decide what we would rather not see again. We might tell the world itself of these new visions. We might picture for the world the completion of promises made but not yet fulfilled. And would not this, then, be our expressions? Our sciences, or our works of art?

And what is a work of art? It is the outcome of precisely this described power developed. In a work of art, man is expressing, through categories that he has learned to control, his appreciation of this newly discovered world. He makes manifest the awe, delight, and terror it inspires in him.

But the art that is produced is not itself the educating act in our now limited sense. It is not the deliberate, organized effort at enabling anyone else to develop a capacity that he did not have. It is simply man tangibly expressing himself, sometimes to himself, sometimes to others in the context of the world in which he is living. It is the expression which is persuasion, illusion, and revelation. In this sense art is always more appealing than education. That is why people, both children and adults, prefer play to school. Play is akin to art; and play, especially for children, has little to do with education. This is why children love to go to the cinema but not to the classroom. This is why children love to watch television, but not to do homework. This is why the "lover" in the classroom is preferred to the teacher.

Of course, the knowledge of this leads to—and has almost always led to—the innocent recommendation that it would be logical and clever to make education fun. Unfortunately, when pursued, it does not take too long before education becomes eliminated in the name of the fun. This is what newspapers do. The excitement of the reporting displaces the subject itself. The use of supposed esthetic powers becomes so obsessive that children and readers are simply esthetized. It is argued, though not in these terms, that it is possible to esthetize them enough so that they cease being conscious of the learning that needs to go on. Since they can be expected to drift off into the delights of the esthesis that derives from play and from reading, education, in some miraculous way, will occur. This would be excellent if we then proceeded to the problem of assuring that the educational task were indeed being pursued. But, unfortunately, the esthetic becomes its own end.

The word "esthetic" is the positive form of the word "anesthetic." Perhaps this should recommend itself. When we talk of an esthetic state, we refer to the sense of having been transported out of time and place. We are no longer obliged to observe the quantitative character of the sustaining world. It is the state of mind-feeling which legitimizes a response to the quality of an existence in timeless, spaceless, indeed, dimensionless worlds. If the reader can remember when he was so completely absorbed in music that he lost all sense of time and place and of people around him, he will know what is meant by *esthesis*. When a play is so overpowering that the theater itself dissolves and the only thing that exists is the body and the feelings of the spectator, and the drama unfolding on the stage, the state of esthesis has been reached. Any of the forms of a complete love act, whether physical or emotional, are intensely esthetic in this sense. Time and place simply disappear. Only the qualities of events, in their immediacy, become the total context of our lives.

But, unhappily, when time and place disappear, education has to disappear too. Categories, because they are concepts without spacial or temporal dimensions in the literal sense, appear to be akin to the esthetic. The aim of education is not only to make these categories available, but also to heighten the very cognition that is suspended in the esthesis.

Symbol-using and the thinking act.   In an effort to show both the difference between expression and education and the ways of the inhabitants of the new world of education, we are going to have to offer a detailed description of the thinking act—the category-making and the category-using (or the sorting-out) activity. In pursuit of this it will be wise to observe the directions recommended in the opening chapter. There, you will remember, we attempted to distinguish between the questions that an observer, even a critical observer, and the questions that a philosopher will ask about the same action. In pursuit of the meaning and the requirements of the act of thinking, we will be talking not as psychologists, or brain specialists, but as philosophers. We will be concerned not with offering validatable descriptions of the process called thinking, but with the effort of constructing systems that will make clear what we generally mean by "thinking," and also with what we ought to mean if we are to verify and to make possible the improved educative act itself. I have written elsewhere[3] that the dilemma we have long faced in education concerning this matter of the improvement of thinking arises from the disagreement about what it is we should measure and work on in the interests of advancing education. Thus, philosophy is not an alternative to common sense, or to scientific undertakings, but is rather the construction of systems for the clearing and improving of the understanding. It is the means of the distinguishing goals so that both science and common sense can be included in the human venture.

Another distinction, made familiar to us through Plato, should be drawn. Our concern here is not with the motive or purpose for thinking, however important this concern may be at some other time. Purpose and motive both imply substance and direction for thinking; more neutral is the effort to recommend the logical process of thinking. The importance of this distinction should be evident, for applied to the field of education it provides us with reason to differentiate between nurturing the process of thinking and initiating students into acceptance of substantive answers. Socrates sought to understand virtue, not what or who is virtuous.

Now, how shall we determine the character of so ephemeral an event as thinking? There is nothing that we can actually point to; no process that can be observed, no wheels spinning and turning out something we can indisputably identify as a fact produced by thought, or mind. The best we could possibly do is to use the term "thinking" as a characterizing term. That is, we can observe the behavior in its sequence and in its consequence, and we can decide that some of it can be advisably called "thought-determined behavior." Against the same criteria we can call other manifest behaviors by other names, which we would then accept as behavior in which "thought" played no determining role.

Again, as was suggested in the opening chapter, symbol-making and symbol-using seems, according to most analysts of the problem, the most likely behavior to which we would ascribe the term "thinking." This suggests two very obvious things. First, symbol-making and symbol-using are behavioral matters, whether they appear in

[3] Cf. Marc Belth, *Education as a Discipline* (Boston: Allyn and Bacon, 1965). Also "The Study of Education as the Study of Models," *The Alberta Journal of Educational Research,* 12(1966): 203–23, reprinted in *The Social Studies: Structures, Models and Strategies,* eds. Martin Feldman and Eif Seifman (Englewood Cliffs, N.J.: Prentice-Hall, 1969).

ordinary conversation, or in non-verbal symbol systems built to represent something in nature or to reflect certain feelings or expectations. Second, we must also recognize that although symbol-using and symbol-making are fine candidates for the behavior to which we can ascribe the term "thought-determined," not everyone who uses or makes symbols could be described as "thinking," or of being "thoughtful." For parrots, myna-birds, monkeys, and other subhuman creatures also make and use symbols, but cannot, or ought not to be said to be "thinking." So there must be another event to attach to this mode of behavior to make the distinction meaningful.

Observe that we are taking what is commonly accepted as being understood in the language of most people, and using this agreement as the material to be examined. The intention is to determine what we might mean and what we could not mean by the use of a given term—in this case, the term "thinking." We are *not* attempting to enter into the tangible world, equipped with specially prepared probes and graphs, in order to drag up to the surface something that has been lying hidden all these years. If we are probing and groping, it is again only in a metaphoric sense, with the language that we normally use, and with the concepts that we normally construe the language to represent, all in order to discern the meanings we generally have employed.

We will not, therefore, be revealing something that was hidden from view all this time. What we will bring to the level of awareness is the number of meanings generally ascribed to a given term or set of terms, in order to make possible some agreement upon which meanings will be most advantageous to us. The hope is to put these in place of the vague and ambiguous meanings we have innocently lived with for some time.

To go back to the probing, then. Most of us would accept that symbol-making and symbol-using are the behaviors which can best assume the qualification "thoughtful," or "thought," or "thinking." But in order to be sure that we do not overstretch the applicability of the term "thinking," we need some additional definition, to give us a warrant for continuing to make the distinction most of us make anyway. We distinguish between parrots and people, men and monkeys in a variety of ways. Primarily, we recognize that when man speaks he is or can be aware of what he is saying. He can alter what he is saying at any given moment in order to bring the past to bear on the future, or the future on his contemplation of the past. Most of us would recognize that neither parrots nor monkeys are known consciously to employ the past or the anticipated future to determine what, when, or how they say something.

We may not be able to see the specific process by means of which a man summons up remembrances of the past or distills his anticipations into some symbolic form in order to make a statement about the present. We only recognize that behavior of some sort has been performed. But if we cannot see it, and we do allow the process (if it is a process at all), to occur when and if it will, then it is quite likely that its improvement is accidental and its development a matter of luck. For this reason, it is worth trying to offer a theory of what is taking place in this so-called "act of thinking." It is perfectly usual to attempt to describe an internal system, or an inner structure or process of an activity, of which we see only external manifestations. If we need to use familiar events as analogues for what we will try to describe and explain, so be it. We do so because it is easier for someone else to follow when we have an analogy to guide us in understanding and describing some inner function.

A MODEL FOR SORTING

Thinking as sorting. Models at work.   Throughout these first three chapters, whenever we have talked about *thinking,* the discussion has been cast in terms of sorting-out processes, or categorizing procedure. This identification of thinking has been supported by the assumption that to think is to distinguish events from one another, to analyze the elements distinguished, to collect them together, and to keep them apart in order to effect whatever it is we wish to do with them. In this way we discern possible meanings and futures. It has been argued, too, that in so doing the indistinguishable in experience becomes distinguishable and can be better comprehended, directed, and projected. Further, it was argued that when the process of education is directed toward a concern for improving these sorting-out powers of its learners, it is at that moment concerned with improving their capacity to think, to make judgments, and to bring order into areas where there is none.

This is quite simple and unstartling. But it is hardly enough to assert just this. For all we would be doing would be rewriting the dictionaries of home and school by adding the term "thinking" as a synonym for the term "sorting." Clearly, more is needed. What is needed now is a conceptual picture, a working model, of the way in which the sorting-out process operates. And along with this model is needed a justification of why this process can be usefully construed as equivalent to the thinking process. This must be cast into the form of an appeal to what is already known if it is to convince us that a description of the one (the model) is a description of the other (the thinking act.)

To do this, and to have it accepted, will accomplish several things. There will have been proposed the kind of procedures with which education ought to be concerned if there is to be any improvement. Moreover, such proposals will have acquired some legitimacy. But just as important, a distinction will have been made between education and expression; between a consideration of educating and a consideration of the ways in which an educated power is put to use.

What is meant by sorting.   Little has to be said as to justify the need to categorize or to classify. Human beings are complex, and represent extremely diverse functions. Each of these functions requires proper conditions if it is to continue and allow life itself to continue. We breathe in a way that is very different from the way we ingest. Proteins and carbohydrates are needed in a diet to maintain muscular efficiency. They cannot be secured by simply breathing in. Nor can oxygen be secured by eating certain foods.

This is the simplest possible example, demonstrating that for human beings the very process of life is a matter of learning to sort things out and classify them as to functions they perform, needs they fulfill, and conditions they produce. To sort out, therefore, is to explore events in nature and in the mind in order to determine what belongs with what, and for what discernible or logical reasons.

This notion is not a new one. It can be found in Plato and Aristotle. But for Aristotle the categorizing activity seemed to be determined by fixed and final qualities and by the functions observable in both man and the matters being categorized. Yet it is not necessary to assume such fixity in order to sort, though one might see why it would be desirable. Events can indeed be used in a variety of ways and made to function differently on different occasions. So, categorizing or sorting-out can be identified as a function which is necessary for human beings, but not necessarily determined by any previously existing fixed forms. To improve the power to do so, therefore, would be to improve the prospects of human existence. This would apply to the social and political arenas no less than to the biological and the psychological.

But how does sorting out take place? Do we just look at events, line them up alongside one another, and allow their similarities to leap out at us and determine our categories? This is, of course, possible, and it appears that this is just what is done on occasion. Certainly symbols of events are handled this way. But then the presence of symbols already marks an advance in civilization. Unfortunately, however, we must recognize that nature does not come to us all packaged and labelled. This is what makes symbol-making a humanly necessary act. If it were self-classifying we would need to do something entirely different to improve the human prospects. We would only need to learn how to read the labels of nature. In all probability we would not even need symbols; this is what was argued in the first chapter.

We will return to this problem in a brief historical survey at the beginning of the next chapter. Now it is necessary to point out another fact. If we agree that nature does not come to us already labelled or finally and intrinsically characterizable, the agreement itself obliges us to alter our traditional view of man's relation to nature. It will also demand a revision of what we consider man's expectations of himself to be, and what role we see him seeking to improve. If it is man who must give nature its labels, then nature itself shows greater powers only as he, man, is able to create more definitive, more discriminating, more fruitful classifications. In doing this, he shows nature in a greater variety of possibilities; for these possibilities are dependent upon the classifications which bring together elements of nature as nature itself does not.

It is for this reason that it is well worth considering the process of characterizing, or sorting. As Michael Oakeshott has pointed out,[4] not until we get beyond the perceptible phenomena of nature will we reach into the experience of science, or, as we may add, into the study of the educational process.

Sorting as the model for thinking.   How, then, do we sort out? It is quite clear that we sort as we explore the perceptual and the conceptual dimensions of the world we live in. We sort out as we describe what we have explored so others may recognize it when they come upon it. We sort out as we discern beginnings and endings of events to distinguish them from other events to which they might be similar or dissimilar. As we propound logical connectives be-

[4] Michael Oakeshott, *Experience and Its Modes* (London: Cambridge University Press, 1933), Ch. 4, esp. p. 170ff.

tween events which do not show connectives, and verify the connectives in those events which do show them, we are sorting out. As we interpret the meanings of events explored and described, defined and analyzed, we sort out. (The logical dimension, Quine says of the act of ascribing meaning, is a matter of translation from one set of terms and symbols to another, and producing the same responses to the same referrents.[5]) And finally we sort out as we explain both the reasons for the categories we have chosen or constructed, and the consequences these categorizations have upon events and ourselves. Inevitably, the sorting-out process must be re-examined in order to discern this result of the use of certain categories. This is the process of evaluation which is as necessary a part of the sorting-out process as it is of the thinking process. For one sorts out in order to account for all that impinges upon experiences, and the inclusiveness must be validated.

Now, following Quine again, if we were to put the term "thinking" in place of the term "sorting-out" at the beginning of the previous paragraph, the whole paragraph would have the very same meaning it now has. In this sense, then, the meaning given to the concept of "sorting-out" would also be the meaning given to the concept of "thinking."

One further point needs to be added here, in order to make the identification firmer. When we sort things out, we describe them, explore and/or observe them, explain and interpret them, analyze and reason over them. We determine their limits, or their definitions, as a result of this process, and we prepare for a later evaluation of the effects of this particular system of classification. But sorting-out, like thinking, is best considered as an activity, or a process. It is the procedure of projecting concepts, or terms upon the recorded but untouched images derived from past or present experiences, and also upon the vaguer images of anticipated outcomes. In the process these images are organized into some unified, modeled concept which then enables us to speak of certain events in the language of a specific and limited category, and not in the language of any other category.[6] We do not use the category of *cognition,* for example, in talking about rocks and crystals. If we do, we are crossing our sortings, as Gilbert Ryle has pointed out, and we may be deliberately producing the

[5] Willard Van Orman Quine, *Word and Object* (Cambridge, Mass.: The M.I.T. Press, 1960), p. 32.
[6] Cf. Susanne Langer, *Mind: An Essay on Human Feeling* (Baltimore: Johns Hopkins Press, 1967), Ch. 3, esp. pp. 58–59.

imagery of the poet. We may also be producing imaginary worlds to satisfy some sentimental habit or developed anthropomorphic disposition. But when we apply a given category to a variety of events, we are obliged, by that decision, to employ the same terms and the same concepts to all of the events. That is the purpose of a category. Indeed, if this cannot be done, if further examination reveals that the same descriptions and explanations are not to be applied to all the events in the chosen context, and where matters readily observable are thus not accounted for, then the events are not to be considered as belonging to the same category, or to the context examined.

All this may seem very obvious, and no doubt a little labored. But it is necessary to make it explicit, for only if it is explicit can we move to the next point—the point that if a category is given full dimension, and if the sorting instrument has been made quite explicit, and given identity in descriptive terms, this category becomes the very model for sorting events whose qualities, characteristics and processes would have no commonality, and probably no value for us.

The force of this identification is quite simple but quite powerful. Seen as a model, with all that enters to make a model what it is (determinability, handleability, tangibility, dimensionality, sequentiality) the processes of sorting-out (and thus of thinking) cease to be random, accidental events. We can come at last to direct our attention to the separate elements comprising the operating model in order to nurture in the learners the specific powers of each element, and the complete power of the unified act. We learn to think (and to sort out), by learning to improve powers of description, explanation, definition, analysis, interpretation, and so on. The models themselves, when they are constructed, or recognized and used, determine the specific character of the descriptions and explanations, explorations and interpretations which may be employed when given experiences are confronted.[7]

Turning back to the problems of expression, we see both the connections and the distinctions that can fruitfully be made between the process of expression and the process of education. A writer must have learned, or will need to learn, to describe as he sets about to record the events which become parts of his novel. The scientist must know how to explain, or will need to develop the capacity to explain, as he attempts to report the behaviors of the unobservable molecules of some gas he is studying. The painter must know how to

[7] Cf. Belth, *Education as a Discipline*, Ch. 3.

explore, or will need to improve his ability to explore, as he probes and then expresses his growing involvement with the symbols of the events he will put on canvas. In short, as we understand what it is that education actually develops in individuals, we come to grasp what education makes possible in the arena of human expression. But to urge that expression is part or all of the educative process is to believe in the inheritance of such specific skills, or to urge the making of statements before the child or the adult has learned the means by which to make them.

We will return to this problem of differentiating educating and expressing when we come to the consideration of the distinction between *sorting* and *the sorted,* that runs through Chapters Four and Five.

CHAPTER 4

Teaching Theory—
Learning Theory

IN the last chapter it was suggested that if the assumption that nature comes to us labeled and categorized is no longer held, a dramatic change in one's view of one's own powers and responsibilities occurs. Along with this, because there is a change in what we can anticipate we will yet be able to do, there is also a change in nurturing procedures; that is, in education.

Let us consider what is meant by this changed belief, and what it is a change from.

EMPIRICISM

Origins of the empiricist theory of learning. Both Canadians and the people of the United States are the children of the same European tradition. We are the offspring of British empiricism. We may all rightfully call John Locke Grandfather Locke, for it is from Locke, who was so eager to reject the notion that we are born possessing ideas, that we derive this belief that at birth we are devoid of any knowledge whatever. This allows, however, great potentiality for development of the control of nature, and a great sensitivity to everything which occurs about us. Encountered events leave their imprint upon us. Such imprints become the internal sources which make us act; these imprints become what we know. Experience writes indelibly upon the blank tablet which is the mind.

Most of us in this tradition have never fully rejected these ideas. Some have propounded variations of this theory. Some have said that it is not enough for experience to write on the blank tablet. If there is to be knowledge, both the matter of inscription and receipt of this inscription must be analyzed further. The blank tablet obviously must be absorptive, but unhappily not all tablets are of the same material. Some will argue that what is written becomes durable because of what else has been previously written. Then, in some remarkable way, what has already been written gives new meaning to what is now being received. What we do reflects what we have received, but becomes altered as new receptions occur. But the transmission must, in some way, precede the receiving, which is not quite what Locke said, but still remains within his empirical tradition.

Another way of saying somewhat the same thing is found in a form of naive pragmatism. If we do a thing often enough in response to experiences, and the doing proves successful, or satisfying, then the very muscles of the body become habituated to doing that thing. Locke's empiricism, behaviorist psychology, and even the early notion of a reflex arc which Dewey analyzed, all are concerned with showing how experiences from outside leave impressions upon the mind, the nervous system, and the cortex of the brain. These impressions eventually produce habitual responses which become the determined behavior patterns of our lives and of the choices we make. But we also believe that if at first external stimuli are required to get knowledgeable action started, after a while we become self-starting. The impressions have become our internalized reservoir of knowledge. As persons we are one with our habituations.

This conception can be derided a little and we can be unfair to it by pointing out that in a curious sort of a way the whole of the empirical, scientistic tradition accepts a vitalistic view of man, or things (more often of things) and an animistic view of the environment. Thus, man becomes alive, vital and motivated when he internalizes what is outside of him. He is passive, placid, inert, quiescent, but absorptive. When he absorbs, especially when he absorbs the right things, (like swallowing a nugget of force?) that force enters the mind, finds a fertile field and begins to bloom. With further nourishment it is transformed into a unity with the being, and the whole person is transformed into vital activity. The intelligence that is then revealed works because what has been internalized is the intelligence which is in the world of experience. It has been refined into properly acceptable dosages, some even in symbol forms, and can be internalized.

This is in most general, and obviously exaggerated terms, an empiricist theory of learning. Within this tradition consider what a teacher means when he says the child must be given a good experience. Clearly, he means that we must take the child from wherever he is, physically, and mentally, and let him see how worthy things unfold, how they work. If he sees things properly, in the required conditions, they will leave lasting impressions upon him. When he thinks, he will be thinking about real things because these impressions direct his thinking. From the world outside of him he will absorb the very categories that comprise the order of nature. Even these categories must leave an impress, or they are not real. In fact, this becomes the test of just what is real. When he talks about nature, he will talk about nature in the categories that nature itself possesses. No empiricist is willing to say about nature that it is disorderly; indeed, that it is anything but orderly, for otherwise he would be unable to explain how the idea of order came into his mind.

But the curious thing is that whether we believe that nature has order, or that we impose upon it that order, the consequence for education is not significantly different. When education is viewed as the procedure for nurturing powers of perception, explanation, and description, it does not matter whether we believe the perceiving, explaining, or describing is an antecedent or consequent reality. Metaphysical preferences aside, the educational effort remains constant.

Nevertheless, the Lockean metaphysics produces educational negations that must be noted, for no empiricist is able to sustain successfully the argument that nature possesses neither order nor disorder. If he did hold this, he could not also maintain that we learn from nature's own order. He must claim that if we want to see how a tree grows, we must go watch a tree grow; that if we want to see how the seasons change, we must watch the seasons change; that if we want to know why people cry, we must watch them cry. If we want to know if something will pain people, we must observe them under conditions in which they must respond; then we will see whether or not they are pained. We must not invent, nor must we hypothesize. We need not invent because nature provides us not only with every truth we need about reality, but also with the evidence of its truth. From all this it inevitably follows that education is the absorption of nature's truth from nature itself. The consequence, you see, is to give little credence to developments that are taking place anyway. Accidental growth occurs, and cannot always be accounted for. In such a context of beliefs, what logical statement could be said to give an account of the functions of the teacher? Continuing the line of reasoning, it must derive from the orderly conception of nature, as well as the conception that man's nature is entirely impressionable, or absorptive. If nature is orderly and man's nature is totally absorptive, the teacher need do nothing more than guide the child into those experiences which will finally teach him, because they have left an impression on him.

What else may we say? We may say that the good teacher never intrudes himself between the learner and nature. The teacher must never talk too much, though he must surely talk so as to help make impressions. It is the child who must talk, and thus help intensify impressions by being actively absorptive. Besides, the teacher, being old and already diseased with egoism and vanity, would only becloud the mind of the "unadulterated" child. Nature, being nature, is never deceitful. Nature speaks in a voice of such limpid purity that we would all be well advised to learn from it. And finally? Attend to nature with increasing diligence, for out of nature comes all the directions needed for our own fulfilment. And since the child is a natural event, whose condition of continuing growth and development is already a categorized natural fact, his intrinsic and social needs, or the very conditions for life itself, are to be seen as the source of the curriculum. This is the terribly consistent conclusion.

In sum, the empiricist theory of learning is predicated on the conception that man at birth has nothing (knowledge or ideas) inside him. Everything is outside. This must be brought inside, but it must be brought inside in such symbolized and capsulated form as to be "digestible." Not only must these be "digestible," but if the metaphor is to be continued, they must be made of the kind of qualities which will dissolve in the cognitive bloodstream. Thus absorbed, they will course through the body of the child and transform him from a primitive wanderer in quest of experience into a sophisticated wonder, rejoicing in his reservoir of impressed knowledge.

If the child is not always as sophisticated as later experiences will make him, still his primitive vitalities are to be more coveted than the diseased qualities of the older people who become teachers and, in misguided ways, intrude upon and destroy that wonderful quality of being a child. Small wonder that we envy children and respect, honor and adore them. But then, the anthropologists have long advised us that we live in a child-worshipping culture. As adults, in fact, we worship our own childhood and its remembered bright promise. And we continue to live with this fantasy, so long as we do not think about our own experiences too closely.

Some problems of empiricist learning theory.   But the problems raised by this empiricist theory of man and nature are extraordinary. Although there is no place here for a detailed exposition of the problems raised by such a theory, it is necessary to say that it has raised far more problems than it has ever explained. Primarily, the dilemma created is that of trying to account for those ideas which organize experiences and give them meanings, but which could not possibly have been experienced. Concepts such as "suitability," or "objectivity," or "consistency," are devised. We cannot, in this context, distinguish the event from what we direct the event to do. Thus, as a theory of education, empiricism is sterile. We all have too many ideas, ideas not necessarily gained through experience or proven empirically to take such a theory seriously.

Why, then, argue it so lengthily? Because most of us are still Locke's grandchildren, and because most of us cling to our common sense views of nature and the child, and do not even attempt to borrow from the developments in modern science and scientific method. Most of us talk about what the world *ought* to be like, in moral terms, and are not too concerned with what science tells us the world can actually be seen to be. On the purely verbal level we acknowledge what experiment and inquiry make available to us. But on the behavioral level, we respond to those early beliefs so unguardedly absorbed.

An alternative approach.   What, then, is the alternative? What comes to mind is the fact that the alternative to internalization is obviously externalization. And thereby hangs this argument. Unhappily, however, we must lead to it through the exploration of a mass of inconsistent and untenable assumptions which are yet held, before the point and its value becomes clear.

Let us begin with the point that children do not need, as Dewey has argued, to be made active. Activity is a part of the very condition of being a child. If there is ever any responsibility on the part of the adult toward the child, it is to encourage him to be a little less active for a little while, or at the very least, to direct his activity so that other events can take place.

Sometimes it is argued that in accepting the adult responsibility to direct the child's activity, the teacher might properly call his efforts "directing learning." But the educational pattern found in empiricism will reappear unless we are careful. The child is directed to what we want him to internalize. This ignores what must never be ignored, lest we encounter even greater problems. While we are directing the child to the experiences we want him to have, we find ourselves faced with the problem of having to deal with those experiences that he has on his own, at every living moment, in and out of our sight. What happens when the experiences that he has come into conflict with the experiences which have been chosen for him? The answer is quite clear. Still under the suasion of the purity of all things natural, we would say that the experiences he has under his own pushing and motivating, in response to his own immediate satisfactions or comprehensions, invariably are more desirable to him than the experiences we want him to have.

In the context of such beliefs, we find a simple explanation of why children generally resist school. Teachers are always forcing them to do the things they do not want to do. If we want to find the first phases of the generation gap in education, it will be located in this relationship. For, except where nature is given its way, the teacher is probably working on assumptions which oblige him to give the learners experiences that are adult chosen and adult-approved. Resistance on the part of the child obliges the teacher to coerce the child, perhaps cajole him, threaten him, deprive him, reward him, or punish him, until the child is willing to admit that he is not ready to make his own judgments competently. Of course, this stands as a contradiction to Locke's romantic side. But perhaps Locke unavoidably produces such contradictions. For, if the teacher is required, according to his thesis, to accept that the child is noble, he must also either accept the idea that the child is a rich ore to be mined carefully, or a formless being to be molded firmly, as he is exposed to mental salvation. He must hold these views or admit to pronouncing a theory which he does not or cannot live with.

If the child is, as seems to be implied, wise with the wisdom of intuition, then he should be permitted to follow this intuitive guide. But to be consistent, if it is really held that he is the noble ore, then we must be concerned to chasten and refine that ore, in order to allow its purest quality to stand revealed. Admit that what a child does is really childish—and childlike; but these childish and child-like qualities are only evidence of the lack of experience. Underneath lies the great vein of potentially mature powers which must be brought forth and given freedom of movement.

But the dilemma remains. What do we do with the problems that the child presents as a result of his constantly absorbing such matters we had hoped he would not absorb? What of his absorbing a language which has no empirical referents? Children are acquisitive. Everything that they are near, everything that floats by, stays with them; pictures, sounds, ideas, inflections, gestures, expressions. Not everything leaves an immediately noticeable imprint. Yet more of these than we can ever imagine do leave their various effects on him. A child left untended becomes a creature to whom all sorts of things have randomly adhered.

This would suggest that whatever innate human characteristics might be like and however resistant they may be to verification, we can suspect that in terms of imprint, nature is not as orderly as the empirical tradition would have it. Perhaps it is, after all, as Russell noted, just one damn thing after another. We cannot even say it is disorderly because if we said that, we must be implying that we know in advance of experience what form it should stop at to be orderly.

But let us assume that we do not know whether it is orderly or not. Suppose nature were just a great Rorschach blot. There is neither order nor disorder in the blot. The question asked of the observer is what order, what sorting of events, does he project into it? What order can be made out of it as he stares at it?

Consider the child and all of the things that he has absorbed. What order can he make or can be made out of them? To look closely at a Jackson Pollack painting is surely a curious, if not boring undertaking. A Pollack painting becomes a test, not only of the painter, but also quite revealingly of the observer. It tests the observer's categorizing ability as he tries to give order to what does not immediately show either order or disorder. For the primary fact is that his work, in epistemological terms, tests the sorting models that are our usual cognitive instruments. Inventive and flexible minds look at a Pollack and point out harmonies, of the expected and unexpected kinds. Only the traditional, the dogmatic, or the cliché-ridden look at a Pollack and consign it to the realm of the meaningless or consider it an insult to the intelligence. Perhaps it is, perhaps not. We do know this, however; there are people who can look at a Jackson Pollack and find in it all of the exultation of esthetic delight that others can only find in so clear a representation of nature as occurs in a Rembrandt or a Renoir. If we insist that the paintings of Jackson Pollack are a hoax, we will be saying more about ourselves and our powers to project order on events, than we are about Jackson Pollack. We may be saying that our ability to observe texture, line, form, color qualities, and relationships of the painting as an object have been left undeveloped or unmatured.

LEARNING—INTERNALIZATION OR EXTERNALIZATION

Learning as internalization, and the dilemma produced. Assume, therefore, that the child does absorb far more than we ever anticipate. But he does not, on that account alone, need to be guided in this absorption. What would also have to be proven is what sorts of absorptions are harmful, and this is a problem of moral analysis as well as empirical exploration. Thus, absorption is not explained quite as simply as the empiricists would have us believe. We absorb a great many things and store them up using the symbols which we have available to us. But they have different degrees of directive force on our behavior.

Although we see our world through our words, the words themselves have no independent existence. Their meanings are affected by our individual histories. We have come to believe that if we do a thing a number of times we will eventually do it without ever thinking about it again. And who would deny that there is abundant evidence to show that this is the case?

If it is the case, and we consider this to be the paradigm form of all the learning that occurs (as so many do), and if the concern of teaching is to make this type of learning possible, then learning is shown to be most effective when we can finally do something without having to think about it. Even Dewey, that least mechanistic of philosophers, argued that learning is most effective when a person becomes totally habituated to doing certain things. Competence, which is freedom from hesitation in the form of greater and greater efficiency, is a function of habituation and of practice. It moves us to the point where economy of action improves as thinking, in the sense of liberating, is less and less necessary. The basic purpose of the Skinner teaching machine concept is to produce in the learner a capacity to give the correct answer rapidly, on cue, without fumbling or hesitating about it. In such context, thinking can only obstruct. Thus, on the basis of the theory of internalization, education is complete when we do not have to think. In fact, thinking itself can be said to achieve its educational objective at the point when it is no longer necessary.

Recognizing the basic contradiction which has appeared here, our problem is to try to find out what capacities we must nurture in order to be able to transform unconscious responses into increasingly conscious, understandable, and controllable powers of judgment. If I may be permitted a personal reference, I recall that when I was much younger, I committed a good deal of Shakespeare to memory. It was the time for internalizing Shakespeare. It may be an awkward way of putting it, but in so doing, Shakespeare was transformed from the written word into a mechanical, oral state, to be reproduced on cue. It was a long time before the words and sentences were transformed into mental images. The words were retained. So long as Shakespeare could be quoted, on cue, without having to worry about relevance, and I was not called upon to explain what had been said, I submit I was well trained. But whether I was educated in Shakespeare remained another question.

We are acquainted with people who know a great deal, who are able to quote, to refer to sources and to footnote them verbally, and on cue. But with dismay we note that, although the power of recall is present, this kind of internalization is inadequate for such deliberative acts as interpreting, explaining, establishing, and extending relevance, or altering meanings and interpretations. These people who seem to be in control of a great deal of learning, but who also show quite clear evidence of mental inflexibility are not unfamiliar. Often they are individuals who have internalized words and their approved meanings as well.

Shall we call the educated man the one who can always dredge up from his memory some version of the past which seems to be relevant to a given problem, even though he cannot demonstrate its relevance? Or shall we ask the educated man to exhibit a little more than this power of recall? It would certainly appear that in light of the necessity to sort out and give meaning to events, or else be bound by previously fixed sortings and meanings, a good deal more should be demanded.

Accepting internalization, it is externalizing that is educationally fundamental. If we have been willing to accept the notion that the thinking act is just that, an act, and that education requires both a teaching and a learning theory, then perhaps education might be better understood if the emphasis were placed upon the act of externalizing judgmental decisions rather than the act of internalizing stimuli, however necessary this may be.

What is meant here by externalizing? Plato argues in favor of innate ideas, the very view which John Locke rejects. But it is possible to make Plato's view more defensible than Locke's by showing that Plato meant that ideas were innate in the sense that they were embodied *in* the language used. We learn easily, and, especially when younger, so effortlessly that it seems as if we are revealing nothing but our inherent powers. Ideas are not only carried in the language which we learn, but *are* the very language which we absorbed when younger, and are still absorbing. Thus, when we absorb ideas, we absorb a language, and when we absorb a language, we absorb the knowledge embedded therein. We absorb these without altogether understanding what it is that we have absorbed.

But in this sense of the term, absorbing is considered the learning of a very limited type. It is the kind of learning which is received in the sense of having the consequences of external stimuli recorded somewhere in our muscles, in the viscera, or in the lining of the brain. But significant, deliberative learning occurs only when we begin to externalize in order to make this reservoir of received sensations apparent to ourselves. It is when we push forward to examine what has been absorbed that conscious learning begins. As Socrates said, when asked what he thought about a particular problem, "How do I know what I think until I have heard myself speak about it?" This is what is meant by externalizing. We speak either overtly or silently to ourselves and to others. As we speak, we find ourselves listening to what we have said. (To avoid speaking may well be the result of a decision to avoid a confrontation of beliefs.)

The difference between the child and the adult, in this matter at least, is the fact that the child frequently babbles without heeding what he has babbled. So familiar is this to us that when the adult babbles in a similar manner, he appears to us to be a child. The inevitable conclusion is that such a person really is quite immature. When a child says something and listens very carefully to what he says in order to discover whether he has said what should be said, or what he wants to say, it is a curious insistence he shows when he adds, "And I really mean it." When anyone, child or adult, suddenly says, "No, I want to change that," we recognize that we are in the presence of someone struggling consciously between the sense of what properly ought to be said and the language in which it would be properly said. In this reflection and deliberate effort to control expression, we locate the maturing mind.

Now, what activity are we referring to by this term "reflect"? We can only mean that a person has explored, has consciously examined the means employed in the act of expression, and in some way has verified the verbal outcomes. He has offered a description and deliberately set about to show that the description is accurate and meaningful. He has explained or interpreted or defined, and offered a justification for each such act.

Thus, to posit a necessary relationship between education and the power reflection develops over expression is to propose that for education to occur it is necessary to externalize all that has been absorbed. It is in this act that we increase the possibility of controlling the acts which identify our humanness. In so doing we comprehend what is meant by and entailed in the concepts that we absorb in the course of our development, concepts that eventually identify our characters, our ways of acting, and our capacities to see a world and live within it.

THE ACHIEVEMENT OF EXTERNALIZATION

Instruments and externalization. A special opportunity presents itself to us here, an opportunity to see how the act of externalizing depends on objectively developed skills.

More often than not we absorb ideas and impressions at random, and on occasion even without particular order, though this is not very likely, perceptualization being what it is. When we set about to externalize them, we are in position to add connections which did not prevail when they were received. It is a familiar observation that when we say the same things over and over again, and concentrate on the details of what we are saying, we have the opportunity to discern novelty in what we have said. Try reading Shakespeare aloud, over and over again. Intensify your attention on the meanings of the sentences, but lessen your interest in the rhythm, sound, and tone of the lines. It will intrigue you how along about the fourth or fifth time, you begin to grasp meanings that you had not "seen" the first or second time.

Look at a painting (itself an externalization of some facet of the artist's life, in which the painter and materials were in a transaction giving meanings and matter both new form and new significance). The fourth or fifth, or perhaps the tenth time, you will surely see something in the painting that you did not see at first. What has happened is that in your own way you are externalizing the absorbed forms of what was an externalization by the painter. Further, as you bring together two specific externalizations, you project upon them relationships that they could not have had separately, in sequential internalization. In the externalization you are engaged in manipulating concepts and perceptions actively. It is the one way to avoid the often self-deceptive ruminating or random imaging which we permit ourselves to call thinking. Once an image is in you, (whatever we may mean by "in"), it is in you. It is what it is, as it is recorded. It is the picture, the diagram, the formed perception of some event seen or anticipated. It is only when you externalize the image that it is transformed and assumes the quality of flexibility. This capacity to externalize permits you to sort out and to interrelate in different positive ways the aspects of perceived data that would otherwise go unnoticed and unconsidered.

Perhaps the best illustration of this is to be found in the brilliant motion picture *Blow-Up*. In that film we become aware of a new significance in a picture that has been taken in a photographer's normal workday. The photographer is stirred only by a vague darkening, a blob in the picture which has no immediate significance, but seems somehow out of place. He makes print after print by means of his special instruments, each an enlargement of the one before. Each one reveals to the probing, conscientious eye of the photographer some aspect not apparent in an earlier, smaller reproduction. The dénouement comes with the most critical or fullest projection required to give meaning to the darkened area. The image, not anticipated in the first view, is that of the body of a dead man. When we internalize, we have done so in a most direct kind of recording. Some event has made its imprint and we have absorbed it as it was imprinted. On externalizing, however, we are involved in presenting to critical view the intrinsic characteristics which the instruments of thinking alone can expose. The analogy, of course, must be treated carefully, but within limits it is intended as an account of how entailments come slowly into view.

Externalization as an objective of teaching.   Here is a second approach. Consider the nature of the experiences that the child has. If he is to see meaning in the face of every new experience, very new event he encounters, he cannot merely record what has gone on. His primary requirement, if there is to be a learning to enhance living, also allows him to summon up from within the reservoir of recorded experiences some images which he can project "alongside" the new impression. In the comparison, meanings are made possible. In these terms, when a child says "I don't know how to explain this," he is admitting that he is not summoning up images or sounds or terms for comparisons. He is not, in short, externalizing. Primarily, it would appear that either he does not know which of his stored images he should use in viewing this newly received event in order to make sense out of it, or that he has no stored images which he can see as relevant to the new images being received.

By implication we have here an interesting recommendation for the purpose of the teaching function. It is a very different function from the view that argues the theory of learning is simply a theory of internalization.

Fundamentally, the intended implication here is that the teacher's concern is to help the students to use the sorting-out categories in the cultural environments available to him. It is a positive act, not a negative one. Teachers do not merely stand out of the way in order to let the children absorb naturally. Quite the contrary; teaching *is* intrusion! That is its very point—it is intrusion for the purpose of fostering in the child the capacity to select from his reservoir some categories already absorbed but which he must now externalize. And in no less a positive way, it is intrusion in order to make it possible for him to see meanings already entailed, or in the comparison between what was previously absorbed and what is presently being encountered.

Much more important—it becomes the responsibility of the teacher not only to help him "dredge up" the categories he may already have, but to make other categories available to him. But it is clear that it makes no sense to achieve this through direct experience. It must be done conceptually. That is, we cannot simply show him things or push him into things or knock him about with things or hand him things. Conceptualization must be utilized.

Categories, of course, are concepts. And thus, the only way we can communicate a category is by communicating the very terms which constitute that category. But how do we make categories available? Not by confronting an empirical event; not by saying: Here is a historical category; I can show it to you; touch it, feel it, hold it in your hand. In order to understand the type of transmission required here, we would need to use as analogy the way in which we make a tool available. First, we construct a die for the tool we have decided upon. From this mold we can make the required instrument. Within the die the tool to be used will be formed. But metaphorically, the die itself begins as a mental image, from which the die-model is made.

Externalization and the altered logic of teaching theory.   An important point should be extracted here. It has already been shown that in the empiricist tradition there is the strong and enduring view that there can be no teaching if there is no learning. We say that teaching is taking place, or has taken place, only if somebody is learning, or has learned. For, unless learning has occurred, how could we know there has been any teaching? But such a view implies that there really can be no teaching (as Socrates ironically, or was it maliciously? argued for a quite different reason, but to this curiously similar result). The demonstrable fact of learning indicates that teaching must have taken place. All we have, then, is teaching by implication. And as it is stated all this is tautological, since what is meant to begin with is that the act of teaching is manifest only in the demonstration of learning. But what, then, of the equally obvious fact that learning does not necessarily depend upon teaching? Are not all children giving continuous evidence that they learn on their own?

Ignoring this last for the time, in this tradition the only thing a teacher is obliged to do is whatever the rules of learning call upon him to do. Therefore, there really is no such an independently definable act as teaching. This is clearly the basis for the fact that we have come to believe that we do not teach, we just guide. We do not teach, we suffer children to have carefully chosen experiences. A theory of teaching, therefore, is only a drawn inference from a theory of learning. When one has grasped the theory of learning and followed its strictures and delimitations, one has arrived at the definition of teaching and by relatively simple deductions.

But within the conception of education as the process of externalization the logic alters. It is no longer valid to say that where there is no learning there is no teaching. The direct source of learning in the child is not the teacher, but in his own developing capacity for externalizing that which is "within" him. Therefore, there can be learning and yet no teaching. But even more significant, there can be a great deal of teaching and no learning at all going on.

From this the act of teaching can be seen as the act of making categories available to one who is about the process of learning; or developing in the learner the capacity for making these categories available to himself. This can be taught in the sense that it can be nurtured in the child's mental behavior. Even if he never learns to use them for himself, they were still taught to him. He has not learned if he makes no use of the sorting instruments, but teaching has occurred. What must be recognized is the fact that the act of teaching is not the act which the learner learns. In a sense the latter half of this book is commentary concerned with clarifying all that is entailed in this basic observation. It is analogous to the problem of gardening. The gardener plants the seeds of the marigold, and waters them, protects them, stakes them, and so on. But, except in an indefinite, very colloquial sense, we do not say he has grown the plants. He has done what he knows or thinks needs to be done. But the seeds grow as a transaction takes place between elements of the seeds and the elements of the surrounding environment. They grow according to rules of that transaction. But the gardener's methods, though they take account of those rules, are quite different. The plant does not imitate the gardener. The difference between action and reaction is more evident in the case of human beings, since there is present active choice-making powers and conditions. The powers of resistance, rejection or propounding alternatives are present in people, although no use of that power need be made. When such powers are put to use, then learning does not occur, but when conditions and the gardener's ministrations are present, marigolds cannot choose not to appear.

Of course, the happiest moment is when, in some remarkable way, we recognize that what we have taught and what the child has learned have met at some point in the child's developing powers. But logically and empirically, it is quite possible to do the one and not the other.

The need of a new relationship between learning-theory and teaching-theory. It must be clear, however, that accepting this view does not lessen our concern with learning. This remains as fundamentally important as it has ever been. But now we must be far more discriminating in our claims, for teachers are now presented with two responsibilities. We must learn about learning, but more important, as an independent undertaking, we must also learn about teaching. We can no longer assume that, having learned about learning, we have also learned about teaching. Nor, on the other hand, can we assume that, having learned about teaching, the meanings of learning are subsumed. These are two significantly different fields and they must be studied independently, as we have already shown, and as we shall show in even greater detail. Finally, and of greatest importance, we must study the possible ways there are, or that can be invented, to bring a learning theory and a teaching theory together so that they will be integrated and complementary; so that competence in the one relates to conditions which are needed to produce successful outcomes in the other.

The difficulty in attaining this clarification and integration is to be found in the fact that a psychological dilemma obstructs the view of the logical problem. Ultimately, we are concerned about the student as a student. Even when we avoid the romantic sense we legitimately worry about what happens to his state of mind, to the state of his being, to his life as a whole. As normal and compassionate human beings we seem unable to avoid these concerns. But we must recognize that this only creates additional, often more frustrating problems. The teacher's obligations cannot be clearly defined within the concerns for such vague dispositions. There are other concerns of a more technical nature that are logically primary. It actually comes to a point where we are called upon to make a decision as to functional primacy. Are we teachers or human beings? If this sounds absurd, it nevertheless underscores the problem: How shall we balance compassion and reason; psychology and logic?

The fact is that even as human beings with humane responses sometimes the state of affairs does demand that we recognize teachers' obligations first. At such moments it is more advisable not to let so-called humaneness interfere with the teaching responsibilities. Romance and critical thinking make for unsettled admixtures. When the doctor is called upon to perform a delicate and difficult bit of surgery, he dare not allow his humaneness to intrude or he will never do the surgery. It is not an accident that doctors often will not perform operations on members of their own family. There is too much at stake and human responses are much too delicate, and bordering even on the limits of the uncontrollable, to perform operations at such times.

Trivial as it may appear, the day that it becomes generally recognized that a teacher should avoid teaching his own children, we will have gone a great step forward in the direction of professionalizing the teaching act. Unfortunately, we do and have done quite the opposite. We cling to the romantic view of man epitomized in the latter part of the 19th century, with its sterile sentimentality that the mother is not only the first, but the best, most devoted, and noblest of teachers.

When we construe learning as *externalizing,* we at least have a logical ground for the widely held view that the child teaches himself and he learns from himself. Here we use the word "teach" in the traditional sense. But in a more significant, narrower, and firmer sense, no child really teaches himself. He may become conscious of what he is saying, but shall we be content to say that that is what we mean by teaching as well as learning? Is doing something the same as being equipped with the conceptual means to do something? Is simple consciousness sufficient as a defining criterion for either teaching or learning? Is it not, rather, in each case consciousness of a special kind that is part of these distinct but related phases of education? In learning, consciousness becomes a matter of focussing attention on the possible meaning of words, ideas, dispositions, and beliefs already absorbed. And for this, some externalizing must occur. In teaching, consciousness becomes a matter of focussing on the methodology necessary to produce an awareness of these absorbed beliefs, ideas, terms, and dispositions, as symbol systems for sorting out and giving meanings to worlds encountered.

Children learn a great many things without any teaching at all. Sometimes such learning is as positive and as directive as any deliberately induced. The only problem is that we cannot be sure of the character or consistency of this direction. It may not appear in any predictable or cumulative way. The conception of education as the development of the capacity for continued and intensified awareness and for direction of oneself and one's world is given far greater currency, economy, and dependability in the theory of learning as externalization. The child, having absorbed all the signs about him, (as the tape absorbs the sounds and then, as the living phonograph or recorder, plays back the sounds) listens to them in ensuing time and, having been equipped to do so, begins to "edit" his own tapes. This curious notion of a living and willful tape recorder may be used as a simple model of the theory of learning propounded here. Man is a tape recorder equipped with the potentiality to edit his own records, thereby enhancing his powers of selecting further recordings, and allowing them to direct his responses to what has thus been received.

If this analogy does not, for the moment, persuade, consider again the theory on which this conception of teaching and learning rests. Men are educated as their capacities to sort out experienced events improve. But before we sort out the events of experience, we sort out the classifying and categorizing symbols of the events. And this sorting out depends upon the ability to externalize what has been recorded or absorbed. The "gadfly" notion which Socrates used many times may still be a most fruitful one in education, for it is concerned not with the events experienced, but with the symbols which give those events meanings. When Socrates needles Meno about virtue, he is not concerned with who is virtuous or in what way, but with how the term itself is to be used. The symbol for sorting events, rather than the events themselves, is Socrates' concern. And, indeed, as a teacher, what else could have been his concern?

CHAPTER 5

The Forms and
Uses of Models

IN this chapter we will consider in somewhat greater detail what is entailed in the sorting-out activity which, it has been suggested, may be construed as being identical with the thinking act. We have been emphasizing the need to identify the separate mental operations (observation, description, definition, explanation, and the rest[1]) which, in sequence of some kind, constitute the whole of that act. We now must examine the totality of the act in its variety of forms, or emphases. As the emphasis is placed on one or another of the elements, while still maintaining all of them in some operational relationship, we will find ourselves developing or using the methodologies of one or another of the different established disciplines.

It is worth pointing out again that disciplines are developed to make more effectual, more fruitful, and more discriminating our natural or ordinary capacities for sorting out the events of the world. In every case there are methodologies by means of which ordinary or normal powers are enhanced. Thus, a development of the use of the sorting-out processes (or the methodologies) of the discipline of history is a heightening of the normally developed ability of ascribing meanings to events of the present by applying relevant meanings of the past to them, and showing meaning-connections derived from

---

[1] For a fuller statement, see Belth, *Education as a Discipline,* Ch. 4.

the sorting systems. The outcomes of such a sorting act, which becomes identified as the subject matter of a discipline, are the sorted results now seen as its substance.

ANALOGY, SCALE, AND THEORY

Analogical thinking. The point to be made here is that the organization of the mental acts identified as exploring, describing, defining, and the rest, is a deliberate matter. But though it is deliberate and not done randomly, intuitively, or instinctively, it very often is done unconsciously. The concentration of attention has been placed elsewhere than on the process itself. It is done against some constructed model purporting to be the immediately approachable symbol of the event or events that have determined our inquiry.

The simplest and most frequently used forms of models which any of us employ in such pursuits are called analogies, or analogue models. When students in undergraduate classes are asked to explain, describe, interpret, explore, and so on, some event which they have experienced, some school they have attended, or some belief they have about the character or the motives of a teacher or student, a parent, a political leader, or a friend, they have invariably offered, as their first such effort, some analogue. From this model (which is not altogether recognized as such) they have found direction to write or speak in a specific way, using a specific vocabulary, and have offered an account which the model itself demanded.[2]

Strictly speaking, every analogy is a metaphor. It is the act of treating one thing as if it were some other thing. When analogies are used, we suspend making a certain type of judgment, or rather, we suspend a certain area of disbelief in order to make a judgment. In order to emphasize certain characteristics of the certain relationships or internal activities being described, we ignore, for the moment, the fact that a given classroom we are talking about is not really, say, an art gallery. Recognizing that we are not in an art gallery, we nevertheless mean to be taken seriously in the judgments we make in speaking so. We are treating the school *as if* it were an art gallery not *as being* an art gallery.

There are strengths and weaknesses in this *as if* mode of thinking. When we frankly admit that we are not truly considering the school as whatever it is—terrain, an art gallery, a garage, an in-

[2] I have included one student's essay in the appendix as an illustration of this.

terior decorator's shop, an enclosed pool in the region of the ocean—but continue to behave as if we were, it would seem to reduce thinking to a triviality because we are being fictional.

Some analogies, of course, cannot be taken seriously. There is usually little possibility that we will make the error of treating an analogy as a real event. Yet in at least one sense, even in the obvious there is a strength. When the analogy is so transparent, we are able to recognize that we are deliberately considering some undertaking in the terms that the imagination has accepted or constructed solely for the purpose of reaching out to new meanings and further insights. For, it is primarily by means of analogy that we can bring any two things together and regard them as related or relatable. In condemning pretensions we may speak of man as God, knowing, of course, that man is not God. But to use some conception of God as a model does make it *logically* possible to lay bare a particular man's adequacies or inadequacies by presenting him with an image of the individual perfection he clearly lacks. (Provided, of course, we are clear about the analogical figure.) But the adequacies or inadequacies take on the quality and the force which is attached to the model itself; it is imperative to note this.

The danger in the use of analogy is not difficult to discern. Sometimes an analogy is used without realizing that it is just that. In such cases we treat the event as being literally described and explained in the model. Event and model are one. We talk of men not *as if* they were gods, but *as,* in the same moment, men and gods.

Such an error is naive, though not unusual. Quite often in education, especially in classroom or administrative disputes over the uses of authority, someone charges someone else with using the authority of God. In such a case, the analogy has gone awry. No one *is* God, nor is it possible to simply and clearly identify God's authority. Not by the furthest stretch of the imagination can we expect anyone to be God or to use God's authority, unless we mean to eliminate divine perfection from any future definitions. Thus, when we condemn someone (often by raising a question in the strictly pejorative sense) by charging that "you are making a decision as God would," we are taking our own analogy more seriously than we should. We seek to convict a man on the basis of the model we have ourselves constructed, imposed, and accepted as a literal description. But the person being charged with God-like pretension may have had no such pretense in mind. In his own way he may have been struggling to create a situation which he believed was called for in a given situation. These decisions, instead of being explored, analyzed, or explained in analogical form, were considered as literal efforts of an unquestioning authority. The only possible consequence was that he would be castigated as God-pretender. But whether he believed himself so endowed, or whether it was the observer who erred, is not so simply discovered.

Even more dangerous in the use of analogy is the tendency to equate the metaphoric conception with the explanation of an event, as if everything found in A is to be found in B. No analogy could imply this, because such a claim is not of analogy but absolute equivalency between a known and an unknown.

Analogies are especially cogent if we never forget that they are just that: models deliberately constructed for purposes of seeing more in a situation or an event than we could otherwise, or of seeing what we could not otherwise see at all. It must be clear that when we use a model or construct a model in order to explain something in the world, the model itself is not the world. The model is always something in the foreground, a screen, a pair of spectacles, an especially constructed device by means of which things unobservable become observable. But the model itself is not part of reality, nor is it even a segment of reality being explored. However, the character of the explanation of reality does depend upon the character of the model. This differentiation between reality and characterization of that reality will become significant when the status and grounds of knowledge and truth are further analyzed.

But, for the moment, we must note that since these two are not identical, the model can in no way be reduced to its object or become dissolved into the event being explored and explained. (This applies, of course, not only to analogies, but every form of model.) To remember this is to be free from all of the confusions which await those who forget that it is the reality which is the object of our ultimate concern. Necessary as the model may be, we must not be seduced by it.

It is simple enough to make note of this. It is much more difficult to remain actively alert to the limitations of any model and especially its separateness from that which we are trying to explain. But let us now extend the analysis. The success of any attempt at explanation depends upon the uses of instruments and methodology. Without these, no explanation whatever can take place. If we attempt to build explanations with clues from nature itself, we must recognize that we must agree upon what shall be accepted as clues, and thus what shall be counted as evidence, what shall signify connectedness, what shall be entailed in similarities, and also agree upon what organized rules and conditions will serve as the models to explain whatever it is we are now confronting. These purely conceptual agreements may refer to empirical events but do not derive from them; thus the very status of knowledge, truth, and explanation, is postulational—a matter of agreement among inquirers, having no fixed or positive structure in the empirical world, impervious to man's intrusions.

If we are concerned with equipping children to comprehend the world, to be consistent we must be concerned with helping them to develop a capacity to construct or recognize models that could be or have been used; and also with helping them to develop the ability that makes it possible to agree upon the use of models that have organized the appearance and meanings of the present world.

Scale models and representational thinking, as compared to analogy. Although the most usual instruments have been analogical models, there are more than just this one model form. As these are identified, the differences between the actual substances of the world and the formal ways used to organize those substances will become more apparent.

In addition to analogical models, there are scale models. These are quite familiar to us. On occasion, in writing or presenting a view, we want to illuminate some aspect of an event by presenting a picture, a chart, a graph, a diagram, or a blueprint, anything that appears to be a literal representation of the important features of that event. These are all scale models. They are constructed for the purpose of showing, as closely as possible, aspects of the actual event being examined. This is to be distinguished from an analogy, whose purpose is not simply to reveal and explain the features of anything; analogy is invented in order to recommend that the internal relationships in one event can be advisedly used to reveal, or illuminate, the internal relationships of some other event in order to comprehend it.

When we use an analogy, therefore, we must understand the whole of the analogy in order to be able to clarify the supposed relationships within and among the elements of the event being explored. These relationships, clearly described, become the source of the understanding of this new thing being considered. So an analogy does not have to be anything like the actual thing being considered, as does a scale model.

In the biblical story of Joseph's "coat of many colors," we can find an analogy for a set of relationships between several members of one family. Each patch, like each person, has a quality which is unique. All of the persons are "stitched" together by family "threads," as the separate patches are bound by the sewing thread.

The difficulties we have in getting analogies accepted are curious ones, but they reveal the power of any model used, especially the analogy. It is often rejected for the reason that if it is accepted, the acceptance obliges also acceptance of the relationships described within the analogy. Since this is the very thing being resisted, the analogy itself is rejected.

It is especially important to note that an analogy does not have to reflect the appearance of the object it is trying to explain. This is why, for example, one can use what might be the most absurd concepts as analogies for the most realistic human undertakings. And this is why, too, analogies well created can be dangerously beguiling, even to the most obdurate minds.

Consider, for example, the ballet called *The Green Table*. In highly stylized ballet form it analogizes political, diplomatic, military relationships between nations of the world. It is clearly not meant to be taken literally, and indeed, it could not be so taken. Perhaps it is because of this that the literal-minded are likely to say that it is too fantastic, too exaggerated, to accept it as a fair or true description of the political relationships of nations, or that it describes the truth with amazing exactness.

The Green Table is a ballet in which a group of people go through the formal rituals of diplomacy; the meeting, and bowing, and gesturing, are all analogized in the techniques of the dance. Diplomats encounter one another, sit down at tables together, chide and titillate one another, appease one another, taunt and challenge one another, then suddenly charge against one another. In this last scene is analogized the ritualizations of nations and men at war. It becomes quite clear that what is being analogized in the ballet is the relationship among diplomats from various countries meeting at some international congress. To say that diplomats do or do not behave like that is to be absurd and miss the point. It is charging the analogist, in this case, the choreographer, with creating a literal picture, a photograph of diplomats as dancers. In so doing, it is charged that he has deliberately presented a truth or a falsehood.

But the choreographer could not possibly have meant that. What he is suggesting is that the ritual by-play that he is presenting among these figures is a metaphor of the *relationships* that can be discerned among diplomats who perform their own ritual by-play in the somber council chambers of the world. It is for this reason, that art is said to penetrate more profoundly into the heart of human problems than science. It is the concern of the analogy to expose only the deepest of inner relationships, discernible only in the imagination of the creative mind.

In contrast to this, scale models are only concerned with the re-presentation, in scale, of some part or all of the features or the observable conditions of some event with which we are, could become, or wish to become, acquainted. The most familiar scale model is a road map. It is a scale model of part of a much larger terrain, and is designed to guide a traveler. If you examine a road map, you will see what the scale model makes possible. From it we are enabled to predict what will actually be encountered in a drive.

Scale models are material in themselves, and are primarily concerned with physical things encountered. It would be hard, if not altogether impossible, for example, to draw a scale model of the human personality, as, for example, it is understood in Freudian or Jungian psychology. In order to do so, the tenets of formation of scale models would direct us first to reduce the personality to some physical construct. But at best that would be making a scale of a metaphor and would be an analogical model, for all that it appears to be a scale.

If, for example, as modern behaviorist psychologists seem to be intent on doing, we were willing to reduce all human behaviors to a series of neuro-biochemical processes, then we could indeed draw a scale model of the personality. We would draw, to scale, the measurable input of certain stimuli at points of reception in the organism, plot the flow of electro-chemical impulses which are discharged, and course through identifiable nervepaths to centers which in turn send appropriate "messages" (electro-chemical impulses) to the muscles of the organism to produce some observable behavior. If that is what personality is construed to be, then a scale model would certainly be appropriate.

The coercions and the tests of model-using.   If one were to use a scale model as the model of personality, there is no alternative but to accept the notion that personality is a physical event. But the difference between a scale and an analogue is apparent in the fact that in the latter quantitative measurements are irrelevant, where in the former they are primary. In the analogue the totality of relation-ships and consequent connotations of quality is foremost. In the scale, measurable parts are the instruments of interpretation, exploration, evaluation.

This emphasizes an important fact. The use of the model neces-sarily limits our ability to comprehend the world. We understand in the world what the model tells us about the world, and we under-stand nothing else. Whatever is not explained by the model may be sensed, to be sure, but it is not understood.[3]

Thus, at a given moment, we can see what a given model is trying to tell us about the human personality. But what of other aspects? In this case, what of action motivated at a distance? What about a thought of something that has never been seen suddenly goading us into action? If the model does not take it into account, clearly that model will not suffice as a means of describing, explain-ing, or observing events we are nevertheless sensible of in some way.

But, lest you be deceived, let it be admitted that there has been surreptitiously invoked here another model which was not specifically named. We were not confronting fact with fact, but rather the range of applicability of one model against the range of applica-bility of another model. The question: "What of action at a distance"? was possible only by employing another model to talk about ele-ments sensed which the first model could not represent. To say on such an occasion, then, that you don't know what I am talking about, invariably means that whatever it is I am talking about is not accounted for in your model. To be sure, there is as great a danger in ascribing existence to what does not exist as there is in refusing to acknowledge that which does exist. Although models make think-ing possible, the thinking itself will finally be evaluated in the events actually experienced. But even this is not a readily accepted comfort for the mind.

In the disputes between a Freudian and a Behaviorist we find that each charges the other with having treated some dream quality as if it were reality. But the curious thing is that each one charges the other with being deluded about what each considers irreducibly real. So the Behaviorist charges the Freudian with dreaming into existence superego figures. They have no reality, says the Behaviorist. They are probably mistakes in identification of stimuli. The Freudian

[3] Thomas S. Kuhn, *The Structure of Scientific Revolution* (Chicago: Uni-versity of Chicago Press, 1962) makes much the same point; see esp. Chs. 1–5.

counters by saying that to dream man into the condition of being a machine and nothing else, is to manifest a dangerous need for escape from responsibility. Dispute between scholars turns out to be a dispute between the models each uses to give an account of his world. Such disputes, Kuhn has argued, constitute revolutions in thinking.[4]

At this point no claims are made as to priority or primacy for any form of model. Each one makes different things available and understandable in different ways. Nor is any hierarchical priority for any particular model of teaching being claimed. If one has a preference for Freudian models over behaviorist models, or for behaviorist models over Freudian models, it will be because of the fruitfulness of the consequences of their use. What appears to be the great difficulty for teachers who have made a fetish out of their own beliefs is that they are asked to unfix their commitments just long enough to recognize that the world is as variable as the number of models which can be used to explain any dimension of it. And these increase in variability as the discipline is matured. How trying this can be for the teacher in love with the transmission of Truth and Knowledge, can be readily imagined. Even students quickly learn to expect such dispensations. The teacher who is alive to variabilities is often accused of fence-straddling, of deliberately avoiding the obligation to believe something, anything, because he seems to want to believe everything or nothing. Students give such a teacher a bad time, precisely because they want so much to associate with him, and he offers no footing for this kind of association. Sooner or later they want to know what he, personally, believes. This is one of the most prominent hazards of the teaching profession.

One wonders, of course, why the students ask this. Is it because they want to know what they should believe as long as they are in this particular class? Or is it because they want to know at what point they can dismiss this particular teacher, and not have to take him seriously? It is hard to say. But assuredly, it upsets them to be teased with the assertion that, as a teacher you either believe everything, or you are not sure any longer what to believe. To them, the professor *must* believe. He must profess that belief among alternatives, or he is not playing the game.

---

[4] In Belth, *Education as a Discipline,* I have tried to show that rejection of a prevailing model is in fact the rejection of a way of thinking, and is the basis for all cultural revolutions; see esp. Chs. 1 and 2.

But there is something to be seriously considered in this apparently facetious response. This notion that the teacher must always let the student know where he stands and what he believes may be an unfortunate substitute for the more specific responsibility of competence. The question is not what the teacher believes, but on what grounds does anyone continue believing anything? This is much more justifiably the proper undertaking of education no matter what area of thinking is being explored. How fortunate the student who is suddenly aware that he can approach any given problem, not through the fixed models of a given school of psychology, a given school of philosophy, or a given school of anthropology; but rather by developing a comprehension and control of the variety of models that constitute a discipline. As these possibilities expand he is able to see for himself how incredibly rich in potentiality is every experience, how unexpectedly more meaningful is every book he reads, every mind he encounters.

Out of experiences with earlier approaches to science most of us have been initiated into the belief that the ultimate purpose of scholarship is the reduction of all knowledge to a condition of simplicity. But if the end of education is the improvement of the mind's powers, then subtlety and not simplicity is the goal. We may, indeed, seek clarity, but it is in multiplicity. It is making, as Chairman Mao would say if he were a serious man, a hundred ideas grow where only one grew before. The analogy between flowers and ideas is not inept. They may be seen, to press the point just a little more, as analogues, where each has the inner construction that allows for growth. As each derives sustenance from above and below, each blossoms at the observable extremities.

The net result of the kind of an education suggested here can only be the abolition of boredom forever. Nothing today needs to be quite like it was yesterday. However threatening this may be to those who dread change, it must be very welcome to those who see growth in change. For continued development, a little threat such as the threat of change, is but proof of a promising condition.

The theoretical model.   The scale model—coming back to that now—is that instrument by means of which we make clear the surface of things, the observable aspects or dimensions of the world we experience. We can use scale models and analogical models, as has been shown, though not simultaneously. It is not possible to think two things simultaneously. To use a scale model is to reveal one facet of the world; to use an analogy is to reveal another facet. To use one and then another is to gain added dimension of meaning and understanding.

Even further dimension is added as a third model is introduced. Theory, for example, when formulated into a model, becomes an instrument for explaining what neither of the others could. More than either the analogy or the scale, theory makes possible an organization of data that is not already organized. This is its great distinctive characteristic.[5] We can draw a scale model of an event only if it has already been organized by someone, or exists in some tangible form. The roads, an airplane, a coat, or a ship, each fashioned into a scale model, implies that there is already in existence materials organized to perform some function, to present a given appearance. But when we are concerned with theory, we are concerned with raw data which have no specific order or meaning. And precisely because of this, the data have infinite potential that can be actualized in a model of possibilities, the theoretical model.

The primary functions of any theory is to give order to unordered events. When we say of an activity that it does not yet have a theory, (as we do of school administration, for example) what are we saying? We are asserting that there is as yet no organizing model that will bring all of the acts, all of the observable data involved in this particular event into some kind of relationship which can be given meaning in a context, and submitted to efforts of prediction, explanation, and interpretation. When we say that administration still lacks a theory, we mean that administrators have no way of organizing the multiplicity of their acts into some kind of a unitary, purposeful, directed, explanatory system.

Astrology had influence over people for as long as it did because *astronomy* had not built a theory of the behavior of celestial bodies to which men could give their intellectual allegiance. When astronomy became a discipline and a science, it became the means of explaining and predicting the effects of certain tangible events on the lives of men. If astrology still influences many, it is because, as Kenneth Boulding points out, the model of the universe it celebrates still has psychological appeal for a great many,[6] offering explana-

---

[5] Cf. Peter Achinstein, *Concepts of Science* (Baltimore: Johns Hopkins Press, 1968), esp. pp. 212–226.
[6] Kenneth E. Boulding, *The Meaning of the Twentieth Century* (New York: Harper and Row, 1964), Ch. 2.

tions that intrigue, even if they offer little to organize for test. Astrology is concerned with matters astronomy does not recognize.

What, then, is the function of theory? Primarily, it organizes what is otherwise not organized. That should come as no surprise, as most of our behavior just below the level of deliberation is immediate response to immediate challenge, or stimulus.

The human organism does not wait to think before it acts, and it is probably, but not always, just as well. If we are hit, we strike back. We do not think about it. If we are hungry, we eat. We do not often think about it. If we are thirsty, we drink. We see certain things and we rarely respond in ways determined by the things themselves. We can recognize that our responses to each stimulus depend, more often than not, upon habituation. If we come upon something new, we respond to it in the terms of something that is familiar to us. If it is not familiar to us, we either respond to old memories, or we do not respond at all.

Only when we become embarrassed or concerned or fearful about inadequacies in these modes of response do we try to construct some kind of a model that will organize these events. Only in this way are we directed to newer responses, responses which will take fuller account of the ineluctable in existence. Thus, the second function of theoretical models is direction. We organize data in order to direct conduct.

Between these two functions of order and direction, all the other functions of models enter. The terms of the theory used enable us to describe what we are looking at, allow us to explain what is going on and to make acceptable interpretations, and lead us to define elements of events which would otherwise go undefined.

But describing the functions of theory does not explain precisely what a theoretical model is. A good illustration of such a model would be Skinner's concept of the human being. Even though it appears as an analogue which is then transformed into a scale, it finally emerges as a theoretical model. He has recommended the analogy between man and machine, and underlying this there is a scale model of machine-man, but first he offers some theory. The notion that the human organism is a mechanical event whose internal organs respond to one another as the internal components of any mechanism respond, is an analogue. But the analogy does depend on the theory of mechanics, a theory that accounts for the motion of physical events in nature. This clear-cut account is put to use as an analogy of the motion of motives and needs.

In Freud's theory of the human personality the balance between the pleasure impulse and the pain impulse produces an additional power. Now this, too, sometimes is presented as an analogue, but more often it is treated as the scale of a theory. Though I do not know of anyone who has actually attempted to quantify it, it is sometimes interpreted and explained by employing the analogy of a hydraulic system in which two forces operating against each other generate a third power.

From this we might deduce a further characteristic of a theory. It is a characteristic, however, which is difficult to utilize until we become quite familiar with what is at stake. When we observe the world as a series of unordered events we begin to conjecture about underlying conditions which might explain what we actually see. On what does this particular event rest, we ask? Such a question is directed, apparently, to the presence of something that can never be seen, except in the imagination. Only the innocent can listen to Freud's explanation of the id, superego and ego, and then ask where one would find the id. What kind of instrument must be used to locate it? Only the innocent would say of Skinner's theory, to come back to the first example, "Where do I go to find the cogs that, meshing with one another, run the rest of the gears of the organs for the body?" We recognize that as misplaced metaphors, these can be amusing. But Skinner provides us with a special difficulty. He insists that he has no theory. Indeed, he argues that he needs no theory, because what he describes actually exists.[7] But how one goes about proving the existence of dispositions of the human organism without giving them names is hard to imagine.

Nor does he stop there. He also insists that Freud must have believed in the *actual* presence of an id and a superego in the mind or the heart, serving as the behavioral determinant in man.

In a sense, Skinner's is a technical way of saying something quite familiar to all of us, but with one additional aspect. He is saying that theories are predictive statements about facts not yet demonstrated. But he adds, always by implication, that such predictions, or guesses, are better avoided. Against this I would suggest that to continue to hold the notion that a theory is valid only until it is disproven, or that a theory remains a theory until proven, at

[7] B. F. Skinner, "Critique of Psychoanalytic Concepts and Theories," *Minnesota Studies in the Philosophy of Science*, eds. H. Feigl and others (Minneapolis: University of Minnesota Press, 1956), vol. 1, pp. 77–87.

which time it becomes a fact, is to talk about theory in the basest, most naive sense. It is to confuse theoretical talk with projective, practical talk simply because neither has a discernible referent for the moment.

But theories do not become facts, any more than crumbs of bread become roaches, although many people were taught this several decades ago. It is obvious that crumbs cannot grow legs and become roaches, although it is probably true that they do attract roaches. But, even in this form, there is an interesting presupposition; if you drop a crumb, there will be a roach somewhere in the vicinity. If you say that your house has never had roaches, the appearance of one requires some demonstrable explanation. There were no roaches, but there are roaches now; perhaps the crumbs have grown legs, flat body antennae, and have begun to run around. But we know that by the very nature of the case, crumbs cannot become roaches; nor can theories become facts. Such transformations are incompatible with what is known about both cases.

What a theory does.   A theory is a deliberately constructed and described symbolic "sub" world on which the actually experienced world is now said to rest. But it must be understood that even if we did not build the "sub" world, the world of experience would still be there. Children do get frightened of some things but not of others. Parents do become hysterical over certain fancies and not over others. Men do become angry with one another. Whether there is a theory for it or not, these events do occur. The furniture of our world goes on behaving in observable ways, though it may go unexplained. It is because we cannot *see* causes or categories which would be explanations that we are obliged to construct an explanation or an explanatory system. Unless, of course, we are simply willing to accept what is, without needing or wanting explanation.

When we are concerned with theory, therefore, we are not so much concerned with how the thing appears nor even with the inner, but still discernible transactions within events used to explain appearances. We are really concerned with the event itself and with its career, formative character and heritage. We are concerned with offering an account of both the inner and outer phases, and propounding a *principle* to explain the whole.

A theory is valid if it provides us with a logical and coherent *account* of what we see. It is invalid if the logic of the theory does not encompass the logic of the behavior of the things observed. Thus, the theory that man is made in the image of God, and possesses within him the spark of that God, a spark that affects his behavior and his choices, is inadequate to account for human behavior. If the logic of man's observable behavior is not accounted for by this, the theory that man is a diminished God simply will not do. Man's actual behavior does not fall within that kind of explanatory system, unless, of course, we employ an early Greek conception of gods as beings who thoroughly enjoyed that easy transition they were able to make between Earth and Olympus, transforming themselves readily from one state of existence to another, and benefitting from both. Now, if that is the concept of the God-Man relationship offered to account for man, then at least some fundamental aspects of the logic would hold, but only if we are willing to play language games and treat myths and empirics alike. But the conception of God—God as divine, God as pure, God as infinitely self-controlled and self-contained, God as pure act, God as pure intelligence, simply cannot be used to account for what we know of man's behavior.

There is an interesting distinction to be made here between theory and myth. Common sense definitions of myth appear to be similar to the concept of theory in this discussion, except for the fact that myth is offered as a statement in which *both* sides of an equation are treated as having the same quality of reality. Thus, in Plato's myth of the cave, the chained men in the cave were as real as the brassy spirits which resided within those very men. In theoretical conceptions nothing more is claimed of the observable world than direct observations will reveal. Thus, a scientist will not look for a real "spirit" to describe when he offers an account of behavior of men or events. Moreover, the testing of theory lies in active intrusion in behavioral matters, with some evidence to demonstrate any changes which have occurred. No such test can be made of mythic constructions, since what it seeks to direct is itself unobservable and wants proving.

There are occasions when we cannot propound or discern in experience the basis for alternative explanations. Only one explanation seems available. At such a point any theory that is proposed is accepted since it is only by means of theory that we explain behavior. The only reason to reject a theory under such conditions is to say that we do not want or need to have human behavior explained. It is what it is, and we shall leave it at that.

PSYCHOLOGICAL AND SOCIOLOGICAL MODELS

The educational exclusions in psychological and sociological models. If we move now to a consideration of conceptions of subject matter, of the teacher, of the educative process, and of the child, and bear in mind the explanatory function of theory, we are in a position to sort out some of the prevailing theories and offer them as models for critical analysis of the various aspects of education. We might even propound a theory of our own.

To have constructed an educational theory on the basis of what is known of the child's behavior in an educational context allows us an opportunity to make a critical examination of relevant segments of the sciences of psychology, sociology, anthropology, or biology. One of the reasons that education has been totally dominated by the fields of sociology and psychology is that each has a theory to explain the behavior of children. Educators as such (meaning, perhaps, general educationists) really have none of their own. As soon as an educator begins to construct a theory, he has several problems to face.

First of all, he has to face the challenges of the psychologist and the sociologist who have laid what seems to be complete claim to all the dimensions of the child's development. Second, the educator has to explain to his fellow educators why these theories are less desirable than the theory he now wants to help build, what he, as educator, could possibly include not already included by both the others. Most educators have so indiscriminately absorbed the models of psychology and sociology that they do not want to be confused by further notions. Why abandon what has been widely accepted, and is apparently so effective in directing daily educational practices?

It is difficult to persuade others that a fundamental principle of any model is that it imposes limits on what will be understood. When we accept a model, we are obliged to accept, within the limits of the model itself, the terms of what can be explored and explained. However inclusive psychological and sociological models might be, they must in principle be limited, in spite of what the claimants may say.

What could an educational theory say about child development that a psychological theory could not and would not? No psychological theory has presented cognition in quite the way an educator will. No psychological theory can, even in principle, be concerned with the methodology, as compared with the more limited *method* of learning. What psychological models lay open to observation and explanation are the facts of response (motivated or unmotivated), integrated or disintegrated behavior, and balanced or unbalanced emotions. An interesting demonstration of this limiting character is to be found in the fact that no psychologist has ever written about education without inevitably diminishing the primary character of knowledge and of cognition. Sooner or later, every psychologist must in principle become anti-intellectual in some educational sense. The very basis of psychological guidance, psychotherapy, psychoanalysis, is the effort at the reconstruction of behavior whether the patient knows this is being reconstructed or not. It is sometimes argued that it would be of benefit if he knew, but it is also generally argued that it is not imperative that he know. It might, on occasion, even interfere with his being brought back to balance or to sanity. Psychological models, therefore, do not view a child's development from the side we seek.

For the same reasons, neither do sociological models. Sociology is concerned with the study of developing in the child a life-style congruent with others in an ongoing culture. Undoubtedly it can be assumed that the sociologist hopes that the child will learn to take the best possible advantage of the resources in the society about him. But sociology is not concerned with increasing this power. Rather, it is primarily professionally concerned with developing a theory for discovering what are the effective interactions, responsivity to social obligation, and efficient transactions between social forms and individual powers. It would be hard to find any sociological theory that is concerned with giving an account of the meanings and the nature of the processes which enter into the use of social forces for the reconstruction of culture. Since this seems to run almost completely counter to sociological theory, what is to be done with theories concerned with means by which societies themselves are altered?

The force of theory in the thinking act.   It is hard to study the act of thought by means of analogy, scale, or representative models. It can only be done on the basis of the construction of a new *theory*. It is of fundamental importance, however, to remember that every theory ever held was constructed at some point in time by someone. This is the force of theory in the thinking act. However durable it is, however completely persuasive it is, however widely it has been accepted, however seemingly unarguable and irrefutable it is (so, for example, the Theory of Gravity might be deemed), it is nevertheless a theory. While it is constructed to explain the real, in principle it itself contains real qualities of mental phenomena. That is, though theory has no physical dimensions, it is at the basis of behavior. It is the deliberately invented picture of a subterranean world that does not exist. The myth of the Greeks' nether world where Persephone was required to live for six months every year, becomes a charming analogy of Theory, though it does not otherwise have the status of a theory. The analogy needs translation.

The myth states that half of one's life one must spend in pure thought, constructing a world that can never actually be visited. The other half is spent in the outer world. To this outer world we bring the strength of the imagined other world, the strength of imagination itself, since there is no other world except in our imaginations. Surely, Persephone must have been the most urbane of Greek women. She lived easily in these two worlds, consorting well with each, enjoying the fruits of both. So much so that when some outer-world lover tried to rescue her, Persephone was angry and bereft. She had come to love that quiet and darkened world. And was it not her knowledge of that world that finally deepened her understanding and her appreciation of the outer world? Would she not have been deprived of a vital sense of the outer had she been drawn completely away from the other?

As a myth, the charm of the story is limited. As a theory, this concept of man's status in the world of ideas and the world of overt action still has the power to explain and to influence choices.

MATHEMATICAL MODELS: A NOTE ON SYMBOL WORLDS

There is a type of concern with symbols that very quickly develops into such a technical complexity that it all but defies any brief analysis. Yet the very complexity gives a hint of the importance of such models. The timorous avoid the perils of confronting such complexities lest they become embroiled far beyond the realms of simplicity. The brash swim out, hoping the undercurrents do not sweep them beyond control too quickly. For the necessity of swimming across the currents that connect two segments of the one world cannot be overlooked. This is, after all, one world, in spite of all the distinctive universes into which we divide it. The universe of experience is interpenetrated by the universe of discourse so that they cannot be, in any real sense, extracted from one another.

But they can be *thought* about separately. In fact, to be able to think about them separately makes it possible to treat the unitary whole with greater intelligence and sensitivity than if we treat it in its total immediacy. It is for this reason that the intent of the opening chapters, was to show how the control of symbol systems finally meant the better understanding, organizing, explaining, evaluating, of the totality of experience.

Now, such a concern directs us, at last, to a consideration of the very symbol systems in and of themselves. Something happens when symbol systems are constructed that is not very mysterious, though it is sometimes unexpected and undeniably surprising. For when a symbol system is created, the system itself seems to take on a life of its own, become a world of its own, internal to itself, with roads, and signs, and rules, and directions to be followed, and directions for what cannot take place. But this "taking place" must be understood. It means "taking place" in the world of those signs, rules, directions. In this case, it is the world of mathematics. It is a world of symbols where each symbol is treated as a unitary notation, and these notations can be connected together by rules of relationship we call logic. The resulting statements are treated as formulas, or models of relationships, and what else we might be able to say about those relationships, or about later phases of those relationships, must already be clearly implied, or built into, the forms of the original statement.

Every such world begins with postulates, or axioms, and with some definitions. It also contains, at the outset, rules of the relation of notations to one another. Whatever else can be said can be said only if it is entailed in the original combination of definitions, posits, and operating rules. And because this is so, the mathematical world is generally more precise than any world we encounter in existence. (That this neatness sometimes hides unexpected complexities and confusions is part of the history of mathematics, and part of the excitement of its advanced study.)

To give but the simplest possible example of what I am saying, take the illustration which Frege gives in his *Foundations of Arithmetic*.[8]

8 Gottlob Frege, *The Foundations of Arithmetic,* trans. John L. Austin (Oxford: Blackwell, 1959), pp. 7e–8e.

If we define 2 as 1 plus one; and 3 as 2 plus one and 4 as 3 plus one, then we can say that 2 plus 2 is equal to 2 plus one plus one. Then, $(2 + 1) + 1 = 3 + 1 = 4$. But 1 and 2 and 3 are already specific, or particular numbers. What we need is some demonstration from a general rule that we can handle these numbers in ways directed from some larger rule. So let us assume the law that
$$a + (b + c) = (a + b) + c.$$
So long as we maintain constant values for the letters used, the rules recommended produce valid outcomes and relationships in later phases, and show new possibilities to us.

This acceptance becomes a model for every addition which we want to make. There is much more to even so simple a matter of "proving" addition to be valid, but it will serve us for the moment.

The matter, however, that is most relevant to us is to be discovered in the fact that this perfect world (or almost perfect world) of mathematics does not reflect, or mirror, or represent the world of our experiences at all. It is a purely conceptual world, with a dynamic character of its own, bespeaking only the relationship of the symbols which we have constructed within the relationships we have recommended. The temptation to see in this world the mysterious perfection of the empirical world is a dreadful one. But when we can see the experiential independence of mathematics we recognize that the models of mathematics (and every formula in every branch of mathematics is a model for a given set of conceptual operations) explain nothing about the world of nature or of man. What it explains is the conditions of the very models which are its formulas. In this, then, mathematics might even be considered as "self-explanation," or "self-evident," or, in logical terms, "tautological."

But when we also consider that mathematical models, as any models, are instruments for organizing events other than themselves, and for endowing those events with meanings that are elements of the model, we can begin to see the role such models play in human experiences. From the precision of the model we are able to speak with like precision of the world of our encounter. Of course, we are limited in what we can say about that world by the terms of the models. But of that of which we can speak, we can speak with precision. If we speak of the external world in terms of unitariness, of relationships of addition and subtraction, of either/or, of positive and negative, of if, . . . then, of commutation and distribution, and avoid concern, for that time, with what we might call the qualitative dimensions of existence, then we can indeed speak with precision about that world, because the models themselves are precisely constructed.

The study of such models, in and of themselves, as with the study of any language, in and of itself, makes it possible to talk about the world in ways that are not otherwise open to us. That all of the sciences have moved more and more in the direction of "mathematization" is only a demonstration of the quest for greater and greater precision in their explorations of the empirical world by means of the models of the conceptual.[9]

LINGUISTIC MODELS: AN EQUALLY BRIEF NOTE

The last of the model forms, linguistic models, are those by means of which we treat a problem of human existence not so much by means of language but *as* a language. As we learn to parse a sentence, so we learn to "parse" human transactions. In that way we recognize relationships, dependencies, predicates, object, subject, and so on, among human beings, between men and things, and between men and ideas. To be able to see human relationships as a structured language is to be equipped to see the most surprising meanings in this relationships. To be able to give to the events considered the legitimate predictability found in ordinary sentences is to have a powerful instrument for avoiding many types of confusion.

The use of a language model makes it possible to treat an event that you observe as you would treat a sentence. Experience may be construed as language models allow. Vision and ethical beliefs can both be analyzed as language is analyzed. Indeed, it is possible to consider that everything that men do comprises a language. We can develop such conventions that would make every act, every gesture, a mode of communication. Within these we might look for subject, predicate, copula, modifiers, operators, prepositions, conjunctions, disjunctions, and so on. And as when we learn to parse

---

[9] This terribly brief section can be enhanced if the reader were to dip into any of the following: Gottlob Frege, *The Foundations of Arithmetic;* Frank P. Ramsey, *The Foundations of Mathematics* (Paterson, N.J.: Littlefield, Adams, 1960); Bertrand Russell, *Introduction to Mathematical Philosophy* (London: G. Allen and Unwin, 1948); or Friedrich Waismann, *Introduction to Mathematical Thinking*, trans. Theodore J. Benac (New York: Harper, 1959). For a fine introductory work, see Herbert Fremont, *How to Teach Mathematics in Secondary Schools* (Philadelphia: Saunders, 1969).

a sentence, we discover a meaning in relationships that could not otherwise have been observed.[10]

In the modern world, more and more people have come to
view art linguistically. That is, a man acting can be understood as
we would understand man speaking. This can be extended to a man
painting, or sculpting, or building. When we speak, we are saying
something about something. The sentence may refer to something in
the objective world, but not always. It is just as meaningful for us to
refer to whatever may be in our imagination. When we recognize this,
we recognize that we need not look at the mechanism of a sculpture
in order to discover what it is supposed to represent. The meaning
lies in the wholes and parts, in the separate but interrelated parts.
Metaphorically, we look for the syntax and the semantics within
the sculpture. In this analysis we reach to the problem of discerning
the active mind of the individual. What was he thinking about as he
did this piece of work? What he was looking at? What did the artist
"say" in the molding of this or that material? Every work then
becomes a "statement" that a man makes about the world.

Rodin's *The Burghers of Calais* is surely just such a statement.
Is it a statement about means of dress of the Burghers? About their
passions? Their obligations? Perhaps it is not an objective statement
about the Burghers at all. Perhaps it is a subjective statement, revealing the artist's vision. Was he, perhaps, deliberately trying to say
something that obliged him to distort the obvious?

Still another illustration of this is Rembrandt's *The Night
Watch,* where the artist painted the elders of Amsterdam in such a
way as to make a painfully clear statement of their pomposity, their
overbearing egos, their superficial devotions, the splendor which
covered but did not hide their irresponsibilities. All this appears in
the one painting when we consider the painting as a language by
means of which the painter "spoke his mind."[11]

These, then, are some of the models which enter into the think-

[10] In the rapidly growing literature of this field several works command
attention; among them: John L. Austin, *How to Do Things with Words*
(London: Oxford University Press, 1963); Jerome S. Bruner, Jacqueline
J. Goodnow, and George A. Austin, *A Study of Thinking* (New York:
Science Editions, 1962); Rudolf Carnap, *The Logical Syntax of Language*
(London: K. Paul, Trench, Trubner and Co., 1937); Ernst Cassirer, *An Essay
on Man* (New Haven, Conn.: Yale University Press, 1956); Benjamin L.
Whorf, *Language, Thought, and Reality* (New York: Wiley, 1956).
[11] A most impressive work is Nelson Goodman's *The Languages of Art* (In-
dianapolis: Bobbs-Merrill, 1968). It ought to be read in connection with this
particular conception.

ing act, some of their distinctive traits, limits, and type of thinking they make possible. These are models at the most general level. Any act of thought, no mattter how it is particularized, must use one or more of these. This will become more apparent as we move to a consideration of specific models used in specific disciplines, and apply this to the burgeoning discipline of education.

CHAPTER 6

Models of the New World

WE now turn to a more direct consideration of models of education. These had been mentioned very briefly as we developed the thesis of a distinctive theory of teaching. But we now need to concentrate on five such models. In so doing we will, it is hoped, be developing a somewhat more inclusive structure, placing these models into a larger context in order to provide a firmer basis for some of the claims that have been made about the role, the form, and the quality of the act of teaching. In the chapters which follow we will be returning continuously to each model, filling it in until a complete picture has been set forth by the end of this work.

MODELS IN DISCIPLINES

The model as a carrying agency. The conviction that the model of education is distinctively the educator's, that is, the teacher's, and not that of any other discipline should be apparent in this work. Indeed, it is obligatory for the educator to employ a specially constructed model of education to communicate to students the particular models which comprise each specific discipline.

The basic question which education must confront is the question of how both knowledge and judgment-making procedures are to be transmitted. How do we communicate to children, or to learners of any age, the understandings which would enable them to comprehend the world they experience, and undertake the direction of their own lives? How can we nurture in them the capacity for making such judgments as will give meanings and control to experiences? Surely we have come to recognize that understandings are not simply locked into words and passed on by pronouncements, written or spoken. Words are not enough; we must assure ourselves that the words form complete and meaningful wholes, that is, sentences. And we must assure ourselves that the words do carry, in their contexts, the meanings which we want them to have. Moreover, we must be certain that the meanings we want to transmit are actually transmitted. Words do not have meanings intrinsically. When they mean something, they mean something other than their own sounds and appearances. They are not like diamonds and emeralds which hold a glitter within themselves; if words themselves glitter, they have a different cash value than the meanings ascribed to them in the context in which they are placed.

Words are symbols of something; of things, relationships, states of mind, desires, expectations, or such. They derive their specific meanings only in the larger context of symbols which define their focus and the limits. The whole sentence, therefore, is a system of symbols, and within that sentence-system each word derives the meaning that the sentence allocates to it.

The whole sentence becomes a model of the event that it is symbolizing, much as a road map is a model of the terrain it is symbolizing. Within the road map we find standard "terms." We find lines of one thickness representing major roads, of another, lesser roads, of yet another, minor or unpaved roads. Other symbols represent railroads, roadworks, roadcrossings, intersections, distances between places, the places themselves, the size of the cities and so on. Somewhere on the side of a well prepared map, we find a "dictionary" of terms, providing a scale for measuring distances set down for use, definitions of symbols used, and anything else needed if the symbol of the entire event is to be completely understood.

We know, too, that out of context, the symbols which have meaning in the model, the map, have no meaning at all. When the defining context has been removed, there is no way of discovering the meanings intended. The heavy red line which symbolizes a major expressway within the map is simply a visible mark outside of that context. It may be used to symbolize anything at all in some other context. If we are concerned with transmitting to a traveler an understanding of the map, we must make him aware of the model as a whole, within which each elemental symbol plays some role.

Precisely the same obligation holds true for the transmission of the meaning of a sentence embedded in the model which constitutes a history, a mathematical structure, a psychological treatise, a literary creation, and so on. It is in this sense that every model, or symbol system, is a carrier of meanings. To foster understanding we are required to make available the symbol system as a whole, as it has been integrated, along with its "dictionary" for interpretation and comprehension. To teach history is to teach *a* history; to teach mathematics is to teach *a* mathematics; to teach psychology is to teach *a* psychology. To teach anything is to make available the model of some specific event, the grasp of which makes it possible to understand every element within that event, and the ways in which the whole gives meaning to each element.

Model-bearing models require communication.   But we must recognize that in education just as we do not communicate understanding simply by transmitting sounds or providing the written word to those who would learn, so we do not simply communicate a particular model by the written or the spoken word. The model of some history, or some geography, or some work of literature is itself part of a yet larger model of communication absorbing the learner himself into the total context of inquiry. These encompassing models lead him to develop a competence in the language of the model being studied.

It is as if we wanted to communicate to a foreigner the procedures for electing a head of government in the country. Before the communication could take place, a language, a symbol system must be made available to him, by means of which relevant materials can be communicated. What is required is illustrated in a brief novel, *The Ten Commandments* written by Thomas Mann. In it he relates what he thought was the problem Moses faced in presenting the Ten Commandments to the wandering Hebrew tribes.

The Hebrews, he seems to think, were a verbal society, without any written language. If Moses were to transmit to his people a series of rules for living which were said to come from the God on high, either God or Moses would first have to invent a language, distill it into written symbols, and then teach the Hebrews the symbols and their meanings. As the story goes, it took Moses all of the forty days which he spent on the mountain to invent that symbol system, a system of marks he used to sort out the rules of obedience and reverence which he hoped would secure the nation in its desert sojourn. Moses became the lawgiver by first becoming the symbol-system maker. And this system itself became the model for all future communications.

It is in this same sense that we shall be describing the models of educating. The models of the various disciplines that make the realities of the world available to us need to be made comprehensible and approachable by those who teach to those who come to learn. A model-system will be constructed to encompass the rules, laws, theories, concepts, facts, and model-structures which constitute each of the disciplines.

Every discipline is made of a plurality of models.   Every subject in a curriculum is simply an illustration of somebody's sorting out of events past. In this act of sorting out materials present to us in experience, order and meaning is given to that data. It is thus that every form of every discipline is an illustration of a particular sorting out. Toynbee's history is a model of writing history; Bloch's history is another model of a similar sort of thing; so is Becker's, so is Commager's, so is any other historian's. When we find ourselves wanting to know which history is most acceptable, it is to the model of each that we must first go. What we are looking for is some evaluative instrument, or at least some clue to one to lead us to the supportable belief that we may dismiss all except, say, Finger-print's *History of the Risen Atlantis.* In reaching this we will also have concluded that Toynbee's history is an illustration of inadequate historical thinking, and Becker's is an equally limited, but very different kind of an illustration; Commager's is inappropriate for another reason. Only Fingerprint's remains for us a model of historical thinking in this area of events.

But, alas, there is no such thing as the model of thinking, historical or otherwise. Any such quest for *the* historical approach must have begun with the assumption that nature has set out deliberately to confuse human beings until some valiant, courageous and relentless pursuer will at last confront nature and tear away its illusionary veils, like some John the Baptist, tearing away the veils of Salome, revealing her naked and in truth.

Empirically, it would be much harder to sustain that belief

about nature than to undertake the more uncertain, but much more fruitful recommendation that is offered as an alternative. There is uncertainty in the view that there is no one history, no one model for writing history. Every history, which means every written or otherwise recorded account, presents itself as an account whose credibility depends upon the criteria that are contained in the model used. This does not, of course, mean that every history is as good as every other history. All human beings, behaving in equally human ways, do not manifest behavior that is equally acceptable to all human beings. Criteria of purpose, of intention, of motivation, of defensibility, must be posited and used. It does say that there is not one pattern of conduct that is right and all others wrong.

History, to repeat, is constructed on some historian's model. But there is no single model for writing history any more than there is only one method of science. Models are changed in response to pertinent new data and new intentions. If this is the case, then the view that it is the function of education to communicate historical truths is no longer defensible. Rather, the function of the study of education is to make available to the learner conceptual instruments enabling him to penetrate into the works of any historian in order to discover how the use of his particular model, or models, allowed him to reach his conclusions.

It is with a clear exposition of what constitutes this and other educational models that we are concerned. Several such models will be identified, a little will be said about the conditions of each, and then we will consider what cognitive power each model is designed to foster in any learner.

It is important to reiterate a distinction made earlier. The concern in education is to develop in the learner competence in the use of those models that transform raw data into the subject matters, the substantial content by means of which lives are lived. There is a difference between the model the teacher uses and the model-use that is to be generated in the child. Otherwise we return to the naive view that proper education can be accomplished by fostering in the child the ability to imitate his teacher. But if all we want the child to do is to imitate the teacher, then the less complicated the teacher's acts are, the better it is for the child. And if that is the case, then we are back into the point at which any meaningful distinctiveness about the act of teaching is impossible to establish. Teaching is utterly simple. What we want a six-year-old to be, we must first be ourselves. This is applicable to any age and to any type of behavior, intellectual or emotional. It does not matter whether the child understands what he is doing. What matters is that the teacher and the community agree that this is what we want the child to be, and we must make ourselves perfect "models" to be copied. (The quotation marks here are intended to indicate that this is *not* the concept of *model* which is being used throughout this work.)

THE DIALECTICAL MODEL

The conditions. We begin with dialectic. Familiarly, this is an organized play of conversation. Nevertheless, it is not ordinary conversation. It is a deliberately constructed conversation between two or more people, with a specific objective set up at the outset. In a classroom it is expected that one of the participants is expert in moving the conversation from the level of opinion to the level where opinion can be examined carefully so that what is entailed in a given opinion is identified and may be logically tested. By means of dialogue, that which first escaped the awareness of the individual (who may or may not be the learner) is made evident. The purest and fullest illustrations of this, of course, are to be found in Plato's writings. Once it is recognized what Plato was doing, it cannot but be recognized how completely remarkable is this invention of his.

Plato allowed the people of the Dialogues to begin at any point in an exchange. He did not insist on a formally established, logical, starting point. Any place, any problem, was acceptable. What we do observe, however, is that there was a basic presupposition that no agreement existed among those engaged in the exchange. Therefore, because it is basic to such an exchange, one of the functions of dialectic is to develop agreement. From this agreement can be developed some definition that makes it possible to consider anew and with more critical understanding, the original problem. By means of the dialogue each participant is obliged and equipped to look more carefully into the variety of meanings of the terms used in ordinary discussions and inquiries. We become acutely conscious that the variety of meanings in ordinary thinking seems to produce inevitable contradictions. The net result is that we, as students, are obliged to become more critical of exactly what we say as we try to think through problems, problems that have suddenly become much more complex than they had originally seemed.

The most familiar historical view of dialectic is that it is the term applied to the "soul's dialogue with itself"; that is, with man, thinking. As Plato indicated, or seemed to indicate in *The Republic,* it is the mode of thinking we use to think through to the very principles of events, or problems, or of ideas. Thus, dialectic is generally taken to be a form of thinking within which are produced such possible counter-instances of meanings as to oblige the thinker to produce consistent, logically sound definitions and apply these to specific problems.

But in any critical examination of any of the earlier or middle dialogues, it is hard to avoid Socrates' undeniably formal approach to every problem. When the primary concern of the reader is to identify and fix the substantive conclusion of a given dialogue, it is not hard to understand why dialectic is considered only a form of thinking. But from the concern of education, of nurturing powers that are not nurtured, a new meaning and force of the dialectic becomes apparent.

Though this point is rarely made there is in a dialectic a difference between what the teacher does and what the student is being nurtured to do. Careful consideration reveals that the teacher is not evaluating, or being critical of his own assertions. By a process that looks like an open conversation and the tactic of raising questions in the form of pressing for clarification of meanings, he is obliging the learner to peer into the meanings of his own words. In this sense, he is fostering in the learner a disposition for logical evaluation of statements made. But Socrates, as teacher, never evaluates his own assertions.

Nowhere in the dialectic did Plato or Socrates identify by name or definition the mode of logic utilized. Nevertheless, he provided the student with the sense of a logic that must prevail. When the student learns to use it, he applies it to his own beliefs about problems that cannot be pushed into final resolution or final truths.

Suppose you were to be engaged in conversation on any subject at all. As you began to talk, questions might be raised. For purposes of simple clarification, questions about the possible and probable meanings of what has been said are also raised. Such questions would not have the deliberate purpose of obliging you to show that any particular statement you might make is consistent with any previously made statement, but would be put in such a way as to enable you to see for yourself whether later statements were consistent with earlier ones, entailed in them, or controverted by them; whether they were sufficiently distinct, or too vague and too ambiguous.

What the teacher does directly in conversation, the student is being nurtured to do indirectly. And conversely, what the teacher does indirectly, the student is being asked to do directly. This difference between the direct and the indirect is absolutely crucial. What is done directly? Directly, the teacher engages the student in overt conversation. But the teacher is not simply teaching him how to converse. If the student learns this, he will learn it indirectly and on his own, not through any direct efforts. But indirectly, by means of dialogue, the teacher is exposing the lines of logical inquiry. This the student will be learning to do directly.

If you find yourself unable to continue the dialogue because you discover inconsistencies in your statements, you will also find yourself becoming more reluctant to say anything until you have assured yourself that you are not negating yourself, and that what you are saying does have definition. But does one never put himself through such a dialogue? Perhaps. Plato did say that thinking was talking to oneself. But it is not as simple as the statement would appear to make it. (How far Socrates is to be taken seriously rather than as a great wit has been an interesting question for a long time.)

The previous discussion of learning as externalizing has relevance here. In principle, of course, one holds dialogue with oneself as he materializes vague notions into more comprehensive concepts. But more needs to be said. There is nothing in any externalized idea that gives any direction as to how that idea is to be considered, analyzed, evaluated. But words, it may be argued, do have meanings. That is what makes them words. Therefore, to attend to words in their meanings is to think; and to do so privately is to hold private dialogue.

But aside from the question of whether or not words do have meanings outside the context of a sentence (J. L. Austin argued against this[1]), the issue is whether learning is done by oneself, or deliberately and economically nurtured by others.

Consider this additional condition of the dialogue. In a genuine dialogue, a difference of preferences among possible beliefs is the very basis of an exchange between protagonists. The fact that both have commitment provides the condition for dialogue. It is possible for an individual to take two disparate views in hopes of seeing limits of meanings more clearly. But the power to take both sides with equal

[1] John L. Austin, *Philosophical Papers,* eds. J. O. Urmson and Geoffrey J. Warnock (Oxford: Clarendon Press, 1963).

firmness must be nurtured if any problem is to be worked out in a dialogical fashion. In fact, the ability to offer counter-instances to oneself is one mark of the educated man. It marks the development of mind beyond a passionate and zealous adherence to one view. This use of counter examples is more readily accomplished in actual experimentation than in the soul's dialogue with itself. It is the intention in using the dialectic to teach the student to pursue logically what is contained in any belief, or series of beliefs he holds. It is intended to give him an instrument for learning to be consistent in his beliefs, and to see meanings embedded, but not ordinarily recognized, in opinions. It is, in fact, an instrument deliberately employed to promote the act of externalizing on which we spent so much time two chapters earlier.

Unchanging symbols and changing referrents. Nothing so underscores the differences between formal learning with its deliberate tuition between teacher and student, and informal learning with its ordinary exchanges in ordinary confrontations, than an awareness of the structure of dialectic. The classroom becomes the laboratory for learning to detect and correct errors in the logic of our beliefs, thus improving our ability to communicate with others, outside the laboratory. But this is not accomplished simply by enthusiasm or desire. The power of any disciplined undertaking is measured by the forms of its methods and techniques. We will see this in the dialectic.

The great necessity of dialectic can be seen when we consider that there are always too many words poured out in classrooms, words that serve little, if any, function. They are just blather, disgorged untended, indiscriminately and wastefully, ultimately creating a void where there should be thought. Education will never be a discipline until teachers learn to respect words, to tend them in their labors as the lawyer does in his, as any professional uses his instruments, judiciously, frugally, measuring use against intention and achievement. In dialectic, there is a form for control of expression.

There is a significant psychological dimension in any classroom use of dialectic. In some way the intellectual flexibility of the instructor communicates itself to the student as an emotion-laden state. When a sense of freedom appears it appears as a kind of an atmospheric condition, like a sense of congeniality. During the dialogue we are aware that we are talking about things that are sometimes sacred, sometimes deeply private. We know that some people may become tense and upset by the challenges. But it is important to note that the purpose of dialectic is not to convert someone to a view he does not hold at the outset.[2]

An aura of intellectual respect is fundamental here and auras do not get taught, they pervade. But a pervasive aura does not necessarily produce clarity of thinking. It may make it possible to communicate such clarity, once you have learned to think clearly. It may even be a necessary empirical condition that clears the way for teaching and for learning. But it is *not* the teaching or the learning. And it is the latter, the quest for clarity of thinking, that is the objective of dialectic.

It has been said that conversation which has the character of dialectic occurs only with such problems as are not reducible in the long run to a fixed definition. There are unquestionably, in every discipline we know, areas in which the definition we arrive at, or the assumptions with which we begin, must be arbitrary. These are what they are, not because nature chooses them, but because we agree they shall be so, since no other way of reaching the definition appears to be available.

For example, we would all admit that a table is hard. But before we can agree that it is, we must tacitly or explicitly agree to what we shall mean, or what is generally meant by, the term *hard*. There is nothing, no object in nature, that we can turn to that will reveal to us what is meant by the word *hard*. We must agree on it. Even if there appears to be an inescapable feature of the world which needs to be symbolized, the event itself does not determine the symbol. We must agree upon the terms. These terms become our conventions.

Susan Stebbing[3] gives a charming illustration which is relevant to the role of a fixed convention in a changing world. There was a time when we used the term *hard* to refer to an undifferentiated object firmly resistant to the touch. But now that we have high-powered electronic microscopes, we can examine a completely con-tinuous ·piece of plastic that serves as the top of a table and by focussing on it, we can see that what we really think is unbroken has very wide interstices. We explain its enduring rigidity by the fact that it has a structure of molecules darting about at a tremendous rate of speed. We look through the microscope, then look away and

[2] On this matter of conversion, see Marc Belth, "Socratic Persuasion," *Educational Issues,* Toronto University, 1(1968): 50–66.
[3] L. Susan Stebbing, *Philosophy and the Physicists* (New York: Dover Publications, 1958), Ch. 3.

ask "Did we say this was hard?" meaning, did we say that this was an undifferentiated piece? The answer is, of course, yes. But when looked at through the microscope, we wonder why a pair of eyeglasses lying on the counter does not fall through as it is put down. There is so much space and so little wall.

What is the answer? This depends on our recognition of the problem. A later description calls for a correction of the original conventional definition of the term *hard,* Stebbings says.

But isn't it still resistant?

Yes, of course.

And to the now aided eye, does it not have a great many holes? To be sure.

Then, what is meant by *hard* is that which, to the aided eye, has wide spaces, but to the unaided eye looks continuous, but which in either case it is not possible to put a finger through.

Although new evidence obliged us to change the convention a little, the convention itself remained. What was really altered was our awareness of aspects we had overlooked. Now it is this sudden awareness of what convention has not taken into account that is the concern of dialectics. Such changes in the entailments of the symbolic conventions stand at the basis of political, mathematical, physical, and linguistic thinking, and, according to some, are the basis of philosophical inquiry. In every case, it is found necessary to delve more deeply into concepts and events to see if more than what is now accepted can be meant.

Following this, to foster thinking in learners by the use of the dialectical model is to foster in them a capacity to explore conventional agreements on definitions, on what is and what is not included in our referents, on the ways we think and speak about the world in which we live.

The structure of dialectic.   But let us now consider the formal structure of that dialectic that makes it possible for this power to develop. Taken all in all, they are the teacher's tactics for moving the learner along the path of thinking on his own, enabling him at last to perform the kind of thinking that will equip him so that he can produce conventions acceptable to others, and consistent with the conventions already accepted, or defensible if rejecting older conventions.

The exchange, the dialogue, begins with a teacher asking someone what he accepts as the meaning of one of those philosophical-like questions. What is virtue? What is friendship? What is love? What is beauty? And so on. But of course, these need not be limited to philosophy itself. They are the questions which provide the premises for any discipline, whether it is politics or social affairs, psychology or mathematics. It is the type of question that matters, not the particular one.

When a definition is offered, the next step is to put this to a test of meaning and appropriateness by putting it into a larger context of ideas. The teacher does this by moving the discussion from the introduced, or introductory definitions (and thus giving them the status of recommendations, which they may not have had at the outset), to other familiar definitions, and then asking the individual to consider these additional meanings in light of those first offered. It can be easily documented that every one of the dialogues which Plato has written in which the dialectic is his basic concern (especially, as it has been pointed out, in the early and middle Dialogues), begins in the same formal way, with the same intentions and same developing methodology. To consider any one in detail will in effect be discussing of all of these dialogues.

For example: Socrates asks Meno if he knows what virtue means. Meno says he does. He, Meno, then goes on to say that there is the virtue of women and the virtue of men, the virtue of children, the virtue of leaders, the virtue of warriors, and so on. Socrates responds in what appears to be an encouraged manner, in spite of the fact that having asked for the essence of virtue, he was given all the kinds of virtues that there are. But surely, he adds, there is a difference of levels here, a significant difference between these two levels of thinking, between who is virtuous and what is virtue.

At the point at which the dialectic is concerned with producing educational consequences, the learner is directed to reconsider a first assertion by being obliged to note that the system for classifying the kinds of events and meanings being dealt with will not suffice for some of the new instances pointed to. The need for additional classifications and further analysis that is created is directly the result of the fact that the teacher has employed the model of dialectic as his teaching methodology.

A careful examination of the opening exchanges in each dialogue reveals the fact that the intention is to establish, with the help of the learner, a model of reasoning which would then serve as the logical criterion for the discussion and analysis which is to follow. It is achieved by question and answer, by countering an idea with alternatives, by summarizing from time to time, not only in order to teach the learner how to maintain consistency, but also to habituate him to moving through a maze of different definitions, noting what the various definitions seem to have in common and where they differ. The student learns to move from one accepted statement to another acceptable statement coherent with it.

If we say, for example, that virtue in the form of knowledge dominates the lives of people, then it is fair to say that virtue so defined dominated the life of Socrates. The intention is not so much to teach the child that Socrates himself was controlled by virtue, but that such conclusions must be accepted because of the logical warrant making it mandatory to move from one to the other. The teaching is concerned not with the substance, but with the logical process. It is this notion that is so difficult for many people who are concerned with conclusions or finalities, and not with the methods by which one offers conclusions, to comprehend.

There is sequence among the phases of dialectic. It begins with an appeal to the individual beliefs, opinions, and knowledge ordinarily held and easily articulated. It proceeds with an effort to identify the relationship between the answer and the character of the question with which the dialogue begins. It is assumed that no question of the type raised is without ambiguity, and therefore, no answer can be definitive. Thus, the objective appears; it is the quest for clarity of definition that is sought. And it is achieved by means of a continuous dividing of the problem until inconsistent or distracting elements are identified and isolated.

In order to achieve this end a model of reasoning must be developed. Plato revealed how this could be done by illustrating the question and answer tactics on a simple and familiar problem. The agreements end as the model that will be used to further probe the clinical question raised is established. The illustrative use of syllogisms and hypotheses is added to the procedure of summarizings, moving the analysis along. There is logical movement from proposition to proposition, from definition to definition, until an acceptable definition is reached. And when it is reached, the primary or original problem is now approachable once again, but by methods which promise rational and defensible solutions.

So much, then, for the use of dialogue. It is the method of discourse by means of which an analysis can be made of beliefs for which there are never any final dispositions, in the hope of offering some tolerable solutions. The purpose is to learn how to develop agreeable definitions in order to make further exploration possible. And, as has been shown, it is the model for addressing that phase of every discipline at the point at which it rests on assumptions. In mathematics these are the axioms; in physics, the basic suppositions; in ethics, its presuppositions; in politics, its hypotheses. Each of these, at this level, is open to the exploration which dialectical education makes possible. In fact, no matter what subject is taught, there is a facet of it that becomes more competently approachable when education has applied its dialectical models for those who have come to learn.

THE DIDACTIC MODEL

The methodology of disclosure.   But there are more problems which confront us in our growth of power of thinking. We need to learn to think about the meanings embedded in concepts until the concepts become more precise, usable instruments for exploring the world. But we also need to learn to explore that same world as it appears to us. And for this the didactic appears as the especially developed instrument of teaching. It is the means by which a direct approach is made to some event of inquiry. (The importance of the term *direct* will become evident when we later discuss the function of Paradigm models in *indirect* inquiries.) For didactic is the educational model designed for disclosing what is present in some form. Whatever may be treated as finished or complete, if only for the moment, is the ultimate substance of didactic. For here a teacher is required to develop the skill of opening things up, so to speak. What the students are expected to learn is how to explore, how to find the way things connect together to make the unity that exists. There can be no doubt that in a way the teacher does help to create the very unity to be exposed. But primarily it is his concern to *undo,* or unpack, the event so that the learner will see what the unity is comprised of, and how the parts relate and work together.

When things relate, they do so in some given way. But the recognition of this does not come early, or of its own accord. This fact obliges the teacher to open up events to be considered in such ways that the object examined, while not being destroyed, is exposed for inspection and comprehension. The distinctly educational purpose for this is not so much to make clear facts which were unclear, but to show how complete events are given factual meaning in modeled or structured wholes. Thus, in a didactic on the human skeleton, for example, as integrally structured as it may appear all by itself, enough is added by a teacher doing a didactic to give it the especially intended clarity and emphasis that will make it possible for students to understand the integrated structure, and more, in processive terms, to explore just such events as these.

What is susceptible of didactic treatment? Anything that has already been shaped and identified as having a fixity. That is, anything which has a discernible conceptual or perceptual structure. That means a watch, a house, a system of beliefs, or a political, social, or economic, or religious structure, and the like. Verbal or actual, as long as it is characterized by a structure (even a metaphoric one), an event is eligible to become material for didactic. It means, in short, that anything that man has or seeks to use in experience can, by didactic treatment, be made available for understanding or use.

The difference between the didactic and the dialectic is evident at this point. Didactic is concerned with the *materials* which rest on, or are given meaning by, conventional definitions. The dialectic is designed to consider the very definitions on which the structure examined rests, and to test the merit and clarity of these as presuppositions. But the two models can be seen to dovetail when we observe that one is concerned with the basis of every discipline and activity, and the other is concerned with the finished forms within those disciplines.

As a result of a didactic, the student may learn what is contained in a finished form. But that is not what the teacher is doing as his own purpose. He has already learned the constituted structure he is now exposing. The teacher is dismantling or doing an anatomy of that form so that the child will learn how things fit together to make a whole and what things are a part of that fit. He learns, too, how to do the fitting. The ability to do this depends upon a knowledge of the form's structure.

Didactic, quite obviously, is talk. But as Ryle has pointed out,[4] it is a special kind of talk. It is talk whose purpose is to make discernible what is not yet observable. It must begin with the assumption that there is a teacher who knows what a student does not. It is, of course, desirable that the student want to know, and is thus eager to listen to and to observe what the teacher is able to expose. It is important to note, however, that education does not have to wait

[4] Gilbert R. Ryle, *The Concept of Mind* (London: Hutchinson's University Library, 1955), Ch. 9.

for such desire, any more than the law needs to wait for a man to desire acquittal of the charge of a crime he has not committed. If children do have the right to be educated, and if there is clear necessity for all to be educated in this complex world, then, whatever their particular interests in regard to such matters may be, these cannot be primary. That interest should be enlisted is one thing. But in the technical educational sense, what is primary is the development of all of the powers that can be developed. A child's desire to be ill, even if it is for purposes we might find justified, is not honored as an actual illness by even the most sympathetic of people.

Beyond these conditions, there must be a subject which a learner is unable to explore for himself, either because the capacity for inquiry which he now possesses is inadequate, or because the matter is too complex for his experiences, or both. Taking these factors into account, we find that the process of teaching formed according to the didactic model is both a constructing and a disclosing process. We assume at the outset that what is being explored has a structure, either natural or created. The purpose, then, is to show what that structure actually is, what its inner conditions are, what relationship there is between this inner structure and the appearance of the event being examined, and what process is involved in producing this structure. But all these purposes are achieved in a context that includes more than the structure being explored. It is a context whose design is fashioned for purposes of illuminating special and crucial aspects of the event. It is, figuratively speaking, a matter of inserting specially constructed lights inside a skeleton where they do not naturally appear to show events and connections that would not ordinarily be seen. Thus, the teacher who learns to employ didactic as a model of education must develop the powers of an anatomist, so to speak. He must learn to cut away that which prevents the eye and the mind of the student from seeing what lies within. He can do an anatomy on a living organism, on an inorganic event, or on a series of concepts collected together and structured to comprise, say, a History of the World, a Law of Nature, a Theory of Beauty, or a Philosophy of Government. In each case, when the intention is disclosure, the required model is didactic.

In addition the teacher must be an illuminator of such materials. He must have such competence in the use of verbal and nonverbal instruments as to make it possible to create observable conditions that will direct attention and increase understanding in those who come to learn.

What is the point of this, in so far as the obligation of teaching to think goes? The point is that if the teacher is competent in these tactics, he makes it possible for the student to see more clearly, to describe more precisely, to offer a better explanation of the events being exposed, that he is learning to examine. When there is effectiveness in the teaching, the learner learns how a historian thinks, or a biologist, or a geologist or, may his fates protect him, even how a philosopher thinks. This is the difference between the historian and the teacher of history—a difference reflected in the difference between what a teacher teaches and what a pupil learns.

THE MONOLOGUE AS MODEL

An awkward term for an elusive model.   Now we come to the most difficult and yet the most promising of educational models.

At almost any point in his work, the teacher becomes terribly aware of the fact that he is involved with a human being who is living through such private experiences as might never be reduced to tangible symbols, or open to empirical examination. If he is aware and unpretentious, he may recognize that the learner has more sensibilities than our educational models or methodologies can hope to give positive direction to. There are things that happen to children that we will never be able to cope with, not because there are too many of them in the class, but because with each learner feelings, responses, and vague imagery ensue that fall outside even our most adequate symbol systems. This will occur in absolutely every conceivable undertaking, in play, in study, in ordinary interchange. Moreover, we become aware that there is a kind of impact on the person which an effort at explaining only dissolves rather than enhances. It dissolves that which we do not want to have dissolved. We are always uneasy about those distinctions or sortings that evaporate qualities of persons or events, for we cannot reduce them to their simple elements. These are the habits that we have developed gradually and learned to direct without the controls that consciously developed symbols usually make possible. These habituated qualities are in our impulsive responses to people, in the immediately felt quality of the world.

No words seem able to capture totally the qualities of those experiences. When transformed to knowledge, in sentences, they become public, only to heighten in us the private sense which has *not* been translated. As children, we respond to the world of sounds and sights and movements, and the world affects us to the degree that our childlike powers of absorption allows. These absorptions take on the forms and coloration of our earliest models of acceptability, of the approved symbol systems inherited at birth. As we grow older, those same stimuli may influence us very differently. Awareness of this psychobiological fact imposes on education the responsibility for being concerned with deliberately improving powers of reception, disposition, qualitative expression, and identification of self and with equipping the learner for choosing the self he would rather become. It is quite likely that human beings strive in many ways to push these responses toward consciousness, toward externalization, in order to take direct control of the understandings, the responses, and the development which result. But such efforts multiply the force and the effects of the responses, deepening rather than reducing them. And if we, as learners, grow beyond them, it is because other similar responses have replaced them, and not because we have, as the Positivist would claim, forced abandonment of what is not measurable.

Here is an autobiographical illustration of this state, chosen because of its obvious and dramatic character. When I was quite young I read *Jean-Christophe* by Romain Rolland. From that time on, although I was not aware of it immediately, the quality of the character that the great French writer had invented and developed with such extraordinary power and beauty, the sense of the tragedy and glory, wonder, passion, anguish, and the excitement, in this boy's growing up, first in Alsace-Lorraine, and then in Paris, and my living through his world of music, through the loves that he felt, won, and lost, altered my own disposition. Not for a long time did I come to recognize how I had, in fact, changed between the time I had begun the book and the time I had finished reading it. Without being aware of what had happened, the sounds I heard seemed different, the faces of people I looked at had different qualities. I began to look for different things in people. But most of all, I found a different, more vital, yet less definable sense in myself than I had ever felt. People I had appreciated I suddenly found crude and gross, because they were reflections of certain characters that I had despised in the novel. Others to whom I had paid little attention suddenly came to be remarkable, courageous, pure, ideal.

To some degree, everyone goes through a variation of this experience. Sometimes it is because of a book read, sometimes it is because of a motion picture or play seen. Sometimes it is because of a person encountered. It can occur at more sophisticated levels, in coming upon a new theory of science, a new conception of a model of history, or a mathematical system more intellectually satisfying than any yet encountered. It can even be the result of a new insight into nature itself, or a new conception of God, or man, or society. This response is not limited to works of art. It may occur in the sudden recognition of any new dimension of the world which borders on our own identity. The mind suddenly grasps, and we feel our identities stretched out in new excitement of anticipation. Some greater or lesser transformation has taken place, and we are more than we have ever been before. We find ourselves, without even being aware of it, talking another language.

The curious thing about such an experience is that when we go through it, we think we have come to a great stage of self-fulfillment. We are one with the person who caused the new state, but we say to ourselves that we have always been like this. We identify with him because he has made concrete our amorphous visions. That is why we love him—we have found in him ourselves. Later explanations of these awarenesses in chemical, biological or physical systems do not completely eradicate the memory of those feelings. Sometimes we find someone so engaging and appealing that he immediately becomes the image to reach out to. Or perhaps a new vision of some aspect of reality has been disclosed to the understanding, and in that knowledge a new vision of oneself is generated, buoyed by intelligence yet apparently flying beyond it.

In any case, there is here a clue to the solution of an educational problem. In education, one of the conditions of learning at the cognitive level is to find a deep and growing ability to enrich the powers of something we call the inner self; either the inner self that we already feel we are, or the one that we want to become.

In an awareness of this the teacher must deliberately present to children from the reservoir of literature and the other arts, from the sorted and developed forms of empirical reality, from the constructions of history, such characters as one suspects children might think themselves or want to become, men and women with whom they can identify. If enough of these are made available in the very spirit of the novel or the play, the record of history, the constructions of speculative philosophy, or the findings of science, we will have made it possible for one who learns to learn to think to himself by communing with some sense of self objectified in the luminous figure, desirable world, or new possibility for living. It is at such a point as this that imagery plays its remarkable role in the educative process. It is in imagery that the world becoming appears to those who learn.

There is a basic presupposition to this as an educational undertaking, but one we have already talked about earlier. That is that children are absorptive. They envy the power which they see in others but do not have themselves, and the world they do not possess, but long to. To nurture in them the power to develop in such directions is to have enabled them to think of themselves in the language that, for example, Christophe used to think of himself.

This seems to be so basic a tendency in all human beings that we need not question it, however we may need to explain it. We can only wonder how the role of educator can, in objective patterns, make these subjective availabilities greater, wider, deeper, and more susceptible of being absorbed by students in ways that can then be shaped and directed. For this we need to generate educational models of embodiment whose primary purpose would be to make it possible for learners to hold genuine monologues, to talk to themselves in a cognitive, but not exclusively verbal, form.

As an educational model it will be recognized that the monologue is more limited than either dialectic or didactic. It is limited to what could be called the biographical concerns. All art is in a sense biographical and autobiographical. There is an approach to history that is biographical. Every esthetic undertaking, even including physical education, is truly a biographical study. Many believe that every moral judgment is an autobiographical statement. And is a psychological expression or inquiry anything but a biographical probe into the history of feelings of men? What is needed, then, are instruments for detecting our own biographies in the many dimensions of the litany of our beliefs.

If we must explore much of the world biographically, the world recorded in the beliefs we hold, in order to nurture in the child the capacity to think of himself as something other than himself, the teaching model to be used will have to put primary emphasis on nurturing the abilities for interpretation. We are involved here with felt and observed behaviors which bespeak inward desires, perceptions, expectations, imaginings. If growth itself is to be secured, the need for education as externalization is clearly necessary.

In technical terms, it is sometimes given the form of a mind-body problem. In humanistic terms it appears, as with I. A. Richards, as the problem of the interpretation of expression.[5] In education, the goal is a model of teaching which transforms absorption of feeling states into ideas that are objectifications of such states by providing symbols for increasing awareness of the objectified self. Further analysis of this will follow; the aim here is an introduction of each of the models.

THE PARADIGM

The conditions of comparative thinking. The educational model of paradigm partakes somewhat of the character of the didactic in that it is concerned with events that are objective, and which stand before us. The difference between the two begins with number. There are times when we need to use some event as an illustration of a class of events. This differs from the didactic in which the event we are examining is an event in its own terms. This particular event may, afterward, be recommended as a case within a class of events, but at the outset it is treated as a specific event. Thus, the didactic is concerned with a specific matter—the historian examined in his own work, or a specific theory, however general may be its applicability later; while by means of paradigm we will be concerned with history as such. We sometimes look at a given work in the interests of recommending it, paradigmatically, as a model of history; when we do, we are recommending that it be considered a clear and effective case of how history, any history, is to be written.

In didactic every illustration is an illustration of some specific thing. From the didactic exploration as such we are not logically able to generalize about other such things. But when embarked upon paradigm teaching, we are deliberately concerned with the matter of writing rules to include cases of which this case is a representative. If there is a relationship between the two, it lies in the recommendations that connect specifics with the class of events to which they belong. But a concern for a class of events differs in several important ways from a concern with a member of that class. When we are concerned with the type of class rather than the specific member, we must do something more than just dissect the individual. We must distill from many examples those characteristics that make it eligible

[5] Ivor A. Richards, *Interpretation in Teaching* (New York: Harcourt, Brace and Co., 1938).

for membership to a class. That is, we must sort out what characteristics it possesses that every other individual shares with it.[6]

So, for example, Toynbee's History, Carr's History, Collingwood's History, Commager's History, and Schlesinger's History, have some things in common, but not many. One thing that they do share is the concern with the records of the past. If so, then we may argue that a paradigm of history will include consideration of evidence of the records of the past as being an irreducible part of the study of history. The treatment of records may differ, and criteria as to what is to be accepted as a "record" will also differ, but the role of records as evidence is part of the paradigm.

Perhaps an illustration of what is not part of the paradigm will clarify this issue further. A cause-effect theory seems part of every case of history, but an orderly time sequence within this theory is not. There is little agreement that what comes later is always caused by what came earlier. In fact, it is just as often argued that what will come later has been the cause of what came earlier. Thus, we can accept cause and effect as being part of a paradigm of history without accepting the idea of a linear time sequence.

It could be said, for example, that World War II started because of the dread anticipations that if the United States did not step into the war, it would fall under the domination of Germany. But, of course, not all historians can agree that an event in the future could cause something before it happened. This would be as curious to them as Alice thought the Looking-Glass world was curious, where one first screams, and then is stuck by a pin. And yet it is at least open to consideration and analysis that more of history was caused by things that never happened than by things that did; certainly by things which did not exist at the time they were said to have exercised causal effects. This argument is very defensible. It does not eliminate the notion of causality in history, but by rejecting the notion that cause precedes and impinges on effect spatially, it does eliminate the notion that history is a space-time-unfolding event.

The paradigm as an educational model has concern with a more abstract level of thinking than didactic. To most students the most familiar form of paradigmatic education is to be found in connection with John Dewey's notion of how we learn to use the method of

---

[6] Cf. Kuhn, *The Structure of Scientific Revolutions.* He argues that it is from the paradigm that particular problems are identified and pursued. In this case didactic derives from some paradigm and is not to be reduced to it. Chs. 4–6 are valuable.

science. He offered in his descriptions in *How We Think* and in *Democracy and Education,* the steps of what he called the *scientific method of thinking.* These comprise an analysis of intelligence at work. Particularities do not appear in his description. Although the steps appear to be specific directives, they are not really so, a fact he has often and confusedly been attacked for. He pointed out, for example, that thinking begins when we sense a problem and try to locate the disruption which has produced that problem. He did not tell us what specific impediments create what particular problems. He was concerned only with distinguishing the generic traits that constitute the class of situations known as *problematic.* These may be physical, psychological, social, philosophical, or political. If there is a problematic situation or condition, it will be possessed of certain traits which can be described almost in rule-like fashion.

Going on with his development of his case of thinking, Dewey recommended that we need to try to discover the basis for the disrupted conditions that make situations problematic. He suggested that what makes something a problem is that somewhere in its normal course, behavior or action has been arrested by something intruding upon it and blocking it from continuing in its usual patterns. Anything that disrupts has the power of producing problems. But he did not point to a specific situation to show the features of disruption and the problems which ensued. When he illustrated, he showed *relationships,* not specific features.

The next inclusion in the scientific method is the act of collecting as much evidence as possible of the normal way the event functions to ascertain what the impediment might be. With enough such evidence, a hypothesis can be projected. This is a hunch of what might be, or ought to be, altered in the situation to remove the impediment and allow action to continue. This is hypothesis.

Then experiment is introduced to see if application of the hypothesis will produce the anticipated outcome. If the conclusions drawn corroborate the hypothesis, then it can be inferred that it is safe and proper to act upon the hypothesis. If there is still some failure, the process must be repeated until some final, warranted statement may be made.

This, Dewey said, is the method that the scientists have found so effective. It is, moreover, a method which he was convinced would be equally effective in realms other than the scientific. He saw this scientific method as being applicable to any problem. For, as he argued, what is science concerned with, but the problems in the

environment around us? Any problem, therefore, should be susceptible of resolution when one uses this model of intelligent resolution.
But for our purposes, it is interesting to note that Dewey offered this
model of thinking within the larger concern of education, of *teaching*
to think.

It becomes the problem of the instructor to employ paradigms
in order to nurture in learners a capacity to universalize thinking, to
make a thought more applicable than just to the area in which it
originated.

The materials of paradigm, and the level of their abstraction.
The material of paradigm is all of the empirical events encountered, but
not merely the events as such. The materials paradigmatically treated
are the systematic beliefs that give events the meanings they have.
Thus, paradigm as an educational model is concerned with enabling
those who learn to encounter the cognitive contexts, the systems of
knowledge and belief which make it possible to consider the empirical
events as lawful entities carrying theoretical meanings.

Consider, as a very simple illustration, the boy who has learned
to fix a flat on a Ford and now finds himself driving a Volkswagen.
In order to fix a flat tire in the latter, he will have to universalize
his particular knowledge of how to fix a flat in the Ford. From ideas
of what cars have in common, he distills some conceptions of what
to do. He begins to recognize what he might not have considered
heretofore: how to open up the hubcap, where to look for the nuts
and bolts, the fact that he needs to find a tire tool. (The interesting
aspect of this illustration lies in the fact that most often it is done
unconsciously.) In each case, he discovers the difference between
changing a tire in the Ford and changing a tire in the Volkswagen.
By the fact that he has been able to generalize from the experiences
with the Ford, he is able to identify and to cope wtih the problem
faced in the other. It is in this sense that paradigm can be seen to
lead out of some didactic. If a teacher had been efficient in being a
didact to students, what should appear is the need to move to the
next phase—that of nurturing the ability to universalize from the
particulars that have come to be understood.

One final point should be made. Earlier, it had been pointed out
that, although we might perform a didactic analysis on a dialectical
model, we could not perform a dialectical analysis on that same
dialectical model. But, we could do a dialectical analysis of some
aspect of didactic model. And we can also do a didactic analysis of

some phase of the didactic model. It is of the nature of the didactic, dealing as it does with a constructed or identified event that has an analyzable structure, that one might didactically consider the tools which enable the teacher to take that structure apart, didactically. So it is with the relationship between didactic and paradigm. We can offer a didactic analysis of some paradigm of, for instance, nurturing a level of thinking, or teaching the writing of history, or instructing for painting impressionistically. We can perform a paradigmatic analysis of a didactic model, as we do each time we analyze a specific methodological recommendation for exposing and exploring some event. But we cannot do a paradigmatic analysis of a paradigm educational model. Doing this would only be producing a new level of a paradigm, which would mean an abandonment of concern with the paradigm on hand. If the concern is an analysis of a given paradigm, we can only perform a didactic analysis, which would focus closer attention on the very paradigm under consideration, now treated as a specific instrument.

Consider this brief illustration. It was earlier held that we cannot really hold a dialectical discourse on Plato's dialectical method. The acceptable approach would be to make a didactic analysis of the way in which he organized familiar ideas, introduced alternatives in technical and ordinary expressions so that those who were involved in the dialectic would have a chance to discern more meanings than they did at the outset. To do a dialectical analysis here could only mean to become an active participant in the dialogue itself, contributing to the dispute at the level of any other participant. But the didactic, in this case, makes it possible to treat the dialogue from a higher, external vantage point.

In somewhat similar function, suppose we had before us a Greek statue which was clearly the ideal manifestation of a Greek athlete. If we are to make possible an esthetic analysis of this piece of sculpture, we would have to go beyond this one event, and consider the traits which one might expect to find in such "cases of perfection." Now, the objective may well be to foster an esthetic intelligence in some learner, but the teacher is concerned with constructing a totally different kind of a thing. He is concerned with developing a set of procedures for introducing esthetic judgments, their characteristics, and the ways they are applied. The fact is that teaching esthetic analysis is not of itself an esthetic analysis, any more than teaching science is itself science. The paradigmatic model is of greater abstraction. Even more important, the materials that this paradigm of education deals with are not either scientific or esthetic, but the very structure of cognitive rules, which, employed at some later time, will produce the arts and the sciences.

SUMMARY

The relation between models of education and the thinking act. The discussion of the fifth model we shall reserve for the appropriate point in the next chapter.

Briefly, let us recapitulate the substance of this chapter. We have introduced, in rather different ways, four of the five models which can be construed as serving as a beginning conceptual technology of education. These are models for directing the processes of education, the acts of teaching, and concern the different purposes that direct those educational processes. They differ from one another in a number of ways. They differ because the kinds of data to be dealt with are different in their character, their status as knowledge, and their structure. They differ, too, in what is expected of the student; and finally, they differ in terms of the powers to be nurtured in learners. For it is quite evident that if thinking is one act, as is sometimes claimed, it is so at a very high level of abstraction. At the educational level there are differences that we dare not lose sight of.

Some of these different modes of thinking we have already talked about briefly. A description of what is available to us as having been constructed and has the fixed form of that construction will assuredly differ from the description of, say, a concept which has no objective referent. Historical explanation may have some things in common with psychological explanations, but it will have much that is quite distinct about it. Interpretation in music must assuredly recommend itself as being quite different in character from the interpretation of a legal decision, on the one side, or of scientific consequence in social affairs, on the other.

It would be a fruitful pursuit to undertake a critical analysis of some of these differences, to explore the role and type of evidence that is acceptable in each of these different modes and different elements of the act of thinking. But there is not enough space, and it is not specifically germane to our work here to make such a digression. What is important to note is that the models of education occupying this chapter, and to be further explored in the next, are all bound to the admittedly complex concept of thinking we have set out earlier.

These models are models that are congruent with the elements of the thinking act described, and are each concerned with the total act but intent upon improving one or two of its distinctive elements.

Indeed, the whole point of this work lies in the recognition that teaching (synonymous here with *educating*) categories derive primarily from the thinking act. Other categories do enter, of course, when we are concerned with other than the intrinsic educational act. When, for example, we seek to direct the act itself to some extrinsic purpose, then we must assuredly make ourselves cognizant of the categories by which those outside goals are identified. But in so far as education is seen intrinsically as the act of teaching, then its primary categories for ordering acts derive from that which education is developed to accomplish—the nurturing of the power to think, to judge, to sort out the matters of experience, and to give them meaning and controlled direction.

For this reason, we discover that there are occasions when we must think about beliefs, about "posits," as Quine has called them. In such concerns we may go no further than the form of the belief and its place in ordinary intercourse. When the evidences of the world of experience is permitted to enter our considerations, they serve primarily as illustrations of what needs to be ordered. Much as we would like to, we cannot treat such beliefs as we would treat the hard and resistant furniture of the world whose existence we deny at the peril of the loss of sanity. If that is so, then we need a model for teaching which will enable us to nurture the powers to think in terms of such abstractions as would direct our conduct in a context of arguable beliefs. In the teaching of such thinking we must note the primacy that needs to be given to the uses of reason (as an element of thinking, not a synonym for it), definition, and logical explanation.

When we concern ourselves with learning how to think as physicists, chemists, biologists, and botanists do, (no matter how these disciplines may distinguish themselves from one another, and they do; witness the running dispute between reducing or not reducing biology to physics), we are primarily concerned with thinking in a context in which rules and grammar are limited by the behavior of the things they are constructed to refer to, predict, and organize.

When we learn to think about works which are finished as we encounter them, and are called upon to grasp them, understand their operations, their inner conditions, and the state of their organization, we are called upon to think about events in such a way that our powers of exploration and description are not only the primary elements of the thinking act, but the most precise elements we can possibly develop in those capacities. Didactic teaches us to observe and describe with increasing precision.

When we are concerned with nurturing in learners the capacity to think about themselves and their inner worlds, where known languages seem only to dissolve the very things we want to help them think about, then surely the model we need must be truly different from the models which nurture the other modes of thinking mentioned. If there is an art in teaching anywhere at all, it will be here, in this model of embodiment by means of which we make it possible for the student to *become* someone whose very existence has become a goad or an inspiration for him, to understand and to think as the person he seeks to become, and to interpret what he has seen because he has learned to interpret what he will become.

To put it as simply as possible—by means of dialectical models the elements of reasoning (analysis) and defining are improved; by means of didactic the powers of exploration, observation and description are improved; by means of paradigm, explanations and invention, especially of rules for category-construction, are improved; by means of monologue, the powers of interpretation are improved. (Projection, we will see, is an emphasis on invention in terms of evaluation, or reconstruction.)

It is only as we recognize this relationship between the elements of the thinking act and their use as categories for sorting out and constructing distinctive models of teaching that we will be led at last to the definitive region of deliberate preparation for the study of the educational process.

CHAPTER 7

More about Models
Of the New World

THERE is perhaps no better way to demonstrate the very important difference between a theory of teaching and a theory of learning than to consider these models again, this time not each in isolation, but in comparison.

THE TYPES OF MODELS
AND THE QUESTIONS RAISED

The dialectic and definition. What is the meaning? Let us consider again the kinds of concerns and materials that each of the educational models is specifically designed to handle, this time in terms of their human uses. We find ourselves in need of better sorting principles if we are ever to attain greater understanding and control of a world in which problems continue to arise. In order to be able to cope with these dilemmas, a teaching process that will foster the development of skills sufficient to identify, define, and resolve these problems has to be instituted.

There are situations in which we can encounter no actual baseline of factuality. These would be problems that arise in formulating definitions of such concepts as Justice, Virtue, Goodness. In these

131

abstractions the only way to cope with the difficulty is to sort out its parts conceptually. But there is no one formula or categorial system for sorting out the materials. The very act of sorting out depends upon agreeing, first, upon the need to sort them out, and second, upon the need to accept mutually the categories to be used to sort them out. Categories do not preexist us, except as inert ideas. This is what dialectic as a teaching model is concerned with. It begins with a recognition of the evident fact that there is no clearly defined, universally acceptable, classifying system. There is a need to be taught how to classify and how to come to an agreement about the categories to be used when there are no hard realities that impose such obligations.

To do this we have to learn how to construct recommendations and build hypotheses. We must learn how to recognize what we believe, and what status that belief has. We need to learn to pursue, through an ever increasing awareness of the logic of our activity, all that is entailed in a given belief, and what difference a change in one element makes in the total context of meanings. We must learn what categories are presently used, as well as how to construct new categories that do not introduce contradiction or paradox. From time to time it is necessary to pause and to view in perspective this quest for the meanings and the limits of our classifications. We need to be sure at all times that what we think we are saying is what indeed we are saying; that we are not saying more than we want to, or need to. Because this can be done most fruitfully in personal exchange, we must learn to talk, to communicate with each other.

In this communication we must also learn to listen. There seems to be no sense in talking unless someone is listening. What we are searching for in this process of problem-solving is a definition that turns out to be a definition of a category. Agreement upon a definition makes possible a common inquiry and further resolution of problems shared. But the dialectic has finished when the definitions attained are accepted. Establishment of classifications where none existed becomes a basic goal of education, and dialectic is the unique methodological model used to attain it. The use of the classifications, the sorting-out process, is actually the inquiry beyond the dialectic, though in that process it tests the adequacy of the dialectic.

The distinctly educational objective is to develop the ability to construct sorting-systems, or categories, and to achieve intellectual assent to them. It is *not* the purpose of this model to win arguments, or to persuade to an agreement on the conclusion to some problem.

This is but a restatement of the notion that education ceases to be education when it teaches *what to think*.

The didactic question: what lies within?   A didactic begins with an entirely different presupposition. We perform a didactic on an event that exists in some complete form. We can neither blink away the event, nor blink it into existence. It must have objective character, in the sense that this book existed before you came upon it, and will empirically exist after you have done with it. We do not have to argue the presence of the book into existence.

But categories are not present in the same sense. They do have a reality whose meanings need to be analyzed into acceptability, as the meanings of matter must be argued out and clarified. The presence to our senses of a thing, and the presence of an idea, a category, to the mind, are both invitations to a quest for meanings and explanations. Such presences are necessary if we are to explore internally.

But even in the presence of such realities, we must all too often seek out someone who already knows that which we are trying to know. The very least we may need to do is find someone who knows how to "get into" things. We learn to listen and to follow his accounts. When the complexity is beyond our powers to explore, he will be asked to describe for us what constitutes the internal condition and operation of the event; how it is constructed, what its functions are, what purpose it fulfills, how long it might be expected to endure, and so on.

There is a very special, very limited sense in which a theory can be said to be as real as a table. For example, Plato's theory of education, as it is found in *The Republic,* is as real as the discussion it fosters in a classroom, or among scholars. For this reason, as it was pointed out in the previous chapter, it is possible to perform a didactic on Plato. But it is beyond any of our powers to engage Plato directly in discourse and wait for his answer to a question. We cannot expect him to follow out a line of inquiry which might suddenly be introduced. Then, as it has been argued, we have the evidence that it is not possible to produce a dialectic upon Plato's work.

There is the sense, then, in which Plato's writings can be considered a "finished body of work," whose structure we want to learn something about. We are aware, for example, that a scholar named Paul Shorey knows perhaps all there is to know about the body of work called Plato's Theory of Education. Suppose we were to ask Shorey what there is about Plato's Theory of Education that makes it what it is. We might just as well have asked him what it is about this table that makes it what it is. He sets forth the content of Plato's writings on education. He refers to the books which are parts of the body of Plato's work that support the theory he presents. (Though metaphoric, the word *body* is very advisedly employed here.) He refers to the body of Plato's work and by the proper use of intellectual "scalpels" he makes incisions, cutting open the body of the work so that we can see the Theory "lying" within.

The didactic is completed when the exposition is completed. Dialectic, on the other hand, is not used to disclose what Plato wrote. It is the methodology that Plato invented to explore problems not susceptible to a didactic expositions; those ill-defined, amorphous problems that he thought it so important to address himself to.

Now the two models are placed side by side. Suppose we were concerned for the meaning of *friendship*. A dialectic can be performed to teach how one arrives at agreements on what friendship shall mean, how definitions of it are to be identified and made efficient. There is no place that we can go to find, irrevocably and without any further argument, what friendship, as a concept, must mean. Not even the largest dictionary will help, since that is a history and not a reservoir of doctrines. Such a concept, therefore, is the proper subject of the dialectic.

But Plato's notion of friendship can be the subject of the didactic because in the Dialogues, in the *Lysis,* for example, as well as in others, Plato indeed analyzes, discusses, and gives in a number of ways the meaning of friendship. One might even attempt, didactically, to show how to determine which particular statement is Plato's own by showing which statement is consistent with the "body" of the work. These teaching operations are not reducible to one another. How to enable students to analyze what friendship will mean is one operation; how to enable students to discern what Plato meant when he used the term *friendship* is the other. Learning to inquire into the first type of problem calls for a dialectical teaching model; learning to answer the second calls for the teacher with didactic skill.

If the work being explored is complete, if the event has a beginning and an end and connectives to characterize it for what it is, then only a didactic can be performed on it. If the problem centers on an idea that has a variety of meanings and is constantly the subject of dispute, then it is subject matter for dialectical teaching, the model of teaching used to inquire into and to define classifying systems for sorting out what is unsorted.

THE PARADIGM AND THE QUESTION
OF THE THEORETICAL BASIS

In order to maintain a certain consistency of concern, we will skip over the monologue for now and move to paradigm. The paradigm, it was pointed out, was best understood as referring to a clear case of something. An examination of a paradigm enables us to understand all of those events that derive meaning because they belong to that same clear case. There are aspects of the paradigm that are close to that of didactic. For one thing, both appear to be dealing with existing events. But the difference between the two quickly becomes evident. In a didactic the presence of the event and the purpose of the teaching act limits the inquiry to be made. We do not so much ask *where* the event belongs, as ask *what* it is. In the educational use of paradigm the problem is, first, to discover what theory can be used to construct a clear case to represent the whole range of the things that we want to discover and explore. Second, having discovered or constructed the theory, and the ensuing clear case, we are ready to consider consciously what is contained in this model that will enable us to understand the characteristics of the world it is said to explain. It is by means of the paradigm that we are enabled to discover the fit of things, and the relationship of things to one another. The point is, however, that "clear cases" are heuristic, educators' devices for making specific events discernible, meaningful and comprehensible to learners.

Thus, there is no sense of fixity in paradigm, as there is in the didactic. Teaching may move from paradigm into didactic and then back again to a paradigmatic exposition or analysis of the events that we are trying to understand. The distinction between them appears in the fact that the paradigm does or does not make the didactic efficient and exhaustive.

Consider, for example, a series of houses that are being built by a contractor. What is he going to put into his houses? The buyer, not having direct access to the builder (and even if he does) wants to know in advance what they are going to contain so that he might be able to determine if they suit his needs, and if they will be attractive, and other such questions. The contractor, recognizing this as a condition for selling, decides to build a model house.

If you examined houses in a building project, where, say, fifty units are being built, it would be possible for you to know what your own house would look like in advance. If there are to be two types, each will have its sample.

People have on occasion been able to say, with some satisfaction, that they purchased one of the models. We have come to understand that there is more in this one model than in any of the other houses. The model, in order to give a clear image of the whole series, will be made to hold all that will normally go into every house of the class. For the builder, having created his model, recognizes that in a later construction he would be wise to eliminate one or two little things that do not affect the major character of the house, yet will reduce the cost to his advantage. In the model house he might have included built-in arches between rooms. Someone, looking at this model, might ask if it could be altered so that between the dining room and the living room, where there is now a separation, no separation wall would exist. Can the arches be eliminated? Now, the requested alteration may not be fundamental. The removal of the arch does not alter the fundamental character of the home, and can be compensated for by structural additions in the paradigm plan. It can still be handled within that category of the types of homes which the paradigm has made possible. But to alter the basic plan itself, the paradigm, is to make of it a *new* paradigm; and after that, a different house altogether.

The use of the paradigm teaching model provides for a more fundamental and logically prior undertaking than does the use of didactic. In a sense, the didactic is cleaner and more precise. It is concerned with events as they are immediately present to us; it has a beginning, an internal condition that remains just what it is throughout, and a finality—a conclusive character. It is concerned with events which can be examined in their features and structures. They are fixed in their status, or operations. If we decide at any time to treat the didactic model as if it were a paradigm, we must know that we have turned attention away from the conclusive character of the materials being dealt with, and turned toward the underlying, theoretical, organizing basis from which this and other like events derive their explanatory meanings. Having examined the event by means of paradigm (the word paradigm in Greek, *para-deiknyanai,* means literally: to show alongside), we are going to consider not the things, but the contexts of explanation of things. In the didactic, we examine the event as representing itself and like events. In the paradigm, we are examining the theoretical grounds that account for those things.

When a teacher considers a poem (such as one of Byron's

Hebrew melodies, "She walks in beauty like the night/ Of cloudless climes and starry skies . . .") didactically, he usually means to limit attention exclusively to this poem. What he does, in such a case, is "break it open" exposing its rhythms, the color of its language, the intention, the mode of rhyming, the meter, and so on. Having examined it in all of these dimensions, he has finished with it.

But to teach that poem paradigmatically, in light of all of Byron's poetry, means that he intends to provide an examination of a range of Byron's poetry by an analysis of the characteristics of rhythm, meter, poetic mood, poetic intention as theoretical constructs. The difference and the relationship between didactic and paradigmatic educational models can be briefly summed up as the difference between the facts and the theories which give them meanings, and make them facts.

THE PROJECTIVE MODEL AND THE
QUESTION OF THE POSSIBLE

The projective, or prological model is primarily concerned with two things. First, it is the model teachers use to extend the conception of what now exists to conditions to which it has never yet been applied. Second, it can be used to develop the *capacity* for extending the present into some completed or more extensively fulfilled form at a later time, not yet present to the mind. It thus appears at first to be a model that deals with something already existing. Yet, as with no other model, it directs its attention to that which does not exist, but can be imagined. When our concern is to try to develop in learners the ability to construct what does not yet exist and that perhaps might never exist, but which logically could exist, it is projective models of education that are used.

Generally creative thought begins with a concern with something tangible. We might have before us what is described as the completed effort of some person who has written, say, a novel or a play, painted a picture, written out a psychological exposition, recorded a dialogue, developed a moral theory or a system of mathematics. One of the basic assumptions on which projective models operates is that nothing is ever finally complete. Of nothing can we hold that the last word has been said. Whatever exists can be still further developed. If this cannot be accepted fully, then the notion of projection into the future cannot be accepted fully.

Art shows most clearly the consequences of the use of projective models, but so also does science. The very record of the developing lives we each live, with its character of continual change, is simply a demonstration of the fact that the last word has never been said, and probably can never be said. Whatever conclusions we reach become momentary perches before we or somebody else takes off again. Everything at hand, and every idea encountered seems always on the verge of being extended a little further.

The most interesting illustrations to be offered are the prologues of plays or novels (hence the alternative term "prological"), particularly those of Shakespeare or Shaw, for they show the relationship between what is known, and a future to be presented. In each case we discover that the prologue is a distillation of the logic of the story that is about to unfold. If it is an effective prologue, the logic is so crisp and so definitive that one would have no difficulty in anticipating what is going to happen in the story. We are not told, of course, except perhaps by the merest hint, what the machinations will be that permit it to unfold in the way indicated, but the logic is made clear.

In classical Greek tragedy, when Chorus speaks as Prologue in the plays of Euripides and Sophocles, it tells us about the characters who are going to appear and the tale itself. It gives a clue to the character of various persons in the drama. In *Oedipus,* Prologue speaks of the rash and daring young man who is enslaved by ambition. To grasp the logic of the following drama and the Greek religion, is to recognize this tragic flaw in the character of Oedipus. We know that as the play unfolds, whatever happens is determined within the logic of the established structure. The instrument which sets the tragedy into motion is his ambition.

Oedipus finds himself a young man looking for a kingdom. It has been disclosed by Prologue (Chorus) that, having conquered one kingdom, Oedipus will seek to conquer another and will have to fight the king of that kingdom. He is rash and thinks the fight and the victory to come will demonstrate his right to rule. He attacks. It does not occur to him, although the audience has been made aware of this, that the king might be his father. In the attainment of this ambition, following the logic of Greek culture, all that belonged to the king becomes now the conqueror's. And so Oedipus marries the king's wife, his own mother.

All this is set forth by Prologue. The play becomes intensely satisfying not because it is a mystery, but precisely because it is not a mystery; because it so correctly fulfills its established inner logic.

Nothing is untoward; everything pleases the expectations, and thus gratifies the intelligence. It is what had to be, given the individuals and laws of fulfillment involved.

Curious as it may seem, the methodology of the Greek tragedy of Oedipus can be found in astronomical study. The well-known story of the astronomer who had postulated a logic of the movement of planets relative to the gravitational pull of one another in the distance reveals this. Having observed the planets moving in familiar, described paths, and having accepted the logic of the motion of planets, he projected, on seeing some curious inconsistencies in their motion, that there must be an unknown planet to account for movement that could be observed. Imagine the triumph when some years later that planet was actually discovered.

This, then, is the concern of teaching that uses projective models. Its objective, the nurture of inventive or creative thinking, is primary. It focusses not on the abandonment of logic, but rather on the *construction* of new logics. Thus, the educational objective built into the projective model is that of nurturing the powers to build a logic and follow it out to its possible conclusions. The difficulties are incalculable, to be sure. The scientist who discovered the presence of a planet first constructed the logic of planetary motion. But can we point to the educative process that empowered him to do this? The triumph was not so much in the discovery of another planet, but in the logic he invented. Assuming that logic construction is not an inherited power, it is learned. But more important, is it also taught?

Perhaps a good beginning for solving this educational puzzle lies with the realization that we are not concerned with the power to peer off into the distance and discern something which, astoundingly, has not been discerned before. Rather, we are concerned with developing the ability to see things in new relationships, to account for the unexpected, to construct a different logic of relationships allowing the mind to extend what is known into unexpected paths and meanings. We are concerned with theories of perception—of vision. It is a matter of bringing together things not ordinarily brought together, and then making explicit the logic that would be required to justify that newly sorted out relationship.

Consider a simpler illustration. Barrie's *Peter Pan* is a delightful play, over and above the obviously delicious if quaint dialogue. It is hard for us, out of context, to accept the idea of a play about a little boy who can fly. It is just not to be taken seriously. One suspects that the little boy flying was only the afterthought of the development. The logic of the play, which precedes it and makes it so endearing, does not depend on or derive from the fact that the boy is flying. Barrie, in his other work, revealed himself as a social critic. He was very much concerned with what today we call the lack of authenticity in adult behavior. He was also concerned with the obvious destruction of personality of those growing up. He knew they would become adults who, having grown into adulthood and abandoned the spirit of youth, permitted themselves to be coerced by the sterile moral rules of this western culture that had captured them. They would be content to go to work the best hours of the day; to abandon all of their originality and their spirit, their vigor, their ingenuity. They would dissolve into indifferent cogs in a process, giving trite little memorized answers to sterile little questions, sustaining trivial relationships within barren social structures. Within such social structures imagination and spirit dies.

But what, Barrie must have asked himself, what if one child could know in advance what he was destined to become? What would any sensitive adult have done if, as a child, he knew what was to happen to him as he grew up? To answer this, Barrie gave some of the powers of an adult to an infant. This is the logic of the play.

Peter says that when he was two years old, he heard his father talking to his mother about what he was supposed to become when he grew up. He listened for a time. Then, unable to endure the prospect any longer, he jumped out of the crib and ran away, making them think he had fallen out and been stolen by pirates.

The idea of pirates is a staple of excitement in such a tale. Bring together the untoward, or the impossible and the unexpected with the ordinary, and you have created fantasy. But it is not the fantasy of the irrational. In this case, especially, it is completely and irresistibly rational.

And what of the flying? It can be interpreted as nothing more than the metaphor of the developed power of an adult now given to a child who has steadfastly refused to grow up. The character soars as only a child can soar, but as no well-trained adult can. In this sense, then, the logic is impeccable. It fulfills completely what each of us in his own time has really thought ought to be the quality of the life to be lived. What distinguishes it is its emphasis on the sense of dissatisfaction which haunts us all. Peter was dissatisfied with his future as somebody else proposed it. So he decided to take matters into his own hands; he created his own future. Is this different, in principle, from the scientist who is dissatisfied when he finds that the prevailing view might oblige us to close a door on increasing knowledge because too many believe we have gone about as far as we can go?

A culture cannot stifle the innovative and continue to thrive. This makes the need for imaginative thinking something other than the vaguely identifiable. It is the very instrument or mode of thinking upon which the direction of cultural, social, and scientific improvement depends. This is why it is so crucial an element in the educative process. We are constantly talking about the improvement of society. But just how do we improve society? How do we change things? And at what point does it all begin?

It begins with the deliberate changing of the logic of relationships that is now said to hold between events. The rebellion of minority groups, the rebellion of students against administration, the rebellion of the poor against the rich, the have-nots against the haves, one country against another—these are all predicated on alterations of the logic of relationships that have ordinarily been accepted. Change is sought. It is achieved as new logics of relationships are propounded. The very models upon which our world is built need to be constantly adjusted. And in that alteration, growth and revolution will occur.

College students want a voice in the conduct of their universities, a voice they have been deprived of. Examine the arguments and you will discover that what they have done is to alter the ground rules of the logic of the relationships between faculty and administration, and between administration and students.

When the black in America shouts for Black Power, he does so on the grounds of a recommended reconstruction in the logic of the relationships between black and white. It is this which gives him a rationale for insisting that all blacks must join together and speak with a single voice, as blacks. Only when the many speak in a singular voice, will there be the fulfillment of the logic that has been constructed. The leaders are the logicians. (Abraham Kaplan calls it the "logic-in-use".) They do not call themselves logicians, they do not even call themselves theoreticians. They are visionaries, spokesmen, leaders. But in reality, they are the planners and the constructors of the new logic; they are the inventors of the vision that is grounded in the new relationships internal to the group, and between this group and others.

Clearly the nurture of such power demands an educational model other than dialectic. The scope of its concern is very different from this latter. Dialectically we know the particular problems we are concerned with and we know what we must do in order to reach an agreement.

But the projective model for nurturing thinking has no such immediately identifiable problem as its focus. More important is the distinction to be found in the fact that dialectic does not necessarily lead to overt action. Its objective is the developed ability to analyze and to define. What is done with the conclusion, with the definition, is a decision made beyond the dialectic. But activity is part of projection; fulfillment of the projective logic is part of the logic itself. Thus, projective models extend to a concern with practical intelligence, in the sense that all art and all science entail practice of some kind.

THE MONOLOGIC MODEL AND THE PRIVATE OBJECTIFIED

Consideration of the character and purpose of projective or prological models leads us to make, in contrast, an additional, extended analysis of monologic models.

By means of this model we seek to cope with dimensions or aspects of experience the causes of which are in part approachable only by making inferences from symptoms, not by analyzing the events themselves. It is the model to be used to improve the kind of thinking on matters that must themselves remain private. It is the means for trying to cope with what must surely appear to be unapproachable, the incommunicable world of private experience, as Michael Oakeshott has called it. Our other models are constructed to deal with the world of common experience. They enhance the power of externalizing the effects these experiences have produced upon us and enable us to analyze the meanings of these experiences.

It must also be recognized, if we are to understand the necessity for the development of monologic models as educational instruments, that as we move more completely toward that absolute communicability other models are concerned to reach, and attain the ability to think with more and more scientific precision, we tend to eliminate the realm of private experience. However, all that we are actually eliminating is a consideration of that private realm. Private experience cannot be eliminated in this way. By attributing common names to segments of that world, we tend to cover it over rather than to expose it to greater view and greater communicability.

Our problem is to give direction to the experiences, feelings, reactions, concerns, we know only by indirection, or through symptoms that we cannot demonstrably trace back to some actual world. In response to these processes, the self, or spirit, or psyche, develops. All of these names have been given to this development without actually bringing it into the realm of complete and testable communicability. Nevertheless, it is a realm which must be given direction, lest it stifle every other by growing out of control. This can be done only by use of the same principle of cognition that is used to control every other phase of endeavor.

To control or to improve the powers of perception, in physical terms, the models of didactic or paradigm are probably adequate. They direct attention to the physical conditions of the act of perception, and to the theoretical or conceptual means by which perception takes place. But what of the metaphorical treatment of perception? What is meant, for example, by "mental perceptions" of the soul, or the "essential spirit," or "will" of men? For these we can consider only the symptoms, the outward appearances of behavior, and even then, on a kind of a gamble that the symptoms are indeed symptoms; that they are, in fact, the outcome of some structure operating within the human organism, even though its existence and its sequence cannot be so demonstrated.

But even treated as symptoms, what are they said to be symptoms of? Can we, in any firm way, demonstrate that they are the symptoms of what they are claimed to be? Are perspiration, an eager look on the face, the clenched hand, the broad smile, symptoms of an uncertain self? Of belief confirmed? Of a heart in panic? Of a joyful spirit?

Study of this is incomplete because we want to know what has caused the very behavior we see. We hear laughter, and we do not always see (perhaps we never see), the cause of that laughter. Even when we see a sequence of events, we do not see the cause of the laughter. Someone may say that the laughter is the symptom of happy appreciation of observed achievement. But it is no less possible to interpret this as derision over apparent but not genuine, or only limited, accomplishment. Nor can we eliminate the possibility that it was expectant laughter brought on by this one achievement, or tentative laughter, because the achievement produced nothing so much as a dread of something beyond. In each, a material implication is posited. That is, we talk about the observed as implying some underlying but actual cause that will sooner or later be observed.

What is even more curious is the fact that there is no assurance that, even if we asked a man what he was laughing about, he would be always able to tell us. For there is no actual condition to show that his answer can be taken seriously. Suppose he were to lie to us deliberately, for the purpose of not letting us know how he feels. Suppose he were afraid we might take advantage of his state of mind. Because of the fact that no actual evidence is available, only a series of additional inferences, made in a context of habitual or conventional explanations, will allow us to decide whether a man is sincere or not.

Suppose, as a test, we say something we recall he had previously laughed at. This time he does not laugh. Now we put the two symptoms, or observed behaviors, together. He laughed over something a first time. A little later, when we made another comment on the same subject, in the same vein, he did not laugh. We ponder the inference to be drawn. Either we do not tell a funny story well a second time, or he never laughs more than once at the same kind of joke, or he will laugh congenially once, and feel that is enough kindness in such a situation. There may even be other logical alternatives which not even his own explanation will negate.

We can describe symptoms. But after having described the symptoms, the problem of discovering the inner world of mind remains. Talk might allay your fears, might expose some evidence in order that your dread might diminish, might support you or provide you with ways of escaping the sense of dread. Such an improvement of a "state of being" is, strictly speaking, not the basic problem of the teacher. It may be a humane response to seek to attempt to do this, if it can be done. But professionally, it falls within the arena of the psychological concerns. The educator's problem, on the other side, is to enhance powers of cognition that will ultimately enable the learner to feel more meaningfully than he now feels; to understand in greater depth whatever he now understands. The questions directing the use of the monologue are concerned with what can be done to help a learner to identify more purely that which he identifies impurely, what can be done to enrich his powers of self-exploration, what can be done to equip him to choose from a wider source his own name, his own face, his own passion.[1] This is a teacher's problem, not a psychologist's, not a biologist's, and certainly not the ordinary man's. It is a problem of nurturing thought in order to give a better expression of feelings.

In quest of understanding we must go finally from symptom to other than symptom, to some event which the symptom bespeaks. Yet, in this kind of case, we cannot go to the event itself, for the event itself is unalterably conjectural. What can we do? We must employ our models so that they will enable us to go to sources that in the past have been held to be continuous with what we now identify as a symptom. We are concerned not with improving our working *in* the dark but our working *toward* the dark. We work in the light, with certain ideas in science, or in the arts. We seize upon ideas of the past, or ideas about future. Familiar or not, we know the materials we are working with. But we do not know the powers or the structure of the world which we are working toward within the self. Here only symptom and symbol are left to us.

Nevertheless, they are not insignificant. Nor do we need to come to dead ends because they cannot be reduced to the observable. We can note that in the past symptoms seem to have responded to materials or states ministered in given ways. We can remember that under such ministering in the past the symptoms have altered. Yet we can never be certain, because there is always the chance that the symptoms may have altered for other reasons. This is a fact, it appears, which reveals one of the great inadequacies in modern psychoanalysis. For, in the quest for other minds, other selves, the psychoanalyst is really working in that same darkness, but toward different goals. He does not know when he has really effected a cure. He has responded to the symptoms, but he never knows whether the symptoms have responded or reacted to what he has presented or only to some facet of what he has presented, or, at a cruelly simultaneous moment, to some other occurrence.

Does the psychoanalyst truly know whether the patient has responded to his direct ministering, or whether he has responded simply to the presence of a sympathetic man who is listening? We do know that during psychoanalytical treatment there is a particular period in

---

[1] Lawrence Durrell, in *The Alexandria Quartet* (London: Faber and Faber, 1968), p. 210, writes, "We live . . . lives based on selected fictions. Our view of reality is conditioned by our position in space and time—not by our personalities as we like to think. . . ." and he adds, "Personality as something with fixed attributes is an illusion . . . but a necessary illusion. . . ."

which there is a sudden alteration of the symptoms, and the psychoanalyst finds himself suddenly on the alert. Is it because of something he
has said that the patient is now able to understand his own condition, his own dilemma? Has the patient internalized that understanding? Have his feelings altered, and therefore, have the symptoms
altered too? Or has he just fallen in love with the psychoanalyst? Indeed, why do people fall in love with people? Because they are
near? Surely, it is partly because the doctor talks to them, sympa-
thetically; and surely, too, because he reflects their desires and fears
in such a way that they love him as they love themselves.

It is a well-known joke, which is probably not a joke at all, but
a warning, that psychoanalysts are constantly on the verge of becoming
the lovers of their clients; perhaps not physically, but certainly emo-
tionally. The analogy between psychoanalyst and teacher here is a
curious and defensible one. In both cases the condition with which
the patient is struggling is as difficult for the analyst to identify as it is
for the teacher dealing with the student. Though the relationship
differs in terms of purpose, it may well be similar in terms of effect.
The analyst and the teacher can always make patients and students
love them, and for the same reason. Students in the toils of being
educated, and feeling old values slipping away under the duress of
thinking, seek to cling to their old identities. If they can identify with
the teacher, they love the teacher as they love themselves. And when
they can take on new identity, they love even more the teachers who
seem to have made this possible.

But pity the deceived teacher who takes this as a tribute to his
teaching ability. It may very well be a tribute to the exact opposite.
The teacher may have demonstrated no ability at all. He may simply
have been a passive listener, or a docile transmitter of others'
genius. He may be doing nothing more than introducing ease, a sense
of calm, in a turbulent world. It is this potential confusion of consequences that makes monological models profoundly difficult to use
with assurance or effectiveness, and, at the same time, profoundly
important. The teacher must talk to himself directly, and only indirectly to pupils, in order that they will learn to talk to themselves
directly. The teacher must address himself to the work he wants the
learner to comprehend, but he must not do it didactically. He is
concerned with more than simply exposing students to the things of
which he wants them to know the inner structure. Such knowledge
may, in fact, move the learner further from a knowledge of self.

Nor can he engage them dialectically, thinking that improvement of definition will deepen the inner powers of identity. He might get two people to agree on all sorts of things, but when the agreement is over, the learner returns to his own inward world, often more lonely than ever. Precisely because the agreement was so interesting, but also because, in principle, it cannot be extended into the personal part of his life, the learner goes back to that world more anguished by the contrast, burdened now by an intensified loneliness. Nor can he use the development of paradigm models to reach that world. These are too critically experimental, too concerned with eliminating the unmeasurable.

What is left in this quest of the nurture of self-identifying powers? The teacher must carry on a love affair *with the materials* that he is confronting, becoming almost indifferent to the learner before him. He must transform whatever symptom he has observed into a condition of envy or restlessness, or of impatience on the part of the learner. He must transform this symptom of the student into the urgent feeling of "let me do it!" And even with this, there is no assurance that he has equipped the student. There is only a possibility that he may have motivated him. But there is no absolute way of ever knowing whether or not he has done what he has sought—to equip the student to seek or to create that richer self that he might become. This is the most exhilarating and the most exasperating of all the facets of teaching.

It is exhilarating to have stirred a child into the sense that he can now overcome his own agonies, or to make them more valuable and more articulate than they were. It is exasperating to suspect that we will never know whether he has succeeded. If, in his elation, he tells us that he has done all this, we must be wise and treat it gingerly. There can be no success in this particular area for the teacher, because there can be no finality in anyone's quest for self-identity. Success can only come when the learner has produced some kind of a work in which he has revealed the depth of his new and growing identification. And then, as teachers, we can only wait for him to reveal the next phase of his continual development. Only in the fact of change and its increasing rate can the teacher exult. Perhaps there is enough in this recognition to allow a teacher the sanguinity needed so that he will not seek a litany of completed works as proof of his effectiveness, for although it is possible to measure achievement in the other models, it is not possible in this one.

A FINAL NOTE

In any given day, with any given subject, it is not likely that the teacher will use all five models of teaching, but it is at least conceivable that such might be the case. Each of these educating models is concerned with a different facet or type of conditions, materials, specific skills and powers that we are concerned to nurture in those who learn at the formal level. But it is not only possible, it is mandatory that within a given period, in any nurture of the power to sort out, all five models must ultimately be used. If, for instance, one were to teach a class in poetry, he would find that he could perform first a didactic on the poem; then he might introduce a dialectic on some particular arguable idea in the poem; he could then go on to do a paradigmatic study, locating this poem within a given theoretical design, a complete context of poetry within which this particular poem belongs. At a later moment, he might even do a projective operation, developing an understanding of how the poem *might* have been written, adding even the practice of writing out that possibility. All of these are only a step away from developing a monologic power, in which the learner comes to hear his own voice and his own longing excitement in the words set down.

In terms of the models of education that have been introduced, we may come to recognize that any discipline, as it is distilled into a segment of a total curriculum, may be newly approached and thus newly distinguished. For example, the study of physics has a layer or a phase which is open to dialectical handling, another in which didactic is appropriate, still another in which only the paradigm will serve. Nor is there a question as to the place where projective models are apposite. Only the monologue would seem inapplicable, until we recognize the impact of form and change on one's identity in that changing world.

CHAPTER 8

Models as
Sorting Systems

NOW, where have we gotten to? The purpose of this chapter is to restate, by means of the didactic model, some conclusions and to emphasize the distinctions that have been recommended among the models of education. This can best be done by comparing them with one another in a different context than has been thus far used. We have talked about education as being concerned with enabling people to sort things out, to classify and to organize them. By means of this sorting out and classifying process, we discover meanings in things that we may never have even suspected were present; or we ascribe new meanings to things to which we thought they could never have been applied. Now, if the function of education is to nurture in people this very capacity to categorize, then that is the function of these models, for the functions of education are performed by means of these instruments. Thus, we must examine the various models of education to see how, by their use, it is possible to accomplish those objectives. Perhaps this will all be a good deal clearer if we see the limits of each model relative to the functions of the others.

DIALECTICAL MODELS—CATEGORIES AND
THEIR APPLICABILITY

The dialectical model of education is designed to enable learners to discover what the familiar categories or classifying systems

149

we use mean, what they include and what they leave out. For example, we have recognized that a word can be a classifying system. The word *virtue,* to use this often-used Platonic problem word, can be considered a classifying term. It enables us to sort out kinds of activities to which we will apply the term and which then allows us further to discover other activities or things to which the word is not applicable. So does Plato's use of the term *friendship* and *love,* and *beauty,* and even *education,* and *teacher.* These are all classifying terms. They are the instruments that we use to sort out what is familiar and separate it from events that do not belong within the accepted definitions.

So, we may say, "I am going to use the classifying term *virtue.* These things," (and we offer a list of acts) "that men do fall within the category *virtuous.* These things that women do also fall within it, and so do these that children do. Further, here is a list of things that rulers do that also belong. However, the following things that men and women and children and rulers do" (we then offer a contrary list of acts) "do not belong to that category."

By considering the list of acts against the word, and discerning what appears to be common in these acts, a student is enabled to comprehend, first of all, the applicability of what he is using as a classifying or organizing term. Then, he is able to understand why the things they refer to are considered to be part of this organizing system. When dialectic is used in this sense, the classroom activity performed by the teacher is an activity that, by nudges, urgings, stimulations, and counterings, obliges the student to reconsider, compare, and contrast, in order to discover which meanings a classifying term ascribes as primary in certain events.

Second, it enables him to discover what belongs to this classifying term that he may have thought did not belong at the outset. As an illustration of this particular phase, we are reminded that virtue sometimes is called knowledge or knowledge virtue. In that sense, teachers who know can be called virtuous. We discover that when we more fully understand what is to be included in the term, we also recognize the things that do not belong to it, and things that we thought did not belong to it, really do.

Third, it enables the learner to discover the possibilities for use of all these things when he pushes the category to its furthest possible applicability. If, for example, we use a classifying term such as *democracy* in a sorting sentence such as "A democracy is a place where every individual has the right of private choice," the classifying term *democracy* logically includes the idea that everybody has a right to vote. It also includes the idea that people who are in a minority group must be accorded freedom of action and thought, for if they are not, that right of choice is denied them when the voting time comes.

It includes other concepts, too, that are not readily apparent. The student is urged to continue to probe until he is sure that the classifying term is known by the full range of its inclusions (knowing that that "fullness" may be ephemeral, on the verge of opening at some moment when it was thought finally complete). To learn more about something is to analyze the classifying or sorting-out term until all that it may include stands revealed.

There is a fourth point. Critical analysis of the meaning and the use of a classifying term in the manner just described enables us to discover many of the inconsistencies in our ordinary use of that category. As we narrow or make more definite our classification system, we are able to identify inconsistencies between categories. For instance, in the broad context of America, we are identified both as a democracy and as a capitalist nation. When these terms are analyzed more definitively as sorting-out terms, and we begin to list first, all the processes that may be included in democracy, and then all those which are conventional to be included in and tolerable to capitalism, we are more than likely to discover an incompatibility. Democracy, at a very general or abstract level, is accepted as meaning a free exchange between all inhabitants of the democracy. Capitalism conventionally has a more restrictive meaning for "free exchange," a meaning limited to certain social conventions or quasi-sacred doctrine. This would exclude such concepts as free exchange of the accrued wealth (cultural, economic, educational) of a society seen as a singular political-economic event. A grasp of the two categories, pushed to logical completion, enables us to see inconsistencies within the larger context. It brings to the fore the premises on which each category is predicated, making explicit parts of the category.

Finally, by effective use of dialectic, we are enabled to discover what might have been left out of a given classifying system in ordinary discourse, but which ought not to be neglected. The classifying system (term) *democracy,* at this moment in the United States, is usually interpreted to read that all people who have reached a certain age, identified conventionally as chronological maturity, and have resided in the nation a specified period of time, are to be given the rights of citizenship. The right to vote is entailed in citizenship rights. Of course, there are other specifications that can be mentioned, but these are not considered intrinsic to the concept of democracy. Yet we discover that many people who fall within this age group do not have the right to vote, for reasons such as lack of fixity of domicile and zoning rules, poll taxes, literacy tests, and so on. In such cases the classifying system enables us to recognize how and where it is that the rights of individuals are being proscribed.

The system is also used at times to bring to the fore other kinds of inconsistencies. One such problem is that of disbalance, as with the just raised issue. The right to vote remains restricted from the very people on whom is imposed the responsibility to bear arms, each being proscribed by different age requirements. These are no trivial dilemmas that dialectic lays open to consideration and a re-sorting. In this particular case, the obligation to bear arms left unequated by the right to vote, leaves the categorizing concept of democracy at least indeterminate and unclear, and in certain lights, dangerously inconsistent, indeed, paradoxical.

What, then, is the dialectic as such? It is that teaching methodology by means of which we make the learner aware of the system of sorting out things that he already has, in order to enable him to see where they logically lead, what they oblige him to believe, what the limits are, what inconsistencies the learner is asked to tolerate, and what are the paradoxes to be resolved, or put into balance. Whenever we teach dialectically, these are the awarenesses we are developing. We are nurturing ability to discern the categories or sorting-out instruments in the familiar, ordinary language that bears our concepts.

DIDACTIC MODELS—THE AVAILABLE CATEGORIES

In the interests of interrelating all of the recommended educational models, it would be helpful to assume that every model is concerned with the same fundamental process, that of sorting out or organizing the data of empirical and cognitive experience. It is by such sorting that we are able to ascribe or discover the meanings and the class memberships of what we experience in our daily undertakings. Dialectic enables us to sort out the inner phases of the categories we normally use. Didactic, within such a consideration, can be understood as a concern for the exposition of a prevailing system of categories that the learner may not know anything about, but that the teacher does. It must be made clear that to teach didactically is not limited to telling something to someone who does not yet know it, although this does enter to a degree. Far more important and interesting, it is a matter of *demonstrating* to somebody what sorting-out systems or categories an individual used to produce what is now about to be studied. To prepare a didactic upon so simple a matter as a table, it would not be enough to say that the top is formica, of a brown color, and put together in such a way that it can be used as a table (and on and on in this progressively trivial vein). The full didactic would have to make possible an identification and an understanding of the conceptual sorting instruments that were used to bring this table into existence. Otherwise, it is truly a triviality. In addition to just identifying these concepts by name, the didactic must be concerned with a presentation of the rules that were used to make this sorting-out process an effective one. It is necessary to identify these roles and to clarify how they were made to operate, permitting the system to produce what we are studying. Such a didactic moves an examination of the table into the more determinate disciplines of either anthropology, or architecture, or the like.

To give a didactic in science or in history or in mathematics, or in any defined area, is to present the classifying or categorizing system used by the creator, the inventor, or the discoverer, and to show how the data came to have its meaning in this sorting-out system, and how it effected the results now being examined. In chemistry, for instance, we first give the constructed names of the events we are going to examine. The name is the classifying term. It enables us to handle some particular thing. Each name given to an element or a compound of elements is an instrument of categorizing and making things usable in their distinctiveness. To teach chemistry is to teach how to sort out or to know the system already accepted for sorting out all of the varieties of powders and metals and gases, and to do what the sorting-out rules tell us in order to be able to arrive at a conclusion, either derivable or already derived from following such directions. This, of course, is about as simple an illustration as can be given about extraordinarily complex matters. But, however complex the material, the didactic makes it possible to be handled according to the same principle.

Further, although the data differs, methodologically the same principles are employed in any didactic of history. We are concerned with disclosing the historical sorting-out terms, and thus we would be involved with the same operations as in the study of chemistry. That is, we disclose the terms which have been used to present the historical account of some event, and learn to do what the historian did in reaching the conclusions now being studied.

Consider that we have chosen to expose and describe these three terms which could easily have been used by a historian: *war, government,* and *voting.* These are the sorting-out terms. Presenting them to the student, and doing an "anatomical" exposition of each, including a study of the rules for their use, we make possible the understanding of the history as written. We look through all of the raw materials we can find and see how evidence, to which the rules for the use of the term *war* are applicable, has been treated. We do the same with the term *government.* As we explore the way the history was done, (or written, to put it more conventionally) we may find that at a point there was a further sorting decision to limit the work chronologically from 1800 to 1850. Perhaps the time boundary was introduced for the reason that it made it possible for the sorting to become narrower. Otherwise there would have been too much data to deal with at once. Then, we examine the way the sorting term *voting* was used. Considering how they were brought together, and identifying the further rules employed to establish their relationship, we find that we are revealing an organized picture, a history of war and government in terms, for example, of the right to vote in Canada between 1800 and 1850. It is this type of exposition that takes place when history is treated didactically.

Of course, in advanced forms, more subtle historians use more subtle sorting-out or classifying terms and rule systems. Many historians interweave these in such a way as to give a clearer, more detailed picture of the life and career of a particular group or a particular period; and this imposes on the didactician the responsibility of developing a more penetrating awareness and more skillful ability to expose these more subtle categorizings and their outcomes as historical statements.

We can do the same with mathematics. What is mathematics itself, after all, but a sorting-out system? Suppose we were to teach geometry. We first communicate to the learner the language that sorts out and defines postulates, axioms, theorems, and the various rules and sequences together defined as geometry. Then we show the rules of the logic that relates these terms to each other by giving an exposition of the operators the learners will need to know. We are literally saying, "This is the sorting-out system. These are the rules for using this system. Now I am going to give you a series of numbers. This is our raw material. Using the sorting-out system known as Euclid's mathematics, I will show you how a Euclidian, that is, a geometrician in Euclid's system, would find out what would be the outcome if a given series of numbers were brought together according to the directions entailed in a given operator." As part of a didactic, we may give a geometric problem to be worked on in order to expose more clearly how the angle of a triangle is derived from certain data given. The objective is to make the sorting-out system and its uses available to the student. When he can use it, he can classify raw materials and end up with the conclusions that are already built into the logic of the system that comprises Euclid's geometry. Thus, we see that in principle it is not different from didactic teaching of history or chemistry.

To summarize, the purpose of the use of the didactic is to enable the learner to become aware of, and to learn the uses of, classifying systems which, entered into, produce a given piece of work. More important, didactic entails consideration of the organizations of those created events, ideas, institutions, and works of art, science, or philosophy, each in their formally established structures. In this consideration we lay bare the systematic thinking and acting that produced the products we are examining, and teaching. When successful, didactic has enabled students to sort out and to think as the scholars who have created have thought. By this means, education has expanded the thinking powers of these students.

PARADIGM MODELS—THEORETICAL CATEGORIES FOR EMPIRICAL MATTERS

A discussion of paradigm models begins with the obvious fact of the world as an ongoing event. As we come to know the world, we know it as a series of things sorted out or collected together according to identifiable categories, and made to operate according to established rules. To teach children about this world is to enable them to discover some generic classifying system in operation. By testing this in the face of other materials, the learner is able to learn what happens within this system as it continues to operate.

A paradigm, whose purpose is to make possible scientific explanation and description, is constructed in the following manner.

First, there is the establishment of laws of behavior for a given set of events. These can be drawn from the stored common knowledge of a group (a society) or more judiciously from the works of researchers in a given field, and would represent generalized statements of their findings.

Second, there is the identification of conclusions (facts) that fall easily and discernibly within the laws accepted as established. The quest, thereafter, is the identification of given events; are they further cases of the laws established, or do they fall outside these laws?

What makes for the paradigm, then, is the general statement of the law, supported by clear cases covered by the law.

In light of this we discover another distinction to be made between paradigm and didactic, although it has been implied already. As history deals with particulars, and science with laws applicable to many events brought under the categorical umbrella, the didactic is concerned intentionally with the internal characteristics of both history and science, with the rules for interpreting particulars and organizing and describing events. Paradigm, on the other hand, is an analysis of the features shared by many members, identified as commonalities by some law-established categorical case. In paradigm, therefore, more attention is given to the model of inquiry than the matter examined.

It was suggested earlier that the most fruitful approach to paradigmatic teaching is to commit oneself not only to the use, but to the study of some model of scientific method, to a generic or universal system for organizing, identifying, and directing the control of empirical matters. This would yield a whole system of categories. It gives us a beginning term—*problem*—which enables us to direct the child to recognize what belongs under that classifying term. It is by means of this kind of model that the teacher can direct the perceptions of the student to the fact that when something is no longer doing what it has usually been able to do, it is to be called a problem. By means of this classifying term, the teacher moves the student to look around within a specific situation in order to discover what has ceased to function the way it usually does. But the crucial step is to expose the role of a prevailing explanatory system, and its failure to take into account the matters now to be considered, for what we see lies first in that system, the paradigm.

We construct a paradigm for students. We show that a clock has stopped running. In order to motivate curiosity to find out the how of things, we depict the general condition of the running clock.

We point out verbally or illustratively that the clock usually runs but now it is not running. But what is the problem? The term itself directs us to pick out of a series of events something that is no longer taking place, or something that has intruded upon and probably impeded regular action, but which is not accounted for in our system of expectations. But whereas in didactic we expose the sorting-out of actual particulars as some researcher or creator has done, with paradigm we confront the theoretical constructs some particular individual has himself employed. These are the contributions of scientists, artists, and philosophers at the more strictly cognitive level.

A second classifying term to be analyzed in this same way is *observation*. From what is identified as a problem we move to an exposition and exploration of the specific elements that the theoretical construct has developed an account of. Even knowing that experiment can mislead, we open the back of the clock indicating how to check if the wheels are moving. But it is the nonempirical theory we continue to stress, in order to reveal its role in problem-solving. It may be that for a comparison with what is usually expected in the paradigm of clock-behaviors we will notice a bend in one of the wheels. But the sorting-system which has led us here is one which is concerned with generic statements, not with particular thoughts or things. The bend alone may be sufficient for us, in a didactic sense, but paradigmatically, it is the theory itself that is of concern. The question is not why doesn't the clock work, but where does the theory reach its limitations?

The next phase calls us to examine how to establish a *hypothesis*. Observation leads to a consideration of the problem of deciding what the observed event is a case of. We are working with a law of the running of clocks, and conclusions as to the possible kinds of disruptions that can occur. From these and from observation, we are attempting to determine whether the case before us is already predicted by our law and our conclusion, or whether it falls outside and demands a new law. The tentative judgment we make in this setting is the hypothesis.

This requires a more thorough exposition, for it is the heart of the matter.

Although science must accept presuppositions no less than mathematics must begin with postulates, there must be a time when its presuppositions are put to some proof, pushed to some condition that reveals the limits beyond which the postulate no longer is acceptable. In deductive thinking we begin with a law which is considered definitional in character. A case within that law that claims to be evidence of one segment of the law, can then claim identity with other segments, for we have a closed system of reasoning. If all *A*'s are *B*, and *C* is an *A*, then *C* is also a *B*. But the notion that all *A*'s are *B*'s in such a system cannot be empirical, for that would require a demonstration that even in principle could not be accomplished. We really must accept as a definition that all men are mortal, for who knows in what future period this seemingly irrefutable fact could be shown to be false. It is the very problem of Euclid's axioms transposed into scientific investigation that we face here.

Induction shows no better promise. Quite the contrary. The exactitude of deduction comes from the fact that it is not empirical. And the strength of the empirical, being open as it is to direct observation, is weakened by the impossibility of attainment of absolute truths. The best we can hope for, through countless examples, is the higher degree of probability that the next case examined will be like all the previous cases. In the experiential world no amount of cases examined will lead us to the right to establish an unexceptional law of the behavior of things. If every piece of wood I ever handled burned when I applied a match to it, it is still not sufficient evidence to enable me to say that the next piece will burn. If I claim it as a law, it is because I am defining wood as the "object that burns when lit by a match." If it then does not burn, my definitional approach allows me to say that it is not wood. But inductively I would have to allow the wood to be wood if it fits the case of being wood by other criteria and still does not burn. And if I were further to argue that after a thousand or a million efforts, wood burning allows me to post an inviolable law, I have deceived myself by postulating in advance the very law I am trying to write, and confusing postulate with conclusive evidence.

It is a combination of these two modes of thinking that we can identify as paradigm. From the paradigm we are enabled to move from the model of conceptual inquiry (the deductive system implying class membership for a given event, or group of events), into the active investigation of existences. But the models themselves, Charles Peirce has argued,[1] both depend upon still another form of reasoning, the *abductive,* which concentrates upon the act of hypothesizing

[1] See Charles Peirce, *Collected Papers,* eds. Charles Hartshorne and Paul Weiss (Cambridge: Belknap Press, Harvard University Press, 1960), vol. 1, esp. Ch. 2.

on the particular event being examined. Such reasoning, he has shown, occurs within a context of inquiry, within which the laws of a deductive process and the conclusions of the inductive are both conscientiously used to derive an hypothesis; for a hypothesis is a claim made as to where some specific case belongs. In such an investigation, our findings show the adequacies of our presuppositions, and the validity of extending the conclusions to the new event.

Thus, for example, if I had come to accept the law that all diseases are microbiotic in origin, and conditions described by sniffles, fever, severe chills can be concluded to be colds, which are microbiotic in origin, the case before me would immediately recommend itself as being a cold. (The hypothesis is constructed from our law and previous conclusions.) If, however, the hypothesis that it was a cold was not borne out in further examination, which showed a curious kind of sudden recovery and equally sudden reappearance, we would be confronting a case of something, but not a case described either by the law or the already accepted conclusions of previous examinations. In this case, then, science, being a quest for a more and more critical description and explanation of events before us, has obliged us to recognize that the model of explanation that was applicable until now is not applicable here. It does not, of course, refute the paradigm and the conclusions of previous inquiry. It simply demonstrates the need for another model in order to give a proper account of the case before us by showing the limits of its powers, and exposing the greater possibilities of nature.

At this point we see even more emphatically the uniquely conceptual character of science. Even experiment, although it is concerned with exploring existential matters, describing them more and more precisely, and showing the validity of explanation, does so by proving the models in use, by means of which these acts of explanation occur. For it is in the models of inquiry that our descriptions and our explorations are generated.

Of course paradigm models of education are not limited to this description of the scientific method of investigation, or even of scientific thinking, considered in the narrower sense. It applies to any general method of intelligent inquiry into the problems of any undertaking where the concern is increasingly precise use of concepts and increasingly exact modes of communicability.[2] For, when we teach paradigmatically, we are intent upon fostering the ability to use

[2] Cf. Oakeshott, *Experience and Its Modes,* Ch. 4.

with increasing skill *the process of discovering the classifying system that was used to make a thing go, or to discover what made things go, and after this, to discover how the classifying of terms affected that which is in operation.* This is all part of paradigm thinking. It is, above all, the concern for the development of skill in constructing and handling theoretical models and following their careers in the empirical world.

MONOLOGIC MODELS—THE USE OF CATEGORIES AS METAPHORS

The focus of concern in monologic models is the classifying systems that produce conscious awareness of the several facets of the private self. The teacher who uses monologic models finds himself motivating a learner to think about himself, to come to a knowledge of himself, through unexpected ways and foci. When a student is absorbed into the new world of some creative mind, with its newer promises, probably unfamiliar categories and altered values, his own identity is, although perhaps for only a short time, enriched by this absorption. The richest, though hardly the only, source materials for monologic models of teaching are found in literature and in the arts. The aspects of the human condition that make this model necessary, and that direct the very construction of the model and allow it to occur, are important to note.

None of us has x-ray eyes. We cannot see, as we talk to someone, the past written on his face. We cannot penetrate beyond the surface into the feelings he is struggling with at the moment. We cannot observe the thoughts he is entertaining, the dilemmas he is facing, the resolutions he is offering to himself. The language that is available gives us no assurance that the private world's symptoms are being fully described. Yet we apparently need just such knowledge of another if we are to appreciate our own possibilities, the lives within ourselves, and avoid the self-deception we so easily fall into. So we turn to objectification, to the meanings embedded in literature where the structure itself compels the inner life and the outer life of men to be set out side by side, and we can know the former as we know the latter. In literature, then, where such development is presented to us, we can learn to imitate, to absorb ourselves consciously into, to become embodied within a complete person whose past and future, whose passions and reason as they become clear to us are revealed in the very fibre of the person we encounter, and then in ourselves in a surrogate of that same encounter. For this reason literature becomes a source of education. We come, as students, to think as a persuasive author, or a vibrant and absorbing figure, allows us to think. This is what is meant when we find ourselves saying an oppressive situation is "Kafka-esque" and cynical political behavior is "Orwellian"; or when our own dilemmas, created by guilelessness, innocence, optimism, lead us to say, "I am a Candide, Heaven help me!"

But until we learn to love to read, the existence of this dimension of potentiality remains closed to us, for these metaphors for our lives are not readily available to us in any other way.

Here, as in none of the other models, we learn to sort out the world by means of the vision of creating minds or created figures, without necessarily being conscious at the outset that we are doing just that. We think in the categories which are the passions of others, now made intensely attractive and deeply satisfying to us. But the strong emotional power which becomes the learner's is that which the teacher, with exquisitely measured care, introduces, but is not himself involved in. If he is, then the metaphor itself vanishes, and we find that the teacher is introducing the learner into what he construes to be a literal reality.

PROJECTIVE MODELS—ALTOGETHER
NEW CATEGORIES

Finally, in the use of the projective model in the act of educating, the teacher's concern is directed to the nurture of powers of deliberate construction of new classifying systems used to cast familiar materials into those new relationships. The aim is to foster a capacity to sort things out in ways not sorted out before. The purpose is the development of a creativity that mixes what has not been mixed before.

To learn to do this with the conflicting categories of dramatic tensions, and to be able to project these relationships between fictional creatures is to learn to write a play or a novel.

To learn to develop new sorting-out systems for the materials of the nature and to apply these to concepts of motion and change is to be involved in writing a new theory of physics.

To learn to develop a new sorting-out system for symbols

relative to one another, for the purposes of making newer, more precise inferences from those symbol relationships, is to try to develop a new mathematics or a new logic.

To learn to create a new sorting-out system for the explanatory terms of the lives and careers of people in the past, is to be engaged in preparation for writing a new history.

Essentially, to be involved in the projective model of education is to be particularly and deliberately concerned with that form of thinking that could be called a judicious *mixing* of metaphors. To teach this mode of thinking is to foster the deliberate application of one system of organization to things that are usually bound together by another, more familiar, classifying system, just to see what outcomes are possible.

CONCLUSIONS

The educational models and their defining contradictions.   At this point a few concluding observations are in order. First, it may help in understanding the limits of each of these educational models if we understand their contradictions.

The contradictory to dialectic is mere dispute. It is contradictory because its intention is trying to get students, learners, to understand all that is included in the sorting-out systems they have long used. Mere dispute is designed to produce the very opposite. Since the goal is a debater's victory, the best tactic is to confuse the student about the rules that are part of the sorting-out system. The teacher who is a debater may amuse and sometimes impress, but he has ceased to be a teacher. Plato's *Euthydemus* presents a delightful illustration of this exasperating kind of person.

The opposite of didactic, the aim of which is to make evident a sorting-out system in use in a particular event in order to see how it has produced what it has, is the dogmatic. It is opposed to didactic because through its use the need, or the opportunity to come to know how the sorting-out system works is abrogated. The intention of dogma is transmission of what must be believed, whether it be understood or not.

The opposite of the monological model, whose purpose is the deliberate bringing to the fore of those sorting-out systems that have shaped or may yet shape the private self, is mere *rumination,* the encouraging of undefined emotional states. For a teacher to speak to students through such passion is to attempt to move the learner without giving room for the understanding of the choices producing the vision sought.

The opposite of a paradigm, the model for developing a conscious awareness of the relationship between some given sorting-out system and the meanings of the behavior of the things inquired into and the limitations of this relationship, is total immersion. When one is totally immersed in a situation, it is likely one does not see nor can one examine what one is bathing in. It is like being not only in, but under the water. One cannot study the characteristics, the components, the behavior of water and its elements simply by swimming in it. Immersion prevents the distance and perspective intelligence requires in inquiry, and therefore the identification of the immersing system itself.

And the contradictory to the projective model, by whose means things are brought together in new ways in order to see otherwise, is mere drift, where things just flow in and out of relationships. To encourage dreaming without the obligation to consider that such dreams are used as a new sorting-out system without being so identified is to encourage the substitution of dreams for reality.

Models, sorting terms, and key ideas: a concluding observation. We sometimes hear scholars say that the best way to teach a given subject is to teach what can be called the *key ideas,* or the basic concepts. To all intents, and for all purposes, we are called upon to begin with the fundamental truths of the subject, and then to build on them until a picture of some segment of the real world is complete. Accepting such a recommendation involves the acceptance of a limited number of familiar categories or classifying terms on the assumption that the primarily important data has been organized by these central, or key terms; and from these all other encountered data derive their meanings. So, for example, Philip Phenix has argued that you can teach any subject by finding its key ideas.[3]

Now, just what are key ideas in the context presented here? They would be the key sorting-out terms or the key categorizing terms. Still the result of this approach is to reduce any subject to a specific, fixed sorting-out system of terms.

[3] Philip Phenix, *Philosophy of Education* (New York: Henry Holt, 1958), Pt. 3, esp. Ch. 17.

It cannot be doubted, however, that the key ideas are themselves selected by some teacher-inquirer. Thus, the key ideas are themselves the result of a previously established sorting-out system, and a different sorting-out system identifies different ideas as keys.

What is even more damaging to the recommendation, with its blunt, fixed, and too encompassing form, is the fact that it fails to recognize that every concept is a sorting-out system, with no necessary relationship between any two of them. If they are to be seen as interrelated, they must be built into a logical system whose constructed and accepted rules enable us to account for their relatedness. But education is a matter of teaching a confrontation of all sorting terms, in order to see the consequences that use of them has upon the so-called furniture of our world and upon ourselves. To teach would not be to transmit the key ideas as much as it would be to nurture such powers of intelligence as will enable us to discern the models on which events, creations, and behaviors are fashioned and directed.

Recapitulation of the goals of the various models. Educational models are employed to enable learners to see the sorting-out systems present and possible—the symbol systems that make the world available to us in the forms that it has and in the forms that it could have. One model of education is designed to enable us to consider our regularly used sorting-out systems more carefully than we have; another is designed to enable us to discover sorting-out systems in use that we did not know were in use; still another attempts to enable us to identify the sorting-out systems that shaped us as individuals; still another hopes to enable us to see the sorting-out systems that undergirded the conceptions allowing us to treat the natural things in our world; and lastly, for the moment, there is a model whose purpose is to enable us to create things that never have existed.

All these, related and interdependent provide the compass of the study of education. Each educational model, critically and carefully analyzed, understood and controlled, allows us to distinguish the range of sorting-out operations available to us, and that need to be made part of the cognitive powers of all individuals. They are applied, in proper limits and against the rules of their use, to the completed systems we call the subjects of a curriculum; in history, chemistry, physics, mathematics, geography, and so on. In these undertakings education, disciplined by study and experiment, is taking place. And the outcome among learners is a developing knowledge and control of the sorting-out systems that give man access to coherent and stable meanings, greater possibilities of communicability with one another, increasing control of thought and thing, and the chance to fashion new worlds altogether when old worlds pall or threaten.

CHAPTER 9

The Integration
Of Models and
The Lesson Plan

WE must now devote full attention to the major problem of establishing the ways in which the models of education and the models of the subject matter that we seek to make available to learners are brought together. How are the models of history, or science, or psychology, or literature made available to learners through the educational models which have been identified and analyzed here? If we are to be consistent at all, we cannot leave this, at the last moment, to the notion that at the desired time there will be some surge of intuition during which time the educational models make the models of the various disciplines available to students. There must be a definitive plan that can be examined, evaluated, improved, and put to the test. Without this, everything else has been just logical, metaphysical, or literary curiosity.

In advance of this culminating analysis, let us first make some important further distinctions, in quest of further direction to be taken.

EDUCATIONAL THINKING

The technician and the professional: a balance. Let us begin with a consideration of the difference between the technician and the member of a discipline (let us call him a professional here, though the two terms are not generally considered synonymous). There is a difference that is quite easily detected, but one that it is vital to make explicit. The difference is a matter of the range of knowledge which is intrinsic to the operations identifying each. The professional (or the member of the discipline) operates on the basis of some theory that explains and directs his actions. The technician, much as the disengaged didactic, is concerned with the operating event itself (that is, the didact who leads nowhere beyond his concern for strict exposition).

In an awareness of this last, it is necessary to point out, though it is not particularly startling, that men can perform the most complex acts without being conscious of an explanation for the things they do, or for the way things behave. Training produces extraordinary skillfulness in employing the most subtle and delicate technical instruments. One can learn how to handle the most advanced machinery with the ease that one develops even the most simple of habits. The only difference is in the time that it takes and the number of steps one must cover. In modern heart treatment, for example, the technician can perform with great skill the most advanced operations and therapies and yet not need to know the explanatory theories of the behavior of the human organism—those theories which have led to the development of heart surgery, transplants, pacemakers, the principles of mechanics employed in artificial hearts, and the like.

But without such knowledge the technician is absolutely stumped when the behavior of the body becomes incompetent, inconsistent, or does not accord with his expectations and with his trained skills in performance. He must wait for the deliberations of the theorist, for the discipline-based professional who is competent to evaluate new evidence against what has been known or held until now. The new data needs to be explained and a new theory, or an altered theory has to be introduced in order for some new action to be undertaken.

These facts lie behind this consideration of a theory of models and the corresponding theory of education predicated on such a theory of models. This latter is a theory of thinking in which models are central. Its importance for us is to be found in the conviction that the nurture and improvement of thinking is the intrinsic goal of the educative process. Different levels of models enable us to distinguish between levels and types of thinking. We may, for example, be able to learn to think psychologically at one moment, and historically at another, biologically on one occasion and physically on another. But unless we know what it is that distinguishes these at the theoretical level, we will all be like M. Jourdain, in Molière's *Le Bourgeois Gentilhomme,* who talked prose all his life without ever knowing that he was doing so.

Of course, one might say, as so many have, that thinking is thinking, whenever it takes place; that whenever it occurs, it has a unitary character. Whatever you may think *about,* the method of the action which is called thinking follows the same sequence, and produces the same resulting principles. We go from what we know to what we do not know.

On the other hand we have here recommended an entirely different account of the act of thinking. But it must be admitted that there is truly no reason to accept this account simply because it has been offered. We must do much more than assert this new account. Surely, we must provide a justification, and at points, even a validation that would warrant the acceptance of this new exposition.

Before we do this, however, let us be clear what it is we are going to attempt to justify, and, wherever possible, to prove. I shall be recasting the fundamental thesis about thinking that has been presented in the book thus far into more familiar terms, in order to connect traditional beliefs with the reconstructed presentation here.

The levels of thinking.   Philosophers generally accept the view that there are three quite clear levels of thinking (levels being distinguished as levels of abstraction). There is a level of thinking in which we are concerned with the data before us. Here we are in large measure directed to take account of the details and the elements of the materials we seek to explore and explain, describe and evaluate, define and interpret.

There is a second level, where the characteristics of the materials explored are important, though in a different way than in the first level. Here the concern is with elements of events, not as details in their own character, but rather as the traits of character any given event may share with other events. At this level, for example, we think about the details of an historical event in order to discern in this event characteristic traits, patterns, sequences, and relationships that will enable us to see it as in some way similar, or analogous, equal, or belonging to the class of patterns of growth of what we are studying. We are seeking here such traits as will enable us to use our knowledge of some event to help us to understand another. This is, quite clearly, an integrative act of thinking. Although the details of the events are significant, far more important is the fact that we can integrate what we know with what we do not yet know, but which is before us, and which we are seeking to understand.

There is still a third level of thinking at its most abstract. Here we are concerned not so much with integrating events with one another, or systems with one another, but rather with the construction or identification of the rules which are employed in order to produce that integration of events with one another. In a consideration of rules, and in moving from rules to the source of rules in some theory, we seek to set out the classifying systems themselves. These are the models by means of which we sort out the things we experience, as well as different ranges of experiences, giving them meaning and logically acceptable relationships that would connect for us their histories to their careers and their functions.

The importance of distinguishing these levels is attested in the fact that education as a study is concerned with all of them, in sequence, as no other area of study is. Education is concerned with bringing together the skills required to think about things and integrate the developing abilities of exploring and understanding the different types of events we learn to think about at that first level. But this act of integration, as well as the act of particular confrontation, transcends mere technology only when that third level, the level of the theoretical, is made a conscious part of the range of thinking.

It is interesting to note that one may even learn to think at that third level in a straightforward technical way. One can, indeed, think very abstractly about mathematical problems or metaphysical problems in a technical sense, without having developed the scope of thinking we are attempting to distinguish here.

It is the interrelationship between the three levels, where each supplies to the two others those needed dimensions that will prevent them each from being reduced to techniques alone, that marks the special domain of educational thinking. And it is this relationship that the models of education described sustain and make available to those who would develop the unique capacity called here *educational thinking*.

The levels of thinking and their pragmatic distinctions. Ordinarily a further exposition of the three levels would take the form of a careful logical analysis of what is contained in each concept. But we are intent on something other than an ordinary investigation. It is true that the consideration of education as a scholarly discipline can be satisfied only in that way. But our interest goes beyond that; beyond the logical analysis to the pragmatic end of a programmatic analysis (curious as this may sound). However much we may talk about education, analyzing its central concepts and its language, we must be led, as in a practical science, to the investigation of what it is we are called upon to do, or are in fact doing. In short, we must try to see what kinds of action and what meanings in the world of our experience issue from our analytical considerations. It is in this further exploration that the analysis of the concepts is made complete.

We must examine the relationships between the models of things and the development of models for integrating things. The purpose of this is to discern what it is that the models of education are dealing with, so that we can marshal these various models into such instruments as will produce the consequences we seek in the behavior, both cognitive and non-cognitive, of those who learn.

For this reason it would be advisable to continue the analysis in the material terms of an actual plan of operation. In fact, it might be most advisable to show the relationships among the three levels of thinking by offering an analysis of an archetypical teacher's lesson plan; literally, a model for teaching (in the simplest and least technical meaning of that well-used term).

Let us consider a familiar, though perhaps unexpected case of a lesson plan of the type that will serve our purposes. It will become evident, though, that what will be considered is not normally spoken of as a lesson plan. In fact, it would sound almost pretentious to call it that. Nevertheless, in a genuine sense, a surgeon's blueprint for an operation does serve the same function for him as a lesson plan does for the thoughtful and deliberate teacher.

Whether formally set out in some overt way, or contained in the mind of the surgeon, the fact is that no doctor will embark upon an operation without a more or less definitive plan of what is to be done, what might be anticipated, what alternatives must be kept in mind, and what the outcome is expected to be.

Such a plan would, if spelled out, consist of a model of the organism on which operation will be performed in some form, rendered in such a way that the character of the material to be dealt with, as well as the instruments used for the operation, are clearly indicated and their characteristic behaviors taken into account. The plan must be constructed with the knowledge of the behaving organ, of the character of the instrument, as well as with a view to the proper conditions and functions of whatever is involved, in mind. Further, the plan, whether actually written out or held in mind, must be quite clear about methods to be used, and the anticipated reaction of the organ within the total organism to such instruments and such methods. Such a statement already implies that another model reflecting the integrating functions of organ and organism is present in some form. Finally, the more precise and critical the plan is, the more predictable will be the outcome, and the more comprehensible the failure of that outcome, even if the meaning of the failure may have to wait upon further exploration to be fully understood.

There may, indeed in medicine there often does, occur unpredicted consequences. At any point in its history, neither knowledge of the wide range of behavior of the human body, nor the development of the skills or the methods of surgery is so advanced that all possible outcomes can be anticipated. And yet, new failures are not despaired over. Rather, in a sanguine undertaking, the particular failures are treated as invitations for newer, deeper inquiries into areas not even thought about until then. Every such eventuality presents itself as further instance of the possible. (If this is reminiscent of the paradigm in use it should be no surprise to you.)

If we consider this as an illustrative case of a plan of action, where the knowledge of how certain activities undertaken rests upon a more or less clearly determinate theory, we can see why it is that medicine is so often used as a model for educational planning and analysis.

We are not thinking of that form of lesson plan all too familiar to teachers, ordinarily written out for classroom use. We are not considering the constricting mold so familiar to teachers, that is so often nothing more than a series of dictates of what the teacher is required to "cover" at this moment and at the next, with this material and with that, and to which is attached some kind of imprimatur of authority to assure compliance. The plan we will consider, on the contrary, will be a plan in which the materials examined will be indicated in their character of particulars because critical inquiry, and not administrative fiat, has given it warrant; where the instruments of teaching (the educational models) will be analyzed and analyzable by each teacher; where instruments to be employed are recommended on the grounds of analysis and experiment and are open to continuous test; and, finally, where the integrating models will be understood to have the mandatory force that open and continuously testable inquiry can give.

Except in a kind of "ad hoc" sense, no plan for the performance of an appendectomy can be considered final or definitive. It is simply not wise to insist that at any time we know all there is to know about the appendix, or about the removal of an appendix whose malfunction has affected the proper functioning of the whole body. Nevertheless, medicine is as effective as our commitment to the prevailing plan that its own history has made defensible. Whatever may be learned tomorrow, the event itself does compel action upon what history and experiment has made available to the moment. It is important, of course, to observe that such a plan of operation must be considered authoritative, but not authoritarian. It is not a dictum, sent down from some unchallenged source, that must be followed by all who would be doctors, whether they comprehend it or not. It is, rather, part of a historical continuity, the latest stated point of development in a still continuing, still developing undertaking whose very goal is refined in continued exploration and discovery.

A lesson plan can be far more critically detailed than it ordinarily is, and yet be no more dictatorial than a scientific prescription. This distinction between authority and authoritarian is not very subtle, or original, but it is a good one nevertheless, since it separates conclusions, which are open to challenge, from commands, which are not. It is a plan built on the assumption of preparation and competence in the teacher. It would contain within it the materials constituting the furthest advances of a knowledge of the nurture of intelligence. But, of the most profound educational importance, it takes explicit cognizance of the role which different modes of constructing knowledge play in that nurture. Such a plan in the final analysis is a plan for constructing a situation within which particular thinking and integrated thinking are fostered by deliberate educational ministrations.

This may sound vague, but it is a vagueness unavoidable at this point. The reason for this is that, where in the past we have made a great point of specificity in setting forth the plan as directive, specificity is not possible in a plan treated as dispositional model. On the other hand, what had been left vague and imprecise in the past now becomes very exact. It is this shift that will cause some consternation. Where a so-called "liberal" approach in education has allowed great room for the private and personal preferences of teachers, this leniency has been closed off. If the purpose of education is the nurture of the ability to sort things out, to construct or to recognize constructed categories in order to organize the events of experience until we come to understand and control them, then the primacy given to the dispensing of opinion by any teacher concerning the correct conclusion of any problem is irrelevant. There is a reduction of room for opinion here as in any developing discipline. Such a discipline becomes increasingly controlled by the covering categories that constitute the rules of each discipline.

On the other hand, what was left judiciously vague in the interests of flexibility of what we generally have called "methods" of teaching, is now moved toward greater and greater clarity and precision. The laws of thought are precise whenever they have been set down. They may be no more final than Aristotle's Logic is now recognized to be, but in so far as these are set down, they are precise in their own context.

The uses of data at the educational level of thinking; integrative models. Consider the direction into which we are led when we contemplate the distinctions made in the types and levels of thinking. A lesson plan will, under these auspices, set out the materials to be considered. But these materials are not simply the *conclusions* of someone's history of the world, or of the derived atomic weights of nature's elements, or of the meanings of the novels to be read during a semester. The materials are the *data* that historians, physicists, writers, and other scholars have explored, sorted out, put together. Along with this kind of data, there are also set out in specific symbol notations the ways of thinking used to do that putting together, and producing the conclusions available to us. The conclusions are present, to be sure, but they are present as the consequences of mental activity that is the heart of the educational concern.

What the plan fosters is the understanding and the development of the skill in the thinking that is concentrated in inquiry and analysis. Thus, the materials confronted are of two types. They are matters that can be experimented on and matters that can be reasoned about. They are existential and analytic. What is intended is that students will develop the capacities to think about and control the symbols of these as particular events, whether they are physical or logical. They might be chairs and wooden tables, multiplication or logarithmic tables, or beliefs about war, peace, love and the Tables of the Law. The point is that students are asked to learn how to think about these particulars by taking their characteristics, their functions, and their histories into an account, as these have been represented in the variety of constructions of thinking we call experimental and analytical.

We have already indicated the limitations of technology. Learning to think simply by learning the specific behavior of specific events in the fixed contents of previous explorers-creators can result in a kind of technological skill. The mathematician who can follow the directions of a formula in calculus, putting a set of symbols through the operations required by that formula, however complex these may be, may still be showing a technical excellence only. Mathematical thinking, though it shows this skill, is clearly something much more. The same is true in an exploration or an analysis of any structure, whether it be a physical event, an idea, or an institution. Unless we move beyond the particular into the theoretical level, and concern ourselves with rule analysis and rule construction, thinking finally reduces to developed skills and memory competences.

It is at the point at which we begin to draw out the theoretical model on which the structured materials explored can be said to rest that particular thinking is saved from being reduced to a mere skill of logical manipulations or a competence in following out formulas. In fact, just to recognize this is to prepare the way for comprehending the character and the function of the *integration of levels of thinking*. We recognize that models that transform a given specific set of data into the subject matter of exploration can be used to transform other bits of data into entirely new meaningful matters. The model that a physicist uses to organize the data he has encountered in order to write a law of nature or an instrument for tracing the movement of molecules, can be used by a psychologist who is intent on writing a law of human behavior or as an instrument for predicting responses to given stimuli. Is this not the very basis of behaviorist psychology?

Undergirding all of the particular structures we learn to think about, there are theoretical models making it possible to integrate the widest range of things into manageable systems. It is this synthesizing act which gives genuine cognitive force to the analyses and experiments with which we began, and about which more will be said shortly.

There is still that third level that must be remembered and specified in the plan for teaching. This is the level beyond the use of particular models, or the recognition of the integrating models. It is the level of concern for the construction, confrontation, and evaluation of the models that are finally employed by some searcher in pursuit of knowledge and understanding. At this methodological level techniques play a necessary but not a sufficient role. What is needed is to learn how to analyze the techniques of the first level, and the methods of analysis and of experiment constituting the second level. Here we consider the meanings and logical limits of models, the explanations they make possible, and the measurements they support. We might call this Theoretics, or give it its philosophical term of Epistemology, or we may apply the term Methodology, giving it this clearly limited meaning, as others have done.

The models of education, which we have been considering at length and in their diversity, are models that make possible the fostering of each of these three levels. If education is to fulfill its intrinsic objectives, it must nurture each of the distinct capacities identified here, and weave them together into a single power.

THE APPLICATION OF EDUCATIONAL MODELS

Educational models and the attainment of educational goals. The quality of the lesson plan proposed does not depend primarily on the specific materials chosen for analysis, or on the integrating models to be introduced and used, or even on the methodology to be developed. (Of course, each of these has influence, but not in intrinsic ways.) The plan itself, as a recommendation and a prescription for the nurture of powers not fully present, or not yet present at all, depends fundamentally on the educational models this work has been at pains to identify and explain. Without these, the whole process is simply one of putting the learner in touch with what he must come at last to know, and to show evidence of, in the form of recall. With these models, materials that might be handled in very different ways, with very different purposes in mind, come to be treated as the materials for producing educational results. When, for example, data is handled didactically, the educational purpose becomes not only evident, but quite inevitable. Once materials are organized so that they can be treated paradigmatically, the educational intention not only appears, but is made both obligatory and attainable. Purpose is intrinsic to the model bearing it, and is deducible from it.

But again, the educational models are used to *do something,* that is, to nurture some power. Thus, these models, when applied to data as it comes to us, organized or unorganized, expose not only what is present, but, far more important, transform that matter into instruments for the enhancement of our lives. So it is by means of these educational models, in the presence of the data of our world, that the variety of ways of thinking available or newly invented are nurtured in learners at whatever age.

It must be evident that what is being argued is that the teacher needs to know and to be as completely skillful in the use of educational models as a scientist is in the use of his instruments, as a psychologist is in his means of analysis, or as any member of a discipline is in the models that define his discipline. How these are actually employed in the act of teaching has been the central concern of this whole work. But once again, we must consider the many phases and dimensions of such competence, or reduce the teacher to a mere technician, without knowledge and skill in the use of those integrating models that make possible transactions between the models of a particular discipline and the models of educating.

On the one side the teacher needs skill in the confrontation of theoretical, universal problems, and on the other, knowledge and skill in treating specific undertakings in specific disciplines. This is far from the unhappy, stultifying cliché that the teacher needs to know his subject and to have at least some competence in the "methods of teaching." It means, contrariwise, that the teacher needs to have developed the skills of analysis, synthesis, theorizing, and locating models in use, thereby developing a power to construct models, and to integrate the models of one or more disciplines with the materials and the models of other disciplines. Nor is this simply the borrowing of the skill of the physicist for the purpose of teaching physics, of the historian for the purpose of teaching history, of the artist for the purpose of teaching art. It is, rather, a skill which is bound in some way to the skills and the knowledge found in uniquely educational models. The teacher must know the range of function of his models, and the modes of their employ in phases of the matters he must handle, if he is to perform a didactic, or a dialectic, or any of the other models constituting his own technological arsenal.

But there is yet more involved. Of all of the elements of the act of thinking, those that predominate when we think physically, or in terms of the intellectual operations of the physicists, are the elements of description and explanation. To be sure, it will be explanation of a kind pertinent to physical data, eliciting a commensurate form of description.

How would this compare with poetic thinking as it is usually done? Explanation is, to be sure, of some importance in poetic thinking, but it is not primary. And when it does appear, it is a very different kind of explanation than that of the physicist. In poetic thinking the elements we give primacy to appear as a unique combination of description and interpretation. In fact, none of the arts are primarily concerned with explaining anything about the world in the physicist's sense. The images of worlds and lives poetry is expected to evoke, and the passions it nurtures, achieve the description and the interpretation of that description.

When we learn to think mathematically, what part of the thinking act is given primacy? This would be *reason,* and would appear in the form of the varieties of logic available to us. As mathematicians know, we do not explain anything in nature by mathematics. Nor does mathematics describe anything in any ordinary or poetic sense. It sets forth a type of dimensionality entailed in concepts and relationships that are given symbolic identity. Mathematical formulas are not a description of reality, but they are, par excellence, evidence of the operation of reason within the larger context of thinking and judging relationships and entailments among symbol systems and within them.

Educational models and the concern for cognitive emphasis in each particular discipline. We could go through more of these, to show the way in which each of the disciplines gives primacy to one or two of the elements in special, weighted combination, while permitting the others a recessive but necessary function. Archeology, for example, depends on description and assuredly it requires explanation, but beyond anything the discipline of archeology is the instrument for the nurture of powers of observation or exploration. This is what distinguishes it, say, from physics, whose explanatory function makes it a law-making discipline. Within the total act of thinking the discoverable emphasis in the thinking act tells us what the discipline is ordered to accomplish, what its models are designed to analyze, control, and make understandable.

The types of materials to which we apply ourselves do influence us to emphasize one phase or element of the act of thinking rather than another. That is because the material itself is already given form and emphasis as it comes to us. Nevertheless, there is no prohibition against using the emphasis in one discipline in order to shed light on something that we have looked at in other ways countless times. Thus, at this first level in the developing of an analysis of materials, we do not have just the standard twenty or twenty-four different disciplines which comprise school and college faculties. There are these twenty-four and the additional number we gain by judiciously and deliberately reapplying the thinking act in order to offer up new explanations, description, or accounts of the materials to be examined. We can refer again to the way psychologists have used models of physics in unexpected and fruitful ways. Sociologists borrow psychological models, economists those of mathematics, physicists the models of art. In the borrowing, the borrower finds new meanings because he has followed the required cognitive emphasis of the borrowed model. When the ethician uses social models, he finds himself emphasizing descriptions and social explanations in place of deductive prescriptions that have been his tradition. (The running battle between moral philosophies can be seen to reflect these rebellious model-shifts.)

This deliberate mixing of sorts of things with one another in what appears to be unlawful ways is the source of all that is fruitful in men's explorations of the world and of themselves. Every form of study can, in its own way, arrogate to itself the advances in every other discipline. Without such borrowing, every discipline moves further and further away from every other, in the direction of total isolation and disrupted communication.

Of course, such mixing is not to be arbitrarily done. Unless the borrower makes the proper translations according to the rules of his own discipline, and is aware of the rules that gave meaning to the concepts in the original contexts, he finds himself in trouble. It is only by attending to the rules of transformation that the psychologist may borrow the models of the physicist without also reducing the subject of his study to the inanimate matter that the models of physics address themselves to. What is most metaphysics, after all, but the application of physical models to the non-physical, without having made the kind of transformation that would have avoided the conclusion that metaphysics was a consideration of incorporeal, or insubstantial beings? Such conditions must be heeded, for they give shape and meaning to reality though they may not materialize that reality. The failure to take heed becomes an act of the destruction of the order of thought itself.

THE INTEGRATING MODELS

The integrating models and what they integrate: a basic illus- tration. Now let us consider the intermediary level. It is possible to distinguish four generic models as four integrative classifying systems. At this level the models ought to be kept few in number. Multiplying them leads away from the very clarity which the integrating function is constructed to produce.

In considering the levels of thinking earlier in this chapter we have already hinted at four general classifications that could be used to sort out all of the prevailing disciplines, particularly dis- ciplines which inhabit a school curriculum.

There are, in a metaphoric sense, the archeological models— those models in which we are concerned to dig into something and to expose what lies within, and is otherwise not apparent to the eye.

There are anatomical (or "cutting open") models—those models that accept what is already present to the senses, but go below the "skin" to see actual operations.

There are biographical (or "tracking of changes") models— those models that direct attention to the career (generation and degeneration) of events, human or other.

And, finally, there are constructive (or "building") models— those models that are concerned to project fulfillments or completions of what is presently available.

What is most interesting to note is how the very names suggest the fundamental modes of the exploratory acts we each undertake naturally and constantly.

In these four we may discover that disciplines with seemingly no connections with one another may be seen as being members of one another, and characterized by many common traits. More im- portant, because of this commonalty, certain metaphoric treatments, though conceptually dangerous, are nevertheless quite promising when treated with great care. Judicious use of these integrating models may reveal new realities and create new meanings in the form of new disciplines, fields, and modes of study.

Let us consider, as an illustration, an analysis (a study) of poetry. It is not difficult to demonstrate that there are "archeological" dimensions in poetry that we would do well to attend to. We study the conditions in which the poem was written in order to understand its social basis or the political context. To take the simplest of examples, Mother Goose rhymes have been discovered, after some diligent "digging," to have a significance of an essentially political nature. The poems are now seen as only apparently innocent. More significantly, they were a disarming way of saying mocking things about England in the seventeenth century. These were apparently things that people were not courageous enough to say openly and seriously. Armed with this sorting system, Mother Goose can be discovered to reveal an entirely different character. It might be charged that this is history and not a matter of literature. Indeed; and history is in large measure an archeological undertaking; its raw data are all sorts of artifacts, even literary artifacts. To recognize this as such is to see it through archeological models and methods.

Poetry, at some point of its manifest presence, is not far removed from being a biographical or an autobiographical statement of the poet or of his times. In at least one facet of meaning it is the construction of a new vision of the world. Is this, perhaps, what is meant when the poet Shaughnessy writes: "One man with a dream at pleasure can go forth and conquer a crown/and two with a new song's measure can trample an empire down"? The man with the dream at pleasure may be the poet warrior. And the others, with their new song's measure as their weapons, can trample empires down. Is this anything but the construction of a reality more desirable, more attractive, more enchanting, or more dramatic, more threatening, more hopeful than the one the poet himself lived in?

Is it possible to study poetry seriously without doing an anatomy of poetry—that is, cutting it apart to see the character of its rhythms, its cadences, its measures, the quality of its rhymes, and the color of its words? Surely, there is, in a richly metaphoric sense, an anatomy of poetry.

But please note: everything said deals with the teaching of poetry. It is, in fact, the beginning outline of a plan for teaching. It is not the writing of a plan you can see, or necessarily a plan for reading poetry for one's own enjoyment. It is, rather, a plan for teaching, for equipping someone to think poetically about the world and our own ways. This is what conscious use of the integrating models makes possible. The intellectual developments that are possible within the whole area of one discipline are made available as instruments for nurturing that vital first level of thinking, the level of direct confrontation.

How integrating models make possible a lesson plan. But in order to see how this operates we must consider again the methodology by means of which all this is brought within the ken of learners. Five models have been introduced: dialectic, didactic, monologic, paradigm, and projective, and there are more to be invented.

Each one of these, under careful scrutiny, is seen to be limited by the kinds of materials that it is developed to handle. And yet, it is hard to argue that there is any assurance that such limitations are intrinsic and final. We may learn to use dialectic even in places we normally would not expect dialogue (in teaching mathematics, for example), without offending or deceiving the student. We surely use didactic in order to teach philosophy in a given mode, without intellectually offending students.

It is quite possible, handling the various levels of thinking by means of these integrating models, to write a lesson plan in which we can describe, in almost blueprint fashion, how one is to handle certain concepts and materials (identifying a specific field of study) in modes of analysis indicated, integrating it in determinate ways, with identified materials and by means of the models of educating, setting forth the specific methodology for the teaching act. From the construction and the use of such plans, there will inevitably develop an expertise; for, from such efforts there will appear a continuous line of improvement from teacher to teacher, from planner to planner. With the presence of such clearly specified materials, continuously tested in the experiments whose goals are increasingly clear, teachers are in positions to learn from one another. Such competence develops to a point where, without actual advance testing, the practitioner can review a course of action mentally and decide which materials, in which mode of analysis, can be developed that had not been developed before; and what possible outcomes might be anticipated. Just such a stage is reached by every developing discipline.

Consider, for instance, undertaking the study of biology in terms of the models used in the analysis of poetry. The dangers of such an approach are as appalling as they are obvious. The confusion resulting the application of models of romance to the structures of reality often leads to loss of contact with the world itself. But seeing the various facets of the human organism as so many pulses in a line of verse, seeing this type of organic action against poetic models which have the cumulative quality of beginning and ending, is to bring into sharp focus what is otherwise confused and amorphous. Thinking how the models that we normally employ to analyze poetry will now be used to analyze bodily change, and then deciding how to integrate this with still other organisms, or so-called organisms, such as political or social structures, may indeed produce misleading explanations of serious matters. But the intellectual flexibility demanded and produced is reward enough in the process of education and the purposes for which this process is undertaken. To be sure, we must guard against the confusions of intermixing by using the language of the transported model (of poetry, say) with dictionary precision of its definition. But it must be acknowledged that such fears and such obligations ought not be permitted to sterilize teaching.

Following this, the judgment as to the relevance of an educational model must extend to a consideration of the expectation of the outcome of the lesson; that is, the form of thinking which is its particular goal. But most important, to have written all this down in a system of meanings communicable within the discipline should enable another teacher, who has learned to read and comprehend that same language, to teach the class in the same way and yet not to lose originality or any of the potentialities for new insights made available by working in this manner with students.

The importance of this procedure, simply stated, is found in recognition of the fact that any science is dependable only at the point at which it no longer rests on the whimsical personality of its individual scientists or practitioners. Medicine is an advanced science at the point of its career when one doctor can pick up an operation halfway through and do exactly what the operation calls for. His personality may differ widely from that of the previous physician who had begun the work, but the objectified conditions and instruments are not dissolved by such objective needs and states.

A discipline is composed of an identifiable objective procedure with basic concepts entailing actions to be followed. To the degree that personal preferences can be relegated to the background long enough to follow the theory made manifest, to that degree can the patient trust the science of medicine. This is so in any completed or fully developed discipline. It is so in a physics exercise, in a mathematical problem, in the law. A lawyer who takes over a case in midstream must acquaint himself with what has gone before, with what are being used as precedents, with the pattern set out by the previous lawyer, measured by the logic and the experiences of the profession itself. Law, of course, is not quite as definitive as medicine in most of our experiences, and allows for variations in strategy at many points, but the discipline is not compromised by this. On the contrary, it is a good example because as it appears to us, concepts fundamental to the profession of the law are probably no more definitive or denotative than are basic educational concepts at this time.

If the concern is with the nurture of the power to think, and if the power to think is at all describable, and its elements able to be theoretically postulated, then there is no reason why education should not be moving in this same direction. All disciplines appear to do precisely that.

The phases of planning lessons.   If we are now to begin to develop plans for actual practices or, in advance of this, for rehearsing sessions of the educative act, where shall we begin? The simplest, though perhaps not the best way, is to look first to the materials to be handled. This first step leads to a consideration of the models by means of which these very matters are given form and visibility. Such a step includes the further question of what we want the learners to learn, what scope and power of thinking we want them to develop. There is a range of choices here, of course, but not so great a range that in the long run a group of teachers would be unable to agree upon the modes of treating the materials. The deeper and the surer the understanding of what is included in and what can be achieved by the discernable models by means of which matters are sorted out and shaped, and powers of thinking are nurtured, the greater the possibilities for agreement among the practicing educators.

The next phase of the planning is that of deciding which integrating models shall be used. Here there is the problem of choice among the intermediary or integrating models, where, as is usually the case, more promising models are chosen in favor of the less promising. It is clear that among the integrating models, those generic models that provide an understanding of the combining character of a range of different undertakings, some are more traditional, more limiting, more rigid; others less traditional, less restrictive, more flexible. But whichever model, or models, are chosen, once the choice is made, the acts that it or they direct are quite clear. These are the acts of defining the relationship between the materials considered and the context of events within which the materials can be understood. From such contexts of relationships they take their meanings, and to them they contribute the developing significance of the whole situation. The materials integrated are absorbed into the conceptual activity and are shaped by the models determining that activity.

Finally, there is the question of which educational model, or models, we shall employ in the teaching act. There are not so many that each teacher cannot get to know them all, and in great detail. But it is imperative that we recognize the difference between the models of education which are available, which have been researched, experimented on, refined and clarified, so that their range of effects known, on the one hand; and on the other, the specific methods, those psychological tactics which differ as the techniques used in any undertaking differ with different practitioners. This difference appears always to be overlooked. And thereby we have reduced the whole of teaching to this matter of distinctive techniques, rarely noting that the techniques were techniques of something. That something is the handling of the logically distinct models of educating.

Of course, there is room for the variations of the skills that mark any developed profession and any grown or growing discipline. That is as obvious and as undeniable as the difference between right-handed tennis players and left-handed tennis players, right-handed physicians and left-handed physicians. But the effectiveness of these skills, these artful techniques, is dependent, in the final analysis, on the adequate grasp of the models that enable us to know what it is we are about.

As with medicine, again, the wide range of techniques that may be employed to perform a heart transplant are all finally evaluated against the definitive, accepted model of the functioning human organism and the knowledge derived from this model as to the requirements for the organism to continue to function. Whether we implant the heart of some animal, a mechanical heart, the heart of another human being, a pacemaker, or an instrument that substitutes for the heart, the fact is that the mode of function of the heart and its necessary role in the life process, as these are discerned in some deliberately constructed model of actual and possible operation, sets rules and limits to the variety of incisions, modes of transplants, or modes of stimulation and other treatments which can be used.

The lesson plan, its models, and the non-educational determinants of tactics.   In the actual use of the models of education some teachers may be more dramatic in the use of dialectic, some more ironic, some more beguiling, some more blunt, some more verbal, some more insinuating. But these psychological tactics are not substitutes for, or alternatives to, the logic of that educational model (or for any other model used in a range of qualities). These are only selected responses to the extra-educational domain, to the momentary disposition of the learners as they come to the tasks of education. In the long run, the worth of the psychological ministrations are tested by their support in the logical employments of logical structures. If the stitching which followed the heart surgery falls apart too soon, it may not have been the failure of the sewing, but rather the failure to take into account the conditions, or the materials with which the sewing was done. If the dialectic falls apart, it may not be so much because of the failure of the psychological quality of dialogue, as the failure to consider the structure of dialectic as such. A wide range of psychological tactics can be equally successful. But with a violation of the logic, the educational model and the educational event itself disappears.

THE CURRICULUM OF THE MODELS

Theory and practice in education; the primacy of the educational models. It has been acknowledged that manifestation of great skill in the performance of even the most complex acts does not wait upon a knowledge of the undergirding theories of such acts, or even of the factual character of what is being operated on. This is surely also noticeable in the teaching situation. It is not to be denied that it is entirely possible to be a skillful teacher without knowing the theoretical bases of the acts which constitute education. There is even, quite validly, a genuine question if a knowledge of the theoretical grounds affects in any way the skill of the practitioner as tactician. But this is a very complex question, demanding further analysis of the distinction between educational and extra-educational acts. Yet this much is suggested: the skills of teaching are not what education finally reduces to, just as the skill in surgery, or in recognition of malfunction is not what medicine finally reduces itself to; although in both cases each discipline is enhanced in the skill of its practitioners. In both cases the very structuring of the action to be undertaken will affect the performance of that activity. The definition of health, along with the theoretical aspects that are elements of all definitions, is as much a part of the practice of medicine as is diagnosis or surgery. It is definition, in fact, which will make possible an educational (in this case, teaching) profession and its supporting discipline. It is for this reason that it becomes imperative to know the theory of education within which are included the ingredients for construction of educational models. It is such knowledge that will distinguish the professional educator from the teacher as technician. With such knowledge teaching techniques are transformed into educational powers.

Referring to the brief illustration of teaching poetry earlier offered, it can be suggested that from the point of view of the teacher, the specific models of education are primary. They determine all of what the teacher does within the strictly educational concern. But it is of especial interest to point out that from the point of view of the student, the integrating models are primary. It is in their terms that a learner will finally understand poetry or any other fragment of man's construction of nature's character. The teacher must, therefore, bear both of these facts in mind. He must recognize that it is by means of his teaching models that what is primary for the learner, the integrating models, are made available.

Changing the educational model demands a shift of concern of the materials treated. There is a point here that needs to be made especially clear if we are to show just how necessary is the talk of the many dimensions of education. When the teacher changes the model of educating he has been using and substitutes for it another, the materials he is dealing with take on a completely different character. Some illustrations of this may help to show what is meant. The notion of a class discussion usually implies, in colloquial terms, the employment of a dialectical model. But this is not always the case. It may, curiously, be a didactic that is in use.

In the dialectic, the model itself obliges us to be concerned with the kind of data brought together in statements whose claim can never be finally, objectively, proven or defined as empirically true. If, as teachers, we are going to employ a dialectic in the approach to the consideration of a poem, we begin with the presupposition that there is no final determination of meaning. Any meanings that are developed or definitions that are suggested must be an answer that all the learners in the class, all the people involved in the dialectic, are able to agree upon. On the basis of having agreed, we can then go further into the exploration of this poem, using the terms of that agreement as the rules for a later analysis of conclusions. In dialectic, therefore, what we are concerned with is the poem as each student, at this moment, thinks about it, and is further being nurtured to think about it. The focus of our efforts at intellectual nurture lies in developing the ability to treat in the characteristics of poetic thinking, the *quality* of ideas and beliefs indigenous to poetry and manifest in a given poem.

The basis of this lies in the fact that dialectically what we are concerned with are premises, grounds, and assumptions that are not tangible. They cannot be put to any empirical tests. If, for example, we are engaged in the study of a poem in which the eternal and undegenerating quality of beauty is central, we must first agree, in our study, not upon the truth of the claim, but upon how we shall approach the question of what it is to *mean,* and what we shall agree "beauty" means. When there is agreement on this, we can pursue further questions of the specific definition of the source and the possible erosion of beauty as it is thought of in this or that poem. We can, indeed, measure erosion—but only when we have agreed somehow on what it is that shows the erosion itself. Dialectic is the model for dealing with concepts for which external evidence is simply not ever available.

But if we are going to use a didactic, all this variability disappears. We are no longer talking about the poem in that infinitely open, continuously reinterpretable way. In fact, we are not concerned at all with that dimension of the poem. Didactically, we begin with knowledge of the actual, determinable characteristics of a particular poem. We may involve the students by asking them what they think is the structure or meaning of the poem. But at this point we are not fostering a context for argument. We are stirring powers of observation or recall, because we want the students to note the poem as it is written. Having made that clear, we then go back into the poem to demonstrate, by the evidence in the poem itself, why what we have said is valid. We "break open" ("unpack" is perhaps a better word) the internal content of the poem to show the primary elements or parts of that poem. What we seek to disclose is the way in which structure in poetry produces what are identifiable as poetic effects.

To employ didactic is to produce one cognitive consequence in a class; to employ the dialectic is to produce an entirely different consequence. The former produces the ability to derive knowledge of what is, the latter of what meanings are possible. For that reason it is misguided to think that we can use a dialectic to test yesterday's success with the didactic. When we use a dialectic, we are not teaching the same thing. The outcome is entirely different because totally different aspects of the poem are considered, and for different purposes.

So with every one of the models. The same materials, sorted out and treated by the five different educational models, produce five different consequences in the ability to think and develop understanding, for each is manifestation of yet another aspect, phase, condition, or character of the materials considered.

More important, it is always possible to handle a given set of materials in the five different educational ways. The objective would then be to provide a student with insight into five different facets of the thinking process that he is being called upon to develop, and to show the variety of meanings that any given matter is capable of bearing. And as if this were not enough, we must also recognize that the analysis made was an analysis sometimes of disengaged elements treated as separate datum, and sometimes of a structured event. Sometimes the poem is treated in terms of meanings given concrete form in a series of images, and sometimes it is treated in terms of data that are common to all poetry—sound, rhythm, meter, form, and so on.

Suppose we were to decide, when we made a third approach to the work, that we would show the poem's meanings in the context of a wider setting, say, in a social-moral setting. We know that at the present time the intellectual-emotional climate is such that reading moral meanings of any fixity into poetry produces negations, if not outright rejections from students. We decide not to use the familiar system of moral judgments. We will try to induce an understanding of what might be meant, but instead of the moral language, we will use the language of psycho-social judgments. The use of the language of psycho-social models on such materials will obviously produce an entirely different poem. The words are the same, but the meaning of the poem is not now to be derived from the absolute meanings of its words. A poem, we have learned somewhere in the past, is its sound, and also the imagery that can be produced by its words and the integrating models of interpretation. If we use the models, say, of autobiography, we will get one set of images; of construction, a totally different set of images. Political concepts provide one meaning to a poem, moral judgments another, and psychological language still a third. Change the integrating model of interpretation and the whole poem changes, as it does when we change the educational model.

Changing meanings of content in changed integrating models. This is what is meant when we argue that it is the integrating model that connects the poem as material to other dimensions of life. By the terms of a constructive model, the poem means little in the sense of its content. For learners its meaning lies in the fact that it is an illustration of how one writes a poem, any poem. To argue, at this level, that poetry differs as it is moral, historical, epic, etc. is to mislead the learner into thinking that poetry is distinguished by content, not by form. Constructionist models apply to any poem written, not only to moral poems.

But of course, merely learning the names of these integrating models at these different levels is hardly enough. What we need to know is what each model specifically makes possible and, by this limiting fact, makes impossible. As we get to know more and more of the content of these models and the limitations each imposes, we become more and more precise, first in what it is we want students to learn, and second, in how to get them to learn it.

Again, it is worth repeating, one doctor examining a client and noting that he has need of an appendectomy, does not whimsically decide: "I'm going to use an entirely different model for surgery this time." If the point is to remove the appendix, he must be sure that no disease will occur during the activity and that the patient will recover as quickly as possible. He does not arbitrarily decide that he is going to use a totally new tool in order to do something different, in order to preserve his sacred right of individuality. If he decides to do it in a way not previously considered or analyzed, it had better be part of a research project where the patient is aleady dead, because it is possible that in place of a successful operation, what he is going to produce with his altered model is something other than a cured patient.

If his quest is to produce a new skill, a new technique, a new art, perhaps a new bit of information, whether for doctor or for teacher, his endeavor is something other than cure or nurture. But in so far as the objective remains physical health or mental growth, the demonstrated models that have enabled us in the past to reach this objective had better be employed. Otherwise, we are all still bound by the unhappy conception that teaching is a private art whose goal is "expression." Express yourself in your own way. It does not really matter to me, because I intend to express myself in my own way.

What happens to students, and whole process of education as a result of these attitudes? There is a slow dissolution into mere acts of persuasion, where commitment in the learner proves the force of the passion of the teacher. The student will become one of the unprotected in the face of such institutional coercion.

But if education is our game, then the thinking which sorts out alternatives to passion is our goal.

A quick, not altogether encompassing summary. There are, as far as I have gone, five educational models and four integrating models. In terms of the curriculum, there are as many particular models as there are subjects taught. But within each subject discipline, there may be several distinct models, either because there is disagreement as to what the subject itself is and what it can be expected to achieve, or because some member of the discipline has sought to advance a particular method of inquiry by borrowing the models of some other discipline. As evidence of this latter situation, the study of history, for example, is known to be a much debated affair. The question of what history is (a question, it might be pointed out, that occupies a good number of scholars) produces a variety of theories, and a variety of models which embody those theories. In such cases, the teaching problem is complicated by the great variety of transactions the teacher is called upon to educate in. In fact, in such a field, the number of possible variations a teacher may produce in the effort to nurture in students powers to think historically become so great that there is a need to establish some criteria for selectivity.

In other disciplines, such as physics and mathematics, the variety is not great and the subject is much easier to deal with educationally, but it is varied nonetheless.

A chart might be made in the hope that by this kind of presentation these recommendations would become available, and the range of the many alternatives would immediately be made an instrument for choice. But because it would be too limiting a statement, I will forego it here and suggest that you make one for yourselves. From the *A* group (educational models) will be selected the model by means of which those from some *C* group (models of a subject discipline) will be studied for purposes of nurturing in learners the use of just those models which constitute the modes of thinking of that discipline (e.g. to think psychologically is to be competent in the use of the models of the particular school of psychology you have accepted). But this can be done only if you have first learned to employ the integrating models made available as rules for transforming educational models, which are presented as the fixed conclusions of the subject, into the means for thinking about that same matter in the variety of contexts that make it possible to discern a growing range and depth of meanings.

The educational consequences of such an approach are minds that will never come to an end of growth in comprehension, penetration, and invention.

Appendix

The four essays included in this section were written as classroom assignments in an undergraduate course in Contemporary Education. I might have chosen a great many others, but these four represented analogical, theoretical, cross-representative, and projective models. Each shows the power that attends the increasingly effective use of models in thinking about some event of experience.

A. The first essay was written as an explanatory description of a school the student had attended, especially a description that would make clear the relationships between the students who attended the school and the adults who were in charge of it, and who directed the school and the educational activities. Miss Erwin chose a rather novel event in constructing a full scale analogy of that relationship. I think you will see how the clarity of the event shaped into a model makes for exceptional clarity of description and to some extent, explanation of the school she attended.

A Model of a Parochial School

by

Daphne Erwin

The presence of a parochial school in an open society must by definition make the atmosphere of the parochial school artificial. It cannot present even a semblance of society since it excludes too many modes of thought, differences of opinion, contact among different ethnic and religious groups, to allow for any of the interactions to take place which would be possible in a less limited situation such as public school. The exclusion of contradictory thoughts by the parochial school saves the student from the conflicts which they would cause, but it also leaves the student with misconceptions. The student may have the idea that these contradictions do not exist and therefore all society thinks as he does, or he may recognize that contradictions do exist but through enforced ignorance, his ability to understand the issues will be severely limited because he is unaccustomed to thinking in terms of beliefs which he cannot fully accept.

An effective analogy may be drawn illustrating the relationship of a parochial school to society through the use of Jones Beach State Park. The pool represents Our Lady of Wisdom Academy, a parochial high school, and the ocean and beach combined represent society. The ocean itself represents that form of education provided by society.

The pool at Jones Beach State Park is built in close proximity to the ocean, but any influence from the ocean has been carefully guarded against in the planning of the pool. The initial isolation comes from the surrounding wall which blocks out all sight of the ocean, all noise, and all prevailing winds. The wall not only causes the people inside to be ignorant of what is happening outside but it also causes them to become preoccupied with themselves since they have nowhere else to direct their attention. Admission past this wall is an elaborate procedure. First, a fee must be paid. If the fee cannot be afforded there is no other consideration given to the person and he is asked to leave. If the fee has been paid, he may advance to the next stage which is a purification. Sprinklers are directed toward the person to wash away any residue which may have remained on him from the ocean or sand. The next stage is his commitment. A list of rules and regulations are presented to him to which he must agree to comply. If he has successfully completed each step, he may be initiated by having a stamp placed on his hand. This stamp is not always visible to the naked eye, but it does reveal itself when placed into a simulated atmosphere with a penetrating ultra-violet light. At any moment a patron may be called upon to display his stamp to determine if he is worthy of remaining in the pool. It is relatively rare that a person be dismissed from the pool for not having the stamp. It is indelible and the person himself is not aware of its presence except when specifically asked to display it. It is not unusual, however, that the person be dismissed for disregarding the rules. This is not tolerated since a pool is potentially dangerous and if there is not complete order at all times, a risk is run of endangering someone's life. Therefore, they are strictly enforced.

The area is divided into two pools which separate the patrons according to age, with the younger in the small pool and the older in the large pool. This reduces the risk of any harm coming to the smaller children by keeping them more closely guarded and away from the older people.

The main purpose for having two pools is to provide an area, for those qualified, to bathe. This could be done in the ocean, but it is a belief held by all those in the pool that the ocean and sand are contaminated and hostile. It is considered contaminated because it provides co-existence for all people with an innumerable amount of fish, plantlife and minerals. This they feel is a distraction to the "correct" order which is to keep all groups content among themselves. They feel that if all groups are thrown together, a friction may develop which could possibly injure some of the more delicate individuals, and this must be avoided.

They consider it hostile because they are powerless to exert any amount of control over it. This helplessness which they experience produces an uncomfortable feeling among them, and a deep-seated distrust. The idea has arisen among them that it is the purpose of the ocean to swallow them up and that it is their obligation to take necessary precautions against this.

They also dislike the hindering dirt which they have found to exist in the ocean and on the beach; the sticky sand, the seaweed, and the broken shells which cut; all tend to disrupt the unity and harmony which they feel should pervade a swimming area.

It is because of these ideas that the swimming pool is structured as it is, to provide maximum protection and comfort and safety to the patrons.

The condition of the water is maintained at its optimum level and is constantly being surveyed. The temperature is prevented from reaching any extreme and the bacterial level is carefully guarded. The water is passed through a filtering system which prevents the condition from getting too far out of control at any one time. For increased protection, chemical purifiers are added to the water. Watching the chemical level provides an available objective scale with which the condition can be judged.

To make up for the lack of natural agitation in the water, diving boards are provided. These break up the monotony of the static condition of the pool and they provide a degree of adventure and excitement. The structure of these boards and the manner in which they may be used are strictly regulated. There are three different levels, each accessible from one specific direction. Each level is a progression which the children go through on the basis of age, talent and courage. There is no pressure exerted on the developing children to utilize these boards, and very often there is a gasp from an overly anxious parent as he watches his child suspended in mid-air, unrestrained. There is a deep sigh of relief when it is seen that the child returns safely to the familiar surroundings and readapts himself to his previous state. Occasionally, a child will become overly excited by using the boards and he will neglect the rules which regulate them. If this conduct persists, and he fails to recondition himself, he is asked to leave the pool. If he desires to continue bathing, he must use the ocean.

The area surrounding the pool is made up of smooth granite slabs. These slabs facilitate cleaning and can be periodically hosed down to sweep away any obstructions which may have accumulated, particularly any dirt which has found its way in from the outside. This property of the slabs is an essential one. Any dirt is incongruous to the atmosphere of the pool and all efforts are made to rid the area of it. The greatest enemy in this respect is the sand. Its minute size allows it to work its way through the most carefully designed preventatives. It works as a source of constant irritation and friction. When a sufficient amount has accumulated, it clogs the workings of the filtering system and the sprinklers, and it cuts and grinds the soles of the people unaccustomed to irritation. Preventing this is a major concern of the patrons and administration, and it is toward this job that the major source of energy is expanded.

The administration of the pool is effectively carried out by people called "life guards." Their position demands the utmost respect and their peculiar attire sets them apart immediately from the average patron. The reason for their highly esteemed position is that the very life of each patron is subject to the judgment and protection of the guard. The patrons feel that without him many people would become panic-stricken and confused. They would cease the rhythmic stroking of their swimming, and drown.

Since the work of the life-guard is so important, a special elevated chair is given to him so that he does not receive any of the distractions which would occur if he were on ground level, and also so that he may have a better overall view. If a difference of opinion arises between a patron and a life-guard, the patron is automatically overruled and he accepts this overruling. He assumes that, since the lifeguard has a better view, and since he is dedicated to this work, his opinion must necessarily be more correct.

The life-guards are profoundly aware of the importance of their job, and also of the attitudes surrounding it. They use their undisturbed isolation to devote all their attention to their primary obligation of protecting and saving lives. This dedication and singleness of purpose, they feel, makes them better qualified for their job and more efficient at it.

The chief life-guards are released from their immediate obligation of protecting lives, and their attention is directed to the working of the system as a whole.

Immutability is built into the system. Each specific activity has a designated area with concrete boundaries between each one to prevent overlapping. For example, an area for diving is roped off and separated from the bathing area. Neither activity is allowed in the inappropriate area. The job of the chief life-guards, therefore, is not to initiate changes in the areas, but rather to be certain that they are used only for their designated purposes. By enforcing the preordained rules they are able to maintain order.

Those children using the pools are contented by the comfort and security provided them, without thoroughly understanding what it is in the system which makes their comfort possible. They comply strictly to the rules and they approve of their peers' compliance. They realize that there is a mysterious latent danger in the pool and that they are protected from it by the rules. They do not completely understand the extent of this danger, nor would they understand how to contend with it if they were ever confronted with it, since they are protected from ever facing it.

They are aware of the existence of the ocean by catching glimpses of it while passing to their own area. Few have come into immediate contact with ocean. Those who have experienced the ocean suffered confusion and boredom when transferred to the pool. They were initially surprised by the rigidity of the pool, and the large concentration of people in such confined areas. They were bored by the predictability of activities and the lack of excitement. After a short time, they become conditioned by the orderliness and comfort of the pool, and for the most part, they accept this boredom while gradually numbing their boredom.

Those who never partook of the ocean regard it as crude, and they have contempt for the lack of refinement which they observe in it. The pool, therefore, is a closed system which provides contentment and protection to its patrons. It is little affected by outside activities and consequently, the outside activities are little affected by it. The advantages received by the patrons are directly proportionate to their success in remaining in such a controlled system. The longer they remain, the better conditioned they are to respond correctly. However, the better conditioned they are in these responses, the poorer are their chances to make appropriate adjustments to dissimilar systems such as the ocean. . . .

B.   The second essay was written for an assignment asking students to review a recent book in the field, and to make an analysis either by finding the model implicitly employed by the author, or to construct a model that would best lay bare a significant meaning the work was concerned to set forth. The model form which Mr. Fortunato used was theoretical. Going further, he then demonstrates how an alteration of the model at some point produces a work of a very different kind, one in which certain logical refinements have been made possible.

The Pragmatic Method of Knowing
by
Carl Fortunato

The theory of education offered by John Holt in *How Children Fail* is built on two fundamental postulates: first, that the universe is orderly and follows a basically rational structure; second, that knowledge, which for man is both a symbol and a reflection of the universe, contains certain inconsistencies which are not a part of the actual universe. However, such statements tend toward a philosophical inquiry rather than a model of education. Therefore, the purpose of this paper is to show that what appears as the core of a Rationalist's philosophical study can become the basis for a Pragmatic theory of education. To achieve this end it is necessary to reconstruct Mr. Holt's educational model.

By examining the context in which Mr. Holt makes his generalizations on the universe and man's understanding of it, one begins to infer their possible applicability to an educational framework. Holt reveals his belief in the orderliness of the universe by referring to those children who, because of emotional inhibitions, do not master basic mental skills, " 'What must it be like to have so little idea of the way the world works,

so little feeling for the regularity, the orderliness, the sensibility of things?
. . . those children have come to feel that this universe is an enemy.' "
The bright child, Holt finds, is able to "unite himself with," and place
trust in the universe although it does not for the moment make sense.
Actually, none of Holt's comments has direct pertinence to a working
model of education; in fact, they have more the character of a philosophical orientation than that of an educational theory. These comments
emphasize man's direct confrontation with the universe, the very object
of Holt's citing from Browning's "Andrea del Sarto": " 'A man's reach
should exceed his grasp, or what's a Heaven for?' " However, the emphasis of Holt's philosophical thought is not synonymous with the tone
of his educational philosophy; and the distinction between the two must
be kept clear if one is to accurately derive Holt's model of education.

The second part of Holt's thesis, that knowledge is an imperfect
replica of the universe, provides what is likely to become substance for
the educational analyst. Holt asserts, "If children come to feel that the
universe does not make sense, it may be because . . . there are contradictions between the universe as we experience it and as we talk about it."
Language is therefore a tool with which man fashions his thoughts and
patterns of learning. Man can manipulate language; however, its intrinsic
limitations are set and cannot be changed: teachers can help students
become aware of the incongruities between words and experience,
". . . and perhaps show them [the students] ways of using language that
would to some extent rise above its limitations." Thus, the learner is not
so much learning language as the closed system which, by Holt's definition, it is, as he is learning the connection between language and the
universe. In a sense, the student circumvents human knowledge to more
closely learn its coincidence with reality, not for the purpose of improving
language in general, but for the purpose of expanding his own skill in
using that language. At this point, one can clearly identify the focus of
Holt's concern as the relationship between knowledge and the universe;
but what is more important, by making this clarification, the reader has
isolated the problem of making this relationship more meaningful than
it is at present.

Defining the problem of meaningful external relationships serves
two purposes. First, because it is a basic matter of education, this problem shows, at least at this early stage of development, that a philosophical system can be developed into the grounds for an educational theory.
Then, because it deals with the value of the ties between the objective
condition and the relatively subjective commodity of language, the
problem shows that what seems a foundation of Rationalism can support
a Pragmatic model of education. In order to resolve the problem, Holt
temporarily shifts the focus of his argument to the internal relationships
of knowledge. In making this shift of emphasis, Holt considers knowledge
as an end in itself, and therefore changes the nature of the argument
from purely Pragmatic to combined Pragmatic and Rationalistic. The
object of this combination of philosophies closely resembles the basis of
Rationalism: "A field of knowledge . . . is a territory . . ." or "an intellectual foreign country." However, Holt advocates Pragmatic methods

of attaining this Rationalistic end. Although knowledge is to be acquired and not made, ". . . knowing [knowledge] is not just a matter of knowing all the items in the territory, but of knowing how they relate to, compare with, and fit in with each other." With this fundamental understanding of the structure of knowledge, students can extract new ways of thinking from their original contexts and apply them to totally new situations. The process of using relationships should cause the students to see that ". . . problems and answers are simply different ways of looking at a relationship, a structure, an order." As a result, the good students can tolerate the uncertainty of not knowing immediate facts because he is certain that these facts can be assimilated into easily understandable structural relationships and thereby learned. On the other hand, the poor student, in considering knowledge in terms of the isolated fact, is in constant fear of not knowing because he is not certain he can acquire that fact.

From this increasing tendency away from the philosophical, now arises the more specialized educational problem, how to make the internal structural relationships of knowledge available to the learner. The actual process of learning relationships is one of converting a body of knowledge into the terms upon which the student himself operates, casting knowledge into a form which is compatible with the learner's own lifestyle. Such then is the process of model-making. Holt reveals, "Our learning is not real . . . above all not useful, unless we take these word strings and somehow convert them in our minds into a likeness of the world, a working mental model of the universe as we know it." The actual mechanics of model-making have not, however, as yet been defined. To develop a more mechanical or technical study, Holt must deal with the very nucleus of the model; and so he does, in discussing poor students, ". . . the kind of people for whom all symbols are meaningless; who cannot use symbols as a way of learning about and dealing with reality." Thus, the ability to make models is in a sense the ability to manipulate symbols. This ability to work with symbols is a specialized skill; it cannot be transferred from the teacher and textbook to the student. Instead, the skill is part of the learning act, which is initiated by the student himself. The problem of education has at this point come from the act of learning to the act of teaching.

The act of teaching emerges with the contradiction between the notion that manipulative ability is a skill which the student alone can initiate, and the concept of a formal program of education based on the student's need for a teacher other than himself. The solution of this enigma lies in Holt's statement: "The child who wants to know something remembers it and uses it once he has it." The inference to be drawn is that the educator is one who provides the outward conditions for internal learning. From this inference one can separate the task of teaching into two distinct modes of operations. Before a teacher can give knowledge a form which either enhances the student's existing model or replaces his faulty model with one which is geared more to the child's method of understanding and is, therefore, more efficient, the teacher must obviously determine the model the student presently holds. Hence, this, the process of analysis, is the first operation of the teaching act. Basing his choice of method employed on this analysis, the teacher presents subject matter in such a way that this conventional learning material can be reorganized and used by the student in the construction of his individual world-model. Holt clearly delineates this second phase of the teaching process: "With thought, practice, and luck, we should be able to devise problems that children can do in ways which, being their own, will be of use to them. Such problems could make up a kind of self-adjusting learning-machine, in which the child himself makes the program harder as he becomes more skillful."

The student who is able to foster his own learning is the intended result of Holt's model of education. In this light, one can now re-examine the learning process which has been developed in this paper, and make further refinements in this process. The initial preparation for learning and the ultimate criterion for truly knowing are contained in the same principle: one must know whether he knows or not, be able to recognize the value of an idea, that is, understand how it functions within his world-model, and then he will know how to take full advantage of the power of knowledge at large. Holt believes the power of knowledge has a definite direction; his combination of Pragmatic education and Rationalistic philosophy represents an attempt to make ways of knowing knowledge.

C.   The third essay was in response to an assignment to borrow the model of some mature discipline (or some model within some section of such a discipline) and by proper transformation, determine what could be said about education as a discipline, in its light. This use of models is probably the most common use we all make of models. It is best illustrated in the use that behaviorist psychologists make of the models of physics and mechanics to account for the behaviors of human beings. Further, in addition to explaining conduct, the model obliges the user also to describe the event being examined in the language of the model being employed. As such, the essay of Miss Kalmanowitz turned out to be startlingly effective as an illustration of educational thinking with a severely biological cast.

Education Conceived in an Ecological Model

by

Miriam Kalmanowitz

The educational process conceived as an evolutionary movement aims at the development of potentialities within the child. This fostering of his ability to think furthers the child's willingness to explore, to examine and to judge himself and his world with greater insight. For within this process ". . . each aspect—learner, materials and teacher—alters in the transaction that takes place in each phase, and that with these changes, the functions themselves evolve into newer functions . . ."

If one is to view the educational process as one essentially evolutionary in character, a process whose goals the schools, the institutions of education attempt to carry out, then one can envisage this system as occurring within an ecosystem. Let me at first attempt to explain what an ecosystem is and what constitutes it. Finally, after extensive elaboration about this biological model, I'll describe a specific terrestrial ecosystem—a biome—and its relation to the realm of the institutions of education.

An ecosystem may be defined as a self-contained unit needing an input of energy for its maintenance. This unit or community is found in nature and comprises all of the populations of an area which interact with their non-living environment and with each other. Thus, structurally, an ecosystem consists of abiotic materials—water, gases, light, a specific temperature—and of populations of producer, consumer and decomposer organisms.

The energy flow in ecosystem is very important to their maintenance as a community. The ecosystem must capture energy and utilize it during its interactions between its individual members.

Although the energy captured is transformed into potential energy, some of it is lost due to its conversion to an unusable form (second law of thermodynamics). To make this statement clearer take this example as a demonstration of the flow of energy within the ecosystem. The rays of the sun emit energy which is absorbed by producers. These producers, mostly green plants, via photosynthesis, create potential energy. Some of these plants are eaten by the primary consumers or herbivores. These herbivores in turn are eaten up by carnivores. The other plants and animals not consumed eventually die, their potential energy being lost to the ecosystem. This process continues up until the final consumer, upon whose death the potential energy is completely lost to the system, that is, until the cycle starts again. Within the ecosystem this energy flow must be maintained at a fairly stable level if serious consequences are to be avoided. Energy demands must not exceed the normal level nor may they be decreased.

Another important aspect present in ecosystems is its biogeniochemical cycles. This terms refers to the characteristic pathways in which elements circulate from the environment to the organism, only to eventually return once more to the environment. A possible example of this would be the element in its movement in and out of the living world. Suppose a rock deposit containing phosphorous had undergone extensive soil erosion. Some phosphores may be released, to be utilized by plants and then by animals. When these individuals die, phosphatizing bacteria work to decompose the organism in order to release the dissolved phosphores and keep them re-circulating in the ecosystem.

Ecosystems, or communities slowly change through an evolutional process called "succession." These ". . . communities have a life history during which they go through a sequential period of development, attain some sort of maturity, and eventually may be replaced by another set of producers and consumers . . ."

Organisms within such communities effect changes in their physical and chemical environments. As the environment undergoes metamorphosis, sometimes sped up by such natural forces as floods, fire and changes in temperature, the kinds of plants and animals that inhabit it change also. Thus, natural selection plays an important role here in determining density, natality and mortality rates of all members.

All interactions occurring within the ecosystem have as their roots the evolutionary process of succession and natural selection. Organisms requiring the same materials from the environment had to compete for their survival. At times even two species with identical requirements, will not be able to live in the same habitat (Gouse's competition-exclusion principles). One will be driven away or will have to change its requirements.

Other interactions within the ecosystem are the symbiotic relationships between several organisms. These may apply to any intimate association between two forms regardless of the harmful or beneficial outcomes of the relationship. One of these is commensalism, whereby an individual forms benefits without harming the other. An illustration of this is the "shark sucker" which attaches itself to the unsuspecting host and helps itself to the remainder of the shark's meal. Mutualism occurs when both forms interact in such a way as to benefit each other. An example of this can be found in the ants-aphid relationship. The former maintains and feeds the aphids, while at the same time uses the latter's exudation as nourishment. In addition, parasitism occurs within the ecosystem. It is a relationship whereby an organism will spend part or all of his lifetime (cycle) on or within another organism and use food or tissues of the host for nourishment. Of course, the parasite must not damage its host too severely for its life is at stake, too.

The last interaction occurring in an ecosystem is predation. It is considered as a necessary activity in the community's energy flow. Indeed, it is a very effective method of population control on the part of the prey population, because its victims are the sick, the old, and the less well-adapted.

As time passes the community of interacting individuals reaches a climax stage. As it does this, a decrease in the net production of living matter occurs. Succession has slowed down in the community; however, a balance between the utilization of energy (respiration) and the formation of new organic matter, has been achieved.

Even if an ecosystem had reached its utmost development certain conditions may arise to upset the balance. In most cases these conditions are brought about artificially, that is, by men. For a long time men have tried to manipulate ecosystems by modifying natural environments. Sometimes, his attempts for short-term gains have been rewarded with success; at other times he has only met with failure. In areas such as wildlife conservation, forestry management, rice cultivation (manipulation of marsh ecosystem) some success has been achieved. However, in other instances—the exploitation of the soil via agriculture, excessive timbering, the release of poisonous gases to the atmosphere, in excrescent amounts, the indiscriminate use of insecticides upon plant life, man is disturbing the normal energy relations in the community. By removing or killing one individual (organism) a void is created in the chain of relationships.

This will serve to upset the balance of the community and direct it toward serious consequences.

Now that an ecosystem has been defined and its characteristics described, let us now see how the institutions of education can fall into the sphere of an ecosystem. First, two points must be emphasized about all ecosystems of which our school is a member. Primarily, "the major terrestrial ecosystem—biomes as they are called—are categorized by a distinctive biotic composition and are named according to the dominant . . ." form of life present in the system. Secondly, ". . . the distributional pattern of biomes is determined largely by a combination of the factors of solar radiation, precipitation and temperature. . . ." (in the cases of animal and plant life). Our biomes' name and location depends upon human factors. A central board of administrators, a local board of education and a city planning commission works together to determine a construction site for our school. Furthermore, its name: Teachers Program for the Creation of Intelligent, Mature and Inquisitive Youth (TPCIMIY) is derived from the kinds of participants interacting with each other in this special program of education, students, teachers and guidance counselors.

However TPCIMIY must be a special ecosystem unlike any of the schools that have gone before it. The idea of ecosystem is that it can function in any country on earth which possesses a site favorable to the growth and maturation of both the learner and the learning process.

Although it is in its infancy, TPCIMIY has quite a different atmosphere than preceding ecosystems. The first of its kind, TPCIMIY is a self-contained unit of ten schools, each comprising children of all age groups and all intelligence levels. Every year as new students are admitted, intensive psychological and I.Q. testing occurs. By means of such tests children are grouped in different levels or grades, according to their intelligence and potential capacities. As the school year progresses and the flow of education proceeds in all the classrooms, the students are sorted out two more times. This is to remove those children referred to as educationally atrophied. These must be removed and placed in schools outside the ecosystem complex, schools whose programs are suitable to their capacities. Thus, the classroom situation now uncluttered, unimpeded, can function to maximum efficiency despite the loss of some of its student population.

The interactions between individuals within TPCIMIY are special for this ecosystem. Of primary importance are the symbiotic relationships between the students and their counterparts, and the students with their teachers. Commensalism is reflected in the student-help project. In this project students would tutor classmates of lower intellectual achievement levels than themselves. As a result, if the child's intellectual capacities are motivated even the slightest bit, it is because he has profited from the attention and the knowledge of his tutor.

The continual quest for knowledge and for truth is reflected by other symbiotic relationships and interactions. Mutualism occurs as one aspect of the educational process. Here for the first time the learning process becomes cyclical in character. The teacher assists his pupils in the learning process; they in turn aid each other; and finally even re-educate the teacher in the facts of which he was ignorant. Within TPCIMIY this cyclical process is observed in the many research projects undergone by students, and the faculty of every field. Each of the persons involved in the experiment helps each other in compiling data, interpreting it and eventually coming to an unanimous conclusion.

The purpose of TPCIMIY, through its educational process, is to promote the inquisitiveness of the child, to make him search for the truth, or the models that are the foundations of his world. After adequate exploration, examination and maturation (intellectual) on his part, he is ready to pass judgment upon these truths, and wherever possible, to replace them with more relevant ones. If this is so, another interaction occurring within the ecosystem is vital to the educative process.

Competition occurs here, but not in the same vein as in other schools. In as much as predation, or frequent testing of the students' ability to memorize facts for the sake of memorization has been lessened, competition takes on another meaning.

Competition is no longer the battle for good marks, since the tests are reduced to a mere 4 (3 psychological-intellectual, and 1 yearly achievement tests) and grades have been abolished. Cheating, one of the oldest forms of this competition, no longer exists, and neither do the parasites who have been removed from the educational system. Now competition has as its battleground the quest for knowledge for knowledge's sake. As the inquisitive nature of the child increases, as he matures, he and his counterparts each search for more and more knowledge. In the long run this accumulated knowledge will be put to the test by its application to the competitive experiences of adult life.

In as much as ecological communities do not remain in their infant stage forever, TPCIMIY, too, is not a stagnant educational ecosystem. Slowly TPCIMIY will evolve into a mature organism and will eventually reach a state of ultimate balance between its graduates—those students who have matured and transposed as individuals—and the number of entering students. Never will there be any problem of overcrowding within this system, for evolution and survival of the fittest have played their role well.

Within TPCIMIY the process of education is in itself evolving. Each year panel discussions among students and teachers, school newspaper editorials, student murals and shows, suggest valuable ideas (ways) of improving the quality of education within the ecosystem, making it an enjoyable experience and bringing it up to its ultimate peak.

TPCIMIY, an evolving educational biome, if put into use, could be an ideal model of education. But its likelihood of succeeding is highly questionable, due to the many external human forces which might exert influence on the system. TPCIMIY could possibly succeed if no outside interference is manifested by parents or groups claiming to have substantial power over the Central Educational board that originally created the school. As a result, no anarchy, no disruption of the educative process would arise, that is, unless the shortsightedness, ignorance and prejudice of outsiders exert enough pressure on the system to totally disintegrate it.

D. Finally, the essay by Mr. Gradel was irresistible to me. He had been asked to write a paper on a novel with some educational significance, but to literally take the story apart, and fit it into an entirely new model, whose relationships are not even hinted at in the original. In this way, I had hoped, the student would be able to move back from the work read, and see it in a perspective that would include both the content of the novel and the author himself, as a participant in the creation of that work. What he did was to project a new situation in which the character of the story and the author were both actors in the new relationship. See if this does not develop, with some very real promise, the capacity for literary criticism.

Catcher in the Rye: Salinger
by
Michael Gradel

When I saw the movie, "Schizophrenia," which was produced by J. D. Salinger and directed by Holden Caulfield, I could not help but think of a certain movie produced by William Faulkner. This latter was a four-part narration. More specifically, it was the recording of events of a particular span of time subjectively repeated four times. These four actors respectively played the parts of a castrated idiot, a selfish and dominating brother, a tormented and deluded brother and a relatively lucid servant. These four actors were comparable to four possible types of lenses that could have been placed in the camera that was filming the action. Each of the lenses, due to its inherent defect, added a particular distortion of its own to the filming.

Faulkner could well have used Holden Caulfield in his narrative. His particular type of defect would have added yet another distortive dimension to the film. It seems that a lens free of any kind of defect is difficult to find. The appearance of the lens can be so deceiving. Considering the lenslike mind of the idiot in Faulkner's movie, we have to admit that, due to the extreme simplicity of the lens, there is less subjective distortion of images. Plucking the lenses out of the heads of the other actors, we realize that due to the increased complexity, there is more of a chance for subjective distortion of images.

Thus I come to the movie, "Schizophrenia." The producer, Mr. Salinger, created a work of art with, surprisingly enough, only two hundred and fourteen feet of film and an H.C. type lens; rather complex but defective. Salinger, whose movie was about life, realized that in only two hundred and fourteen feet of film (shown at slow motion, of course) it was impossible to show an actual beginning or an end. The movie could only present a brief segment of life. Realizing also that it is practically impossible to film an objective aspect of life, Salinger resigned himself to the subjectivity of the H.C. type lens. Wishing the title to be appropriate, Salinger realized that the defect of the H.C. type lens created the ideal distortion of life to be filmed.

It wasn't until I had seen three-quarters of the film that I realized that Holden Caulfield was schizophrenic. All I knew was that there was this boy, Holden Caulfield (the main actor), sixteen years of age, who had flunked out of school. I traced his experiences and I sympathized with him at every barrier he met. I despised the phoniness of old Sally; I was disgusted at the prostitution of his brother D.B.'s writing talents; horrified was I at the impersonality and the commerciality of Maurice and the prostitute; bored was I by the useless didactic of Mr. Spencer; revolted was I by the unacceptable behavior of Mr. Antolini.

Caulfield was much too good an actor. The supporting actors could not, for one moment, convince me that Holden's actions were lacking in sufficient forethought or that he lacked the capability of reasoning. As far as I was concerned, this was a very humanistic treatment of a boy who was very lucid and had unfortunately been born into a world full of sham values. I cannot overlook, of course, the fact that the leading actor did direct the movie and thus made it quite easy to make himself look favorable.

Three-quarters of the way through the film a great enlightenment came my way. The part of the film that I am referring to is that part in which his goal in life is made clear. This part of the film was very complex and took me much time to analyze. The camera (with its defective lens) shifted its position and there on the screen became visible a huge field of rye. Inside this field of rye there were little children playing a game. I couldn't see what type of game it was, but I could discern that it was an organized game with rules and all. To one side of this field was a huge white cliff, beyond which I could not see. The camera was concentrated on the area on top of the huge cliff, for here stood Holden Caulfield. He was bigger than all the children there and every time a child strayed from the game and wandered towards the cliff, Holden prevented him from falling over the edge.

This was a little confusing and so my attention wandered for a few moments. I thought of a movie that I had seen entitled *You've either got or you haven't got class,* produced by John Dewey, and based on the book by Karl Marx. I remember in the narration, the discussion of the two warring classes in our society; the progs and the trads. I specifically remember a part, though, in which Mr. Dewey thoughtfully resolved that life is a game with certain rules; and that when a player protests, he is not protesting against the game but rather against the apparent straying from a rule. I thought that the field of rye, first of all, represented a physical environment. The children in the field represented all children and they were playing the game of life only as a child knows it. Holden's role couldn't have been similar to that of an umpire, for he dissociated himself from the game and made no comment on the action of the game. At this point I could think of no further comment. I started to classify

Holden as anti-social since he did not participate in the game of life; but then I realized that he was too old to participate in a children's world.

What I desired to know was the reality on the other side of the cliff. It then dawned upon me that what existed on the other side of the cliff was the adult world that Holden had come into contact with in the one hundred and seventy-two feet of film before this present scene. On this side of the cliff another game was also being played. It was an organized game with rules, but only adults played it. The trouble with this game was that the players were constantly in conflict with one another— verbally and physically. The players felt no spirit, but were merely play- ing to win. They satiated themselves with the materiality of points. They cared nought for the friendship of their fellow players.

Holden Caulfield was, at one time, on the adult side of the cliff, but he couldn't accept their values. He tried to escape to the children's side of the cliff, as was revealed by a part of his monologue:

"How would you like to get the hell out of here? . . . tomorrow morning we could drive up to Massachusetts and Vermont . . . It's beautiful as hell up there . . . We'll stay in these cabin camps and stuff like that till the dough runs out . . . I could get a job some- where and we could live somewhere with a brook and all and, later on, we could get married or something . . . Honest to God, we could have a terrific time! Wuddaya say? C'mon! Wuddaya say?"

Fleeing from adulthood, but unable to re-enter childhood, Holden was stranded in between the cliffs. Wishing to preserve the innocence and warmth of childhood, Holden assigned himself the task of preventing children from falling off the cliff, or experiencing the adult world.

Holden lost contact with the childhood environment and the adult- hood environment. He had no means of identification; his personality disintegrated. Holden Caulfield was a schizophrenic. The movie ends on a positive note, though, for Holden has himself committed to a sani- tarium. I should say, rather, that ended that particular segment of his life.

Bibliography

A. Sources specifically referred to

ACHINSTEIN, PETER. *Concepts of Science: A Philosophical Analysis.* Baltimore: Johns Hopkins Press, 1968.

AUSTIN, JOHN L. *How to Do Things with Words.* London: Oxford University Press, 1963.

————. *Philosophical Papers.* Edited by J. O. Urmson and Geoffrey J. Warnock. Oxford: Clarendon Press, 1962.

BELTH, MARC. *Education as a Discipline.* Boston: Allyn and Bacon, 1965.

————. "Socratic Persuasion." *Educational Issues,* Toronto University, 1(1968): 50–66.

————. "The Study of Education as the Study of Models." *The Alberta Journal of Educational Research,* 12 (1966): 203–223. Also reprinted in *The Social Studies: Structures, Models and Strategies.* Englewood Cliffs, N.J.: Prentice-Hall, 1969.

BOULDING, KENNETH E. *The Meaning of the Twentieth Century: The Great Transition.* New York: Harper and Row, 1964.

BRUNER, JEROME S., JACQUELINE J. GOODNOW, AND GEORGE A. AUSTIN. *A Study of Thinking.* New York: Science Editions, 1962.

CARNAP, RUDOLF. *The Logical Syntax of Language.* London: K. Paul, Trench, Trubner and Co., 1937.

CASSIRER, ERNST. *An Essay on Man.* New Haven, Conn.: Yale University Press, 1944.

DEWEY, JOHN. *Art as Experience.* New York: Minton Balch, 1934.

————. *Democracy and Education.* New York: Macmillan Co., 1916.

DURRELL, LAWRENCE. *The Alexandria Quartet.* London: Faber and Faber, 1968.

FREGE, GOTTLOB. *The Foundations of Arithmetic: A Logico-Mathematical Enquiry into the Concept of Numbers.* Translated by John L. Austin. Oxford: Blackwell, 1959.

FREMONT, HERBERT. *How to Teach Mathematics in Secondary Schools.* Philadelphia: Saunders, 1969.

GOODMAN, NELSON. *The Languages of Art: An Approach to a Theory of Symbols*. Indianapolis: Bobbs-Merrill, 1968.

JAMES, WILLIAM. *Pragmatism*. Cleveland: Meridian, 1955.

KUHN, THOMAS. *The Structure of Scientific Revolutions*. Chicago: University of Chicago Press, 1962.

LANGER, SUSANNE. *Mind: An Essay on Human Feeling*. Baltimore: Johns Hopkins Press, 1967.

————. "Why Philosophy?" *The Saturday Evening Post* 234 (1961): 34.

OAKESHOTT, MICHAEL. *Experience and Its Modes*. London: Cambridge University Press, 1933.

PEIRCE, CHARLES S. *Collected Papers*. 6 vols. Edited by Charles Hartshorne and Paul Weiss. Cambridge: Belknap Press, Harvard University Press, 1960.

PETERS, RICHARD S., editor. *The Concept of Education*. London: Routledge Kegan and Paul, 1968.

PHENIX, PHILIP. *Philosophy of Education*. New York: Henry Holt, 1958.

QUINE, WILLARD VAN ORMAN. *Word and Object*. Cambridge, Mass.: The M.I.T. Press, 1960.

RAMSEY, FRANK P. *The Foundations of Mathematics*. Paterson, N.J.: Littlefield, Adams, 1960.

RICHARDS, IVOR A. *Interpretation in Teaching*. New York: Harcourt, Brace and Co., 1938.

ROBINSON, RICHARD. *Definition*. Oxford: Clarendon Press, 1962.

RUSSELL, BERTRAND. *Introduction to Mathematical Philosophy*. London: G. Allen and Unwin, 1948.

————. *Our Knowledge of the External World*. New York: W. W. Norton and Co., 1929.

RYLE, GILRERT R. *The Concept of Mind*. London: Hutchinson's University Library, 1955.

SCHEFFLER, ISRAEL. *The Language of Education*. Springfield, Ill.: C. C. Thomas, 1962.

SKINNER, B. F. *Critique of Psychoanalytic Concepts and Theories*. Minnesota Studies in the Philosophy of Science. 3 vols. Edited by H. Feigl and others. Minneapolis: University of Minnesota Press, 1956. In vol. 1: 77–87.

STEBBING, L. SUSAN. *Philosophy and the Physicists*. New York: Dover Publications, 1958.

WAISMANN, FRIEDRICH. "The Decline and Fall of Causality." *Turning Points in Physics*. Edited by Alistair C. Crombie. Amsterdam: North Holland Publishing Co., 1950. Ch. 5.

————. *Introduction to Mathematical Thinking*. Translated by Theodore J. Benac. New York: Harper, 1959.

WHORF, BENJAMIN L. *Language, Thought, and Reality: Selected Writings of Benjamin Lee Whorf*. Edited by John B. Carroll. Cambridge, Mass.: The M.I.T. Press, 1956.

B.   Sources not specifically referred to, but which have influenced the work

BELAVAL, YVON. *Philosophers and Their Language*. Translated by Norbert Guterman. Athens, Ohio: Ohio University Press, 1967.

BELLACK, ARNO, et al. *The Language of the Classroom*. New York: Teachers College Publishers, 1966.

BELTH, MARC. "Plato's Dialectic as a Model of Education." *Philosophy of Education 1967 Proceedings of 23rd Annual Meeting*, pp. 224–45.

————. "The Logic of a Discipline of Education." In Harold Full, *Controversy in American Education: An Anthology of Crucial Issues*. New York: Macmillan, 1967.

BROUDY, HARRY S., and JOHN R. PALMER. *Exemplars of Teaching Method*. Chicago: Rand McNally, 1965.

BRUMBAUGH, ROBERT S. "A New Interpretation of Plato's Republic." *Journal of Philosophy* 64 (1967): 661–67.

CASSIRER, ERNST. *The Philosophy of Symbolic Forms*. Translated by R. Mannheim. New Haven, Conn.: Yale University Press, 1953.

CATON, CHARLES E. *Philosophy and Ordinary Language*. Urbana, Ill.: University of Illinois Press, 1963.

DEWEY, JOHN. *How We Think: A Restatement of the Relation of Reflective Thinking to the Educative Process*. Boston: D.C. Heath, 1933.

DUNCAN, HUGH DALZIEL. *Symbols in Society*. New York: Oxford University Press, 1968.

ELAM, STANLEY, editor. *Education and the Structure of Knowledge*. Chicago: Rand McNally, 1964.

ENNIS, ROBERT. *Logic in Teaching*. Englewood Cliffs, N.J.: Prentice-Hall, 1969.

GRIFFITHS, A. PHILIPS, editor. *Knowledge and Belief*. London: Oxford Press, 1967.

GUILFORD, J. P. *The Nature of Human Intelligence*. New York: McGraw-Hill, 1967.

GUTTCHEN, ROBERT, and BERTRAM BANDMAN. *Philosophical Essays on Curriculum*. Philadelphia: Lippincott, 1969.

HANSON, NORWOOD R. *Patterns of Discovery: An Inquiry into the Conceptual Foundations of Science*. London: Cambridge University Press, 1958.

HESSE, MARY B. *Models and Analogies in Science*. South Bend, Ind.: University of Notre Dame Press, 1966.

KAPLAN, ABRAHAM. *The Conduct of Inquiry: Methodology for Behavioral Science*. San Francisco: Chandler Pub. Co., 1964.

KOMISAR, B. PAUL, and C. J. B. MACMILLAN, editors. *Psychological Concepts in Education*. Chicago: Rand McNally, 1967.

LANGER, SUSANNE K. *Philosophy in a New Key: A Study in the Symbolism of Reason, Rite, and Art*. Cambridge: Harvard University Press, 1957.

MORRIS, BERTRAM. *Institutions of Intelligence* (Studies in Educational Theory of the John Dewey Society, No. 6). Columbus, Ohio: Ohio State University Press, 1969.

NASH, LEONARD K. *The Nature of the Natural Sciences*. Boston: Little Brown and Co., 1963.

PARKINSON, G. H. R., editor. *The Theory of Meaning*. London: Oxford Press, 1968.

PHENIX, PHILIP. *Realms of Meaning*. New York: McGraw-Hill, 1964.

POLYANI, MICHAEL. *Personal Knowledge: Towards a Post-Critical Philosophy*. New York: Harper and Row, 1958.

————. *The Tacit Dimension*. London: Routledge and Kegan Paul, 1966.

POSTMAN, NEIL, and CHARLES WEINGARTNER. *Teaching as a Subversive Activity*. New York: Delacorte, 1969.

SAVORY, T. H. *The Language of Science*. London: Andre Deutsch, 1967.

SCHEFFLER, ISRAEL. *Science and Subjectivity*. Indianapolis: Bobbs-Merrill, 1967.

SMITH, B. OTHANEL, and ROBERT H. ENNIS, editors. *Language and Concepts in Education*. Chicago: Rand McNally, 1961.

SMITH, B. OTHANEL, and MILTON NEUX. *A Study of the Logic of Teaching*. Urbana, Ill.: Bureau of Education Research, College of Education, University of Illinois, n.d.

STRAWSON, P. F., editor. *Studies in the Philosophy of Thought and Action*. London: Oxford Press, 1968.

VYGOTSKY, LEV S. *Thought and Language*. Translated by Eugenia Haufman and Gertrude Vakar. Cambridge, Mass.: The M.I.T. Press, 1962.

Index